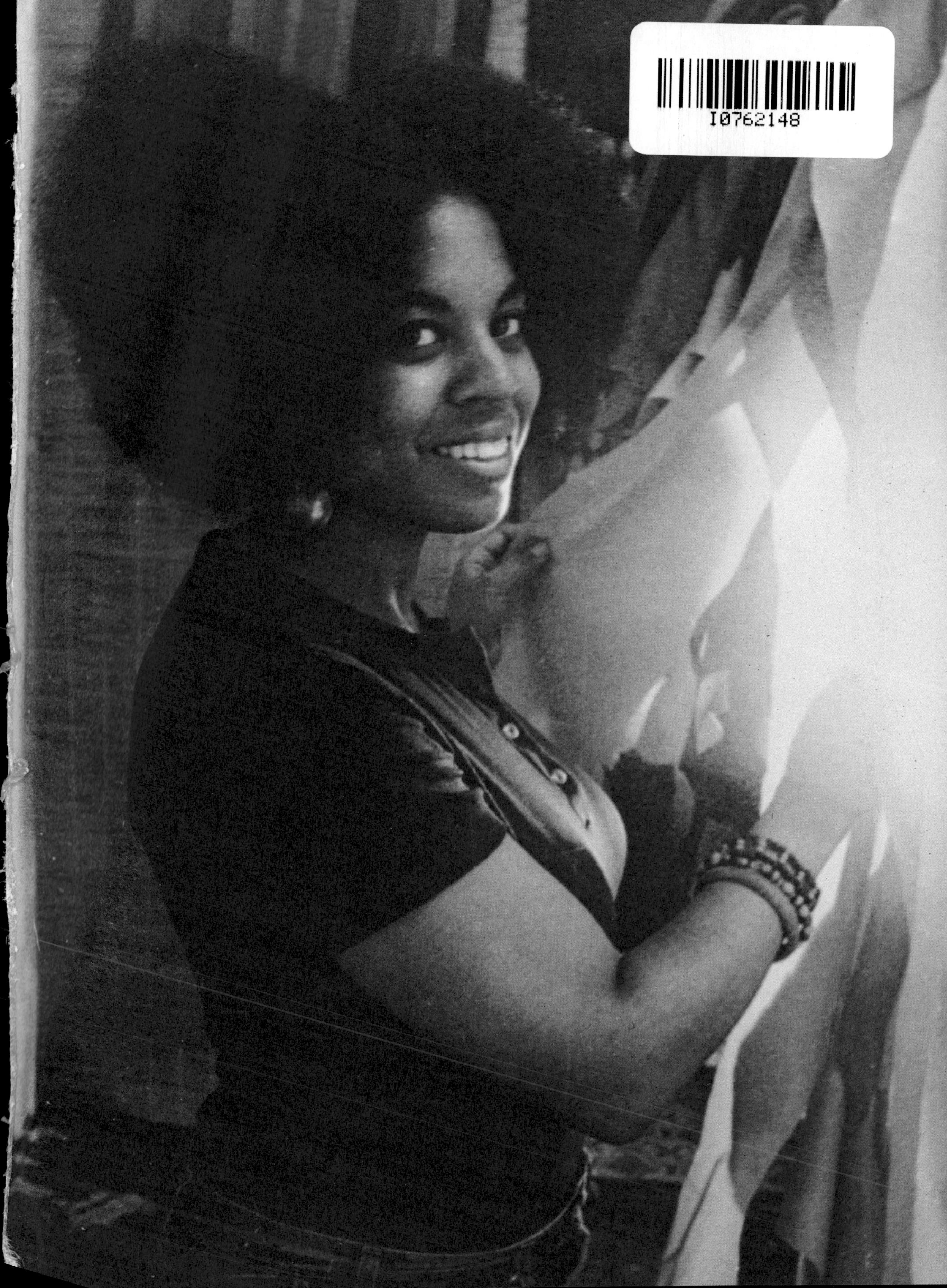

SENGA NENGUDI

SENGA NENGUDI

populated air

Edited by Matilde Guidelli-Guidi and Svetlana Kitto

Dia: HIRMER

THIS BOOK WAS PUBLISHED IN CONJUNCTION WITH *SENGA NENGUDI*, CURATED BY MATILDE GUIDELLI-GUIDI, AT DIA BEACON, NEW YORK, FEBRUARY 17, 2023-MARCH 25, 2026.

SENGA NENGUDI WAS MADE POSSIBLE BY SIGNIFICANT SUPPORT FROM THE ANDY WARHOL FOUNDATION. ADDITIONAL SUPPORT PROVIDED BY FABA - FUNDACIÓN ALMINE Y BERNARD RUIZ-PICASSO, CHARA SCHREYER, AND SPRÜTH MAGERS.

ALL EXHIBITIONS AT DIA ARE MADE POSSIBLE BY THE ECONOMOU EXHIBITION FUND.

THE PUBLICATION WAS MADE POSSIBLE BY MAJOR SUPPORT FROM SUSAN AND LARRY MARX. GENEROUS SUPPORT BY EVERY PAGE FOUNDATION AND JAMES HOWELL FOUNDATION. ADDITIONAL SUPPORT BY ADAM PENDLETON.

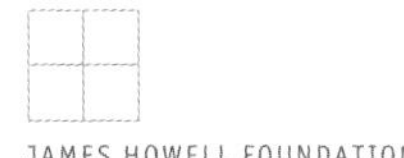

FIRST PRINTING, 2025

DIA ART FOUNDATION
535 WEST 22ND STREET
NEW YORK, NEW YORK 10011
DIAART.ORG

HIRMER VERLAG
BAYERSTRASSE 57-59
80335 MUNICH
GERMANY
HIRMERPUBLISHERS.COM

DESIGN: BOBBY JOE SMITH III WITH HANNES HALDER
EDITOR: SVETLANA KITTO
RESEARCH ASSISTANTS: CHAEEUN LEE, LAURA Y. LUO, AND CHARLOTTE YOUKILIS
RIGHTS AND REPRODUCTION: JENN KANE
PROOFREADERS: KAMILAH N. FOREMAN AND KAREN RASABY
SENIOR EDITOR, HIRMER VERLAG: ELISABETH ROCHAU-SHALEM
PRODUCTION, HIRMER VERLAG: RAINER ARNOLD AND HANNES HALDER

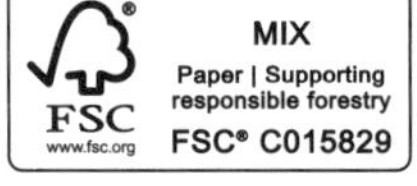

TYPESET IN GARAMOND, GT AMERICA, AND PP EDITORIAL NEW
PRINTED ON 150 GSM MAGNO NATURAL
PREPRESS BY REPROLINE MEDIATEAM, MUNICH
PRINTING AND BINDING BY PRINTER TRENTO S.P.A

PRINTED IN ITALY

COVER, FRONT: *INSIDE/OUTSIDE*, 1977 (P. 83); BACK: SHEET FROM *STRATHMORE SKETCHBOOK*, 1976-77 (PP. 58, 66). FRONTISPIECES: PAGE 8, *WET NIGHT-EARLY DAWN-SCAT-CHANT-PILGRIM'S SONG* (DETAIL), 1996. EARTH PIGMENT ON WALL, SPRAY-PAINT ON CARDBOARD, DRY-CLEANING BAGS, BUBBLE WRAP, AND MIXED MEDIA. DIA ART FOUNDATION. *SENGA NENGUDI*, INSTALLATION VIEW, DIA BEACON, NEW YORK, FEBRUARY 17, 2023-MARCH 25, 2026; PP. 12-13, 248: *SANDMINING B* (DETAIL), 2020 (P. 234)

ISBN 978-3-7774-4607-3

LIBRARY OF CONGRESS CATALOGUING-IN-PUBLICATION DATA
2025934214

NOTE TO READER: ALL PHOTOGRAPHERS WHO COLLABORATED WITH NENGUDI ON HER PERFORMANCES FOR THE CAMERA ARE INCLUDED IN THE CAPTIONS, WHILE PHOTOGRAPHERS WHO WERE CHARGED WITH DOCUMENTATION ONLY ARE LISTED IN THE PHOTOGRAPHY CREDITS.

Contents

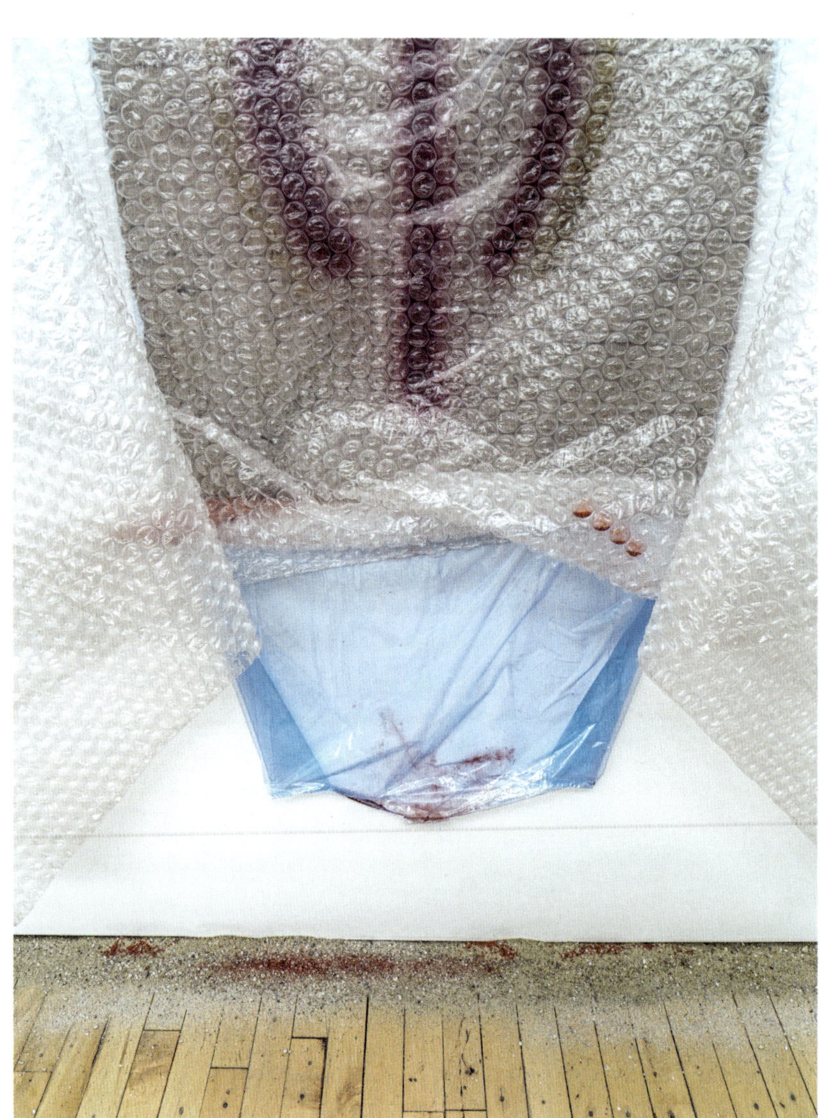

FOREWORD

Jessica Morgan

The idea is the thing.
—SENGA NENGUDI

Smudges and smears of color, pigment rubbed by hand or through cloth, earth in pantyhose applied to a surface to create ghostly impressions of movement or breath: Senga Nengudi's resolutely ephemeral mark making pervades her installations at Dia Beacon. We see the origin of her practice in some of the earliest drawings included in *Senga Nengudi: Populated Air*. Published for the first time in this volume, the suite of drawings *Angst on Pink Paper* (1976), for example, is made with fluid yet minimal precision, red pencil and brown gouache forms on pink paper that summon wildly expressive figures in states of joy and undoing—unsurprising of course for an artist so profoundly invested in movement and dance. At once barely there, in terms of mark and materiality, while also profoundly present through their indelible impression, *Angst on Pink Paper* clearly foreshadows Nengudi's installations *Wet Night–Early Dawn–Scat-Chant–Pilgrim's Song* (1996) and *Untitled* (2023), on long-term view at Dia Beacon, and speak to her lifelong commitment to work that may or may not ever be seen by an audience. For Nengudi, whether the idea ever finds a material form or is only to be momentarily embodied, it is no less valued or acknowledged as work.

Nengudi's privileging of the idea over the object remarkably applies to her own self-presentation. The artist, born Sue Irons, has assumed pseudonyms for her creative identities as sculptor (Senga Nengudi), draftsperson (Harriet Chin), photographer (Propecia Leigh), and writer (Lily Bea Moor). Her refusal to self-define is both disorienting and liberating, unsettling our urge to fix and categorize each other, while giving us permission to do the same. Indeed, it has been Nengudi's mission from the start to remain a beacon of alterity in the face of an ever-increasing economy of celebrity and individualism; this book makes a record of that commitment.

She writes in her poem "Assurances":

i create a peace/
piece
i wipe it out with
my hands, my feet,
my body. it remains
in the fabric of
time threading
through the
millennia
remembered and
forgotten a thousand
times over. yet
there. seen—not
seen—experienced as
part of the air.[1]

Aptly, this is a book of notebooks, sketches, fliers, contact sheets and stills, poems, and choreographic notations or instructions—a collection that reflects this upending of norms of value and visibility. It arrives at Dia after many years of engagement with Nengudi, beginning with her performative contribution to Dia's Artists on Artists Lecture Series at the invitation of Dia's former curator Kelly Kivland. Nengudi chose to speak about Joan Jonas and undertook a memorable multimedia performative invocation that generously extended to a significant encounter with Dia's teens. Nengudi's exhibition at Dia Beacon and acquisitions spanning the 1960s to 2023 (with an impromptu work made on-site) were stewarded by Matilde Guidelli-Guidi, Dia's curator and co-head of the curatorial department. Working closely with Nengudi over the years, Guidelli-Guidi has not only helped bring into being the works at Dia but also guided and researched this volume, uncovering an extraordinary trove of materials, much of which is being shared with a wider public for the first time. We are truly grateful for her work in bringing this to fruition. That process could not have happened without the collaboration and involved creative and editorial oversight of Svetlana Kitto, editor at Dia; together, they shaped this volume with rigor and sensitivity to forefront the multiple registers that characterize Nengudi's life and work. We are grateful to the formidable A. B. Spellman for accepting our invitation and honored to publish his free-verse response to Nengudi's lifelong work. Our thanks go to Bobby Joe Smith III for his deeply attuned graphic design that animates the materials in this volume and shapes the experience of this book.

Over the years, Nengudi has entrusted her papers to the Smithsonian's Archives of American Art, Washington, D.C.; Amistad Research Center at Tulane University, New Orleans; African American Performance Art Archive, University of North Carolina at Chapel Hill; and Just Above Midtown Archives in the Museum of Modern Art (MoMA), New York. We are grateful to Marisa Bourgoin, head of reference services at the Smithsonian; Lisa C. Moore, head of research services at Tulane; and Linda Goode Bryant, Thomas (T.) Jean Lax, and Michelle Harvey, the Rona Roob Head of Archives Services, at MoMA for all their work on the collection, preservation, and facilitation of these invaluable materials. Thanks to Jenn Kane, rights and reproduction associate at Dia, for her indefatigable work obtaining images; and to Fernando Zelaya, design and production assistant at Dia, for his attentive design of Nengudi's personal map of Los Angeles's West Adams neighborhood in this volume; as well as to the researchers who assisted on this multiyear project: Chaeeun Lee, 2024–25 curatorial fellow; Laura Y. Luo, 2023–24 curatorial research intern; and Charlotte Youkilis, 2024 CCS Bard curatorial intern. Thanks to Humberto Moro for his oversight of the program team; Kamilah N. Foreman, who expertly leads every aspect of Dia's publications department; our co-publisher Hirmer Verlag; and to Brooklyn Editions for photography assistance.

Senga Nengudi at Dia Beacon, the exhibition that this volume accompanies, results from an involved process and material research into staging Nengudi's sculptures and installations in a manner that retains the ephemeral materiality and improvisational gestures that inform them. We are deeply grateful to all those who worked closely with Nengudi and Guidelli-Guidi to accomplish this endeavor: at Dia, Emily Markert, curatorial associate; the exhibition design department, then led by Heidie Giannotti with Brian Higbee; the art handling of Joel Bacon, Shane Bryant Henken, Ted Kersten, Cara Kuball, and Aaron Sinift; and the operations department then led by Kurt Diebboll and Curtis Harvey. For their assistance in planning and realizing Nengudi's installations, we are grateful to Sanza Pyatt Fittz

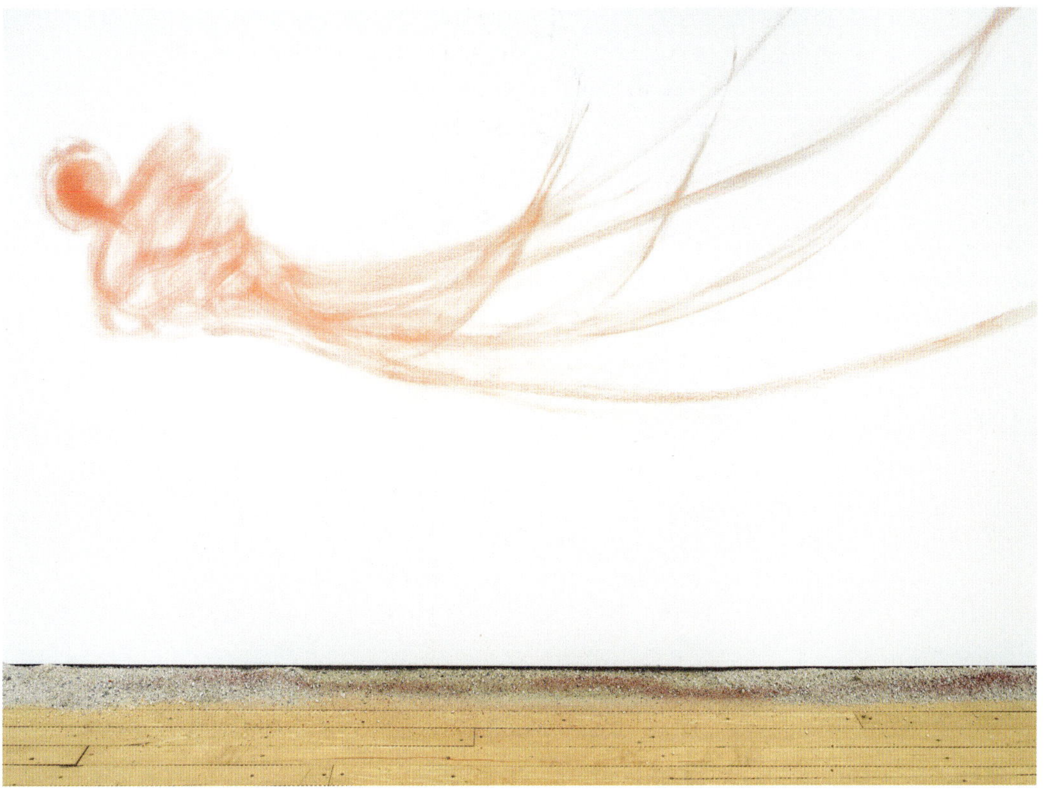

WET NIGHT-EARLY DAWN-SCAT-CHANT-PILGRIM'S SONG (DETAIL), 1996

and JD Sell; Marta Fontolan, Simone Manwarring, and Hannes Schroeder-Finkh at Sprüth Magers; Ian Wallace at Open Format; and Thomas Erben.

Our donors' continued support allows for the realization of projects of this breadth. For their significant support of the exhibition, we are grateful to the Andy Warhol Foundation. Additional thanks to FABA – Fundación Almine y Bernard Ruiz-Picasso, Chara Schreyer, and Sprüth Magers. The publication was made possible by major support from Susan and Larry Marx. Generous support was also provided by Every Page Foundation and James Howell Foundation. Thank you also to Adam Pendleton for his support of the publication. These fundraising efforts were led by our development team, including David Morehouse, senior deputy director; Karey David, director of development, foundation and government relations; Ella Strauss, senior manager, special events, councils, and partnerships; and Kseniya Ignatova-Yates, manager, major giving and campaign.

Populated Air was conceived and crafted in close conversation with the artist, and our greatest thanks go to Senga Nengudi herself who has patiently worked to gather and identify materials and memories, and, most importantly, has honored us with the opportunity to share them with our publics. We are profoundly grateful for being able to work with her over so many years now and into the future.

Epigraph: "Julian Schnabel on Charlie Rose" (February 1, 2008), in this volume, p. 224.

1 "Assurances" (May 1993), in this volume, p. 204.

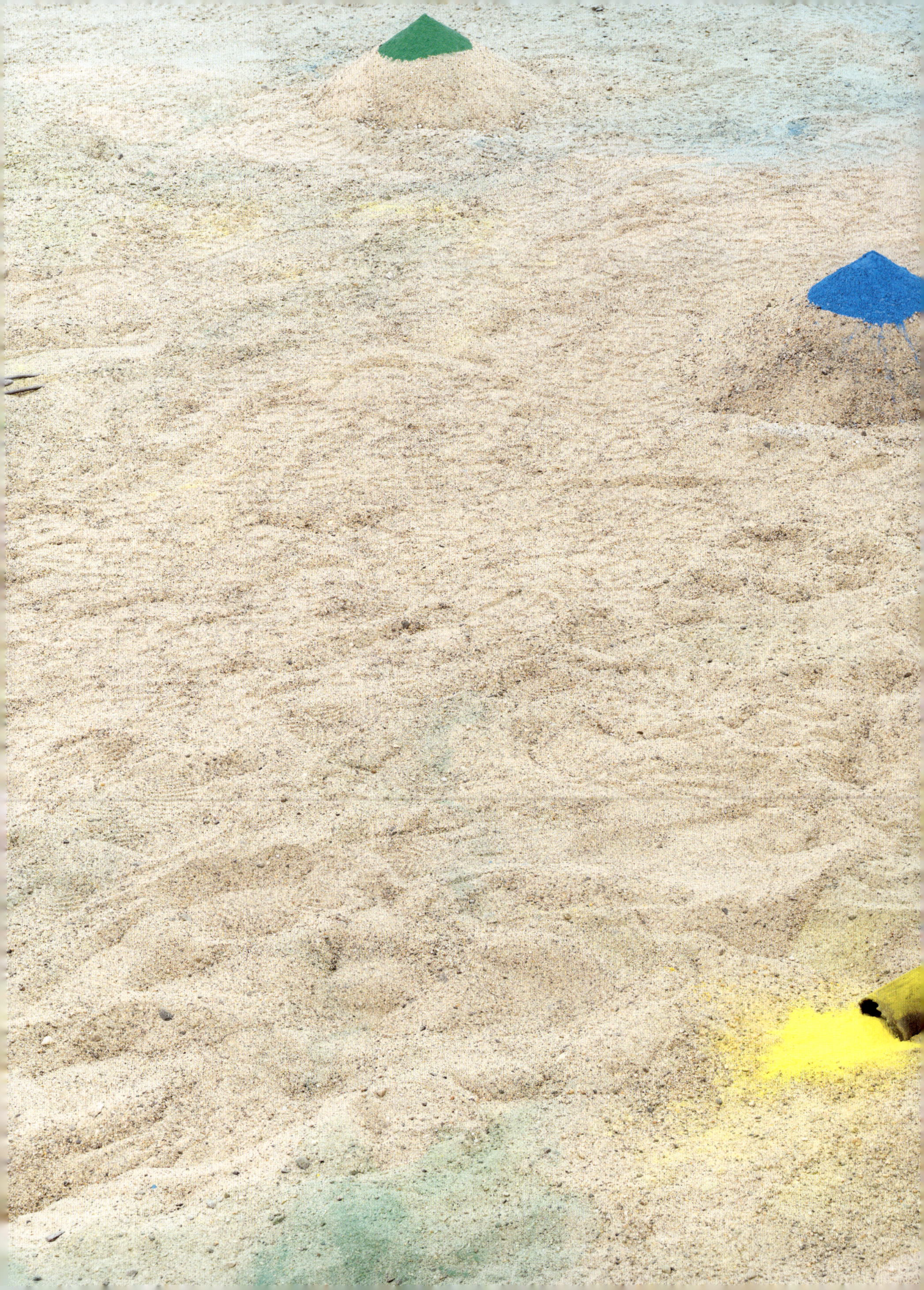

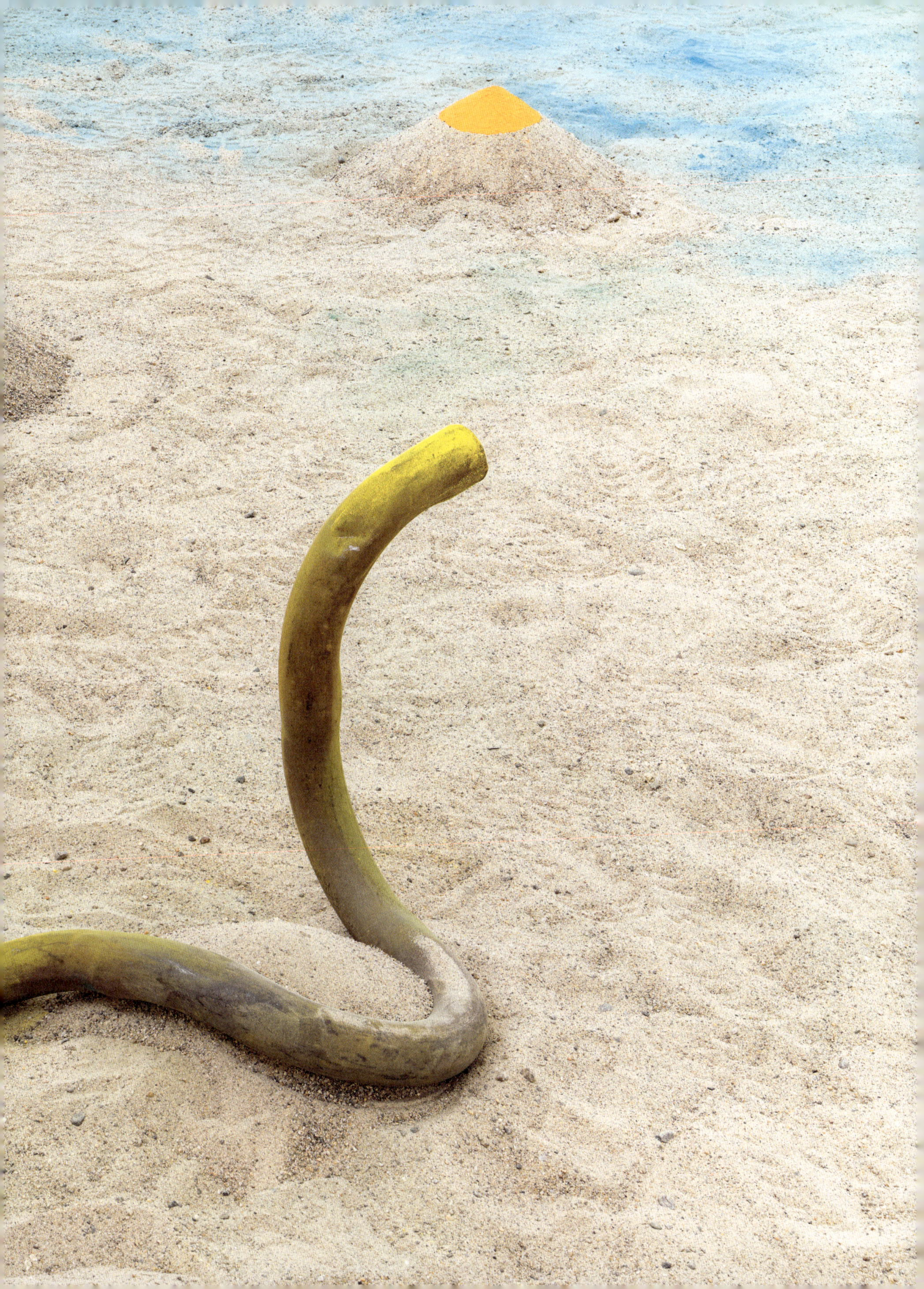

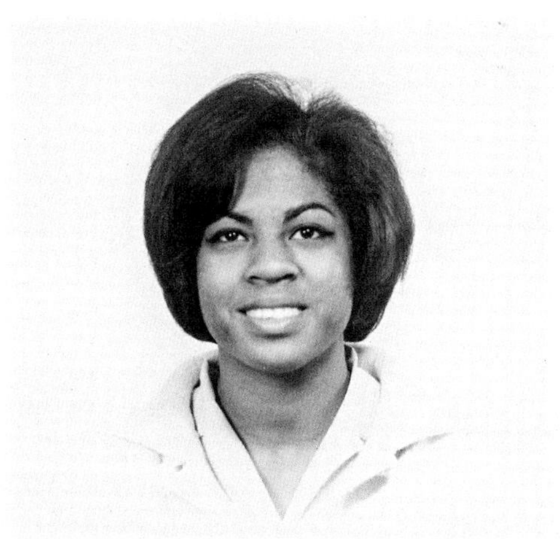

INTRODUCTION

Matilde Guidelli-Guidi

Seated as on thrones
The chorus of before
Call down to us
Be careful, mind your way
This way— this way
—LILY BEA MOOR

"Approach someone and whisper in their ear to do a movement," telegrams one of Senga Nengudi's performance scores. Undated yet stamped with the most liminal of time-space coordinates, "21:59 pm EST," the note is signed: "Subtly, Senga" (ca. 1980s; p. 187).

In its most general sense, *subtlety* denotes that which is diffuse, elusive, and precise; escapes analysis and description; is delicately complex and understated; and is the result of indirect methods. Like a secret always on display, Nengudi's subtlety begins in her play with cultural codes of identity through naming and continues into the capacious range of modes of address in her work, which each time draws the contours of an intimate space for interaction.[1] Whether as a performer or a producer, Nengudi initiated between the mid-1960s and '80s collaborations across experimental dance, film, and music, as well as with local communities, that singularly rechart the maps of Los Angeles and New York's alternative spaces.[2] From Colorado Springs, where she has lived since 1989, she has continued to weave a network of creative partnerships both local and distant that have mutually sustained practices of art and life outside of, yet always in relation to, mainstream institutions of art.[3] Traversed by the currents of improvisation as a means of survival and collaboration, and by ritual as the formal performance of quotidian tasks to reactivate the past, Nengudi's shape-shifting work over the last six decades advances an altogether alternative praxis while attending to the matters of life itself.

Subtlety is locational, too, in that it has to do with where one situates oneself in relation to history. In her life, Nengudi's sculptures and installations went on the record only a handful of times, and her performances have often done without a viewer in any conventional sense.

"I'm an in and out kind of girl," she has said of her infrequent appearances, which tend to skirt protagonism in order to propel presence.[4] Largely realized with the support of her peers and community rather than institutions, her genre-crossing writings, drawings, performances for the camera, and other media work from the past sixty years, a selection of which is presented in this book for the first time, offer manifold expressions of her subtlety in the most sensual operation of the word, done and undone many times over, "yet / there. seen—not / seen—experienced as / part of the air."[5]

WRITINGS

Let's start by going in circles. Nengudi's earliest writings are exercises in observation, alternately turning perception inward to consider her state of mind and outward to events in the world. Written in Los Angeles in July 1965, the poem "Boredom" examines the erotics of boredom as a perpetual dissatisfaction with one's own presence.[6] The only actionable verb here, "to be conquered," is passively drained by a sequence of zero-sum definitions that trade apathy and grief such as, "Boredom is the insane man's excuse for living and the / sane man's excuse for dying." Signed "Miss Sandra," "Boredom" foreshadows Nengudi's lifelong play with personas as a means to circumvent identity and express the metaphysics of youth—the "flirting with things not yet happening."[7]

In 1965, life for the then-twenty-two-year-old artist, however, would have been anything but boring. As an educator at both the Pasadena Museum of Art (PMA) and the Watts Towers Arts Center (WTAC) who was also finishing college at the time, Nengudi was witness to a new era of art experimentation and social practice deployed across the city's institutions, with the PMA catering East Coast Happenings for the upper-class establishment, and the WTAC recently established to foster self-determination and obviate structural neglect in the black community.[8] As an exchange student in Tokyo the following year, Nengudi would compare the Watts Rebellion over police brutality that erupted in Los Angeles in the summer of 1965 to the anti–Vietnam War demonstrations that she experienced on the campus of Waseda University, noting the fallacies of U.S. democracy at home and abroad in a picturesque postcard for an unknown addressee (1967; pp. 48–49). Working within the conventions of postal media, here she explores the complicity afforded by its direct address for the first time.

Twenty years later, Nengudi's radio play *Mouth to Mouth: Conversations on Being—Double Think Bulemia* (1988) infiltrates another media, and the fabrication of stereotypes within it, to broadcast what it means and what it takes for a black artist to "become real within

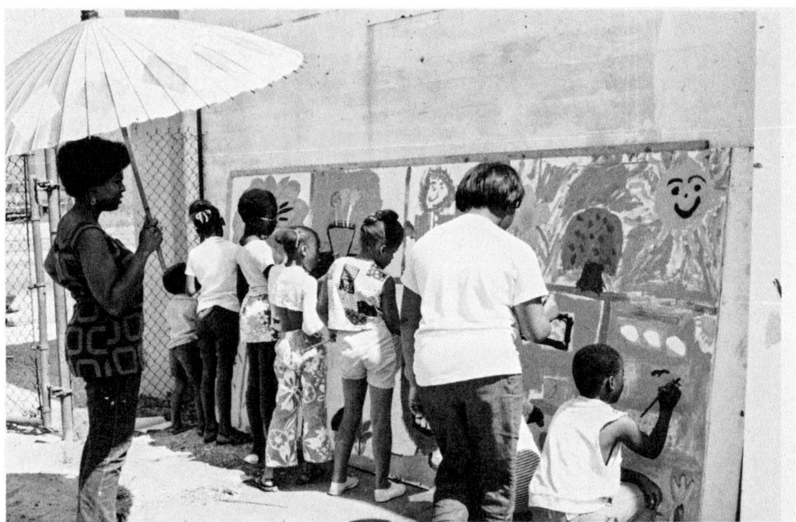

NENGUDI TEACHING A CLASS AT WATTS TOWERS ARTS CENTER, LOS ANGELES, 1965

oneself."[9] Shaping the contours of a state of mind more than a country, Nengudi emcees the worldly and cosmic state of *Bulemia* through scripted conversations with its self-appointed dignitaries, her peers Charles Abramson, Carol Blank, John Outterbridge, Sun Ra, Cecil Taylor, and Kaylynn Sullivan TwoTrees, overlaid with musical interludes by Lawrence "Butch" Morris and other musicians.[10] Her reimagining of W. E. B. Du Bois's double consciousness—a "sense of always looking at oneself through the eyes of others"—vexes the predicament of the visual with the polytempo of the aural.[11]

Employing a range of graphic notations, Nengudi's mature writings have "a feeling of ongoingness."[12] "Space Excursion" and "Time Travel" (both 2004) are prose poems that think through space and time against the realities of history and geometry, probingly moving forward to figure boundlessness or find compromise, to "time travel / Between the lines."[13] Her writing during this period is less observational and more akin to being behind the camera or at the wheel, where motion blurs the lines between seeing, sensing, and afterimage. This is the effect of "Speeding Down the Throughway Boulevard" (1996) where the sight of a white horse while driving, its melancholy figure stark against the whizzing-by of cars, leaves Nengudi breathless with recognition: "the same look and stance must have / come over a slave mother watching / her child being taken away."[14] Intergenerational memory swells in the image, exceeding the order of history and overtaking the narrative flow.[15] Both "Time Travel" and "Speeding Down" explicitly confront the continuum of black death across slavery and its afterlife; Nengudi honors black life by attending to the death of loved ones throughout her work.

Nengudi's writings from this period often reflect a thinking-in-motion about where the art comes from. Sometimes the artist employs drawing as a way to get there without being beholden to the sense-making of paragraphs. *Poetry Plastique* (2004; pp. 212–17) is one such group of works, combining writing and drawing in a mutually generative relationship that sustains art making as a multidimensional practice of discovery.

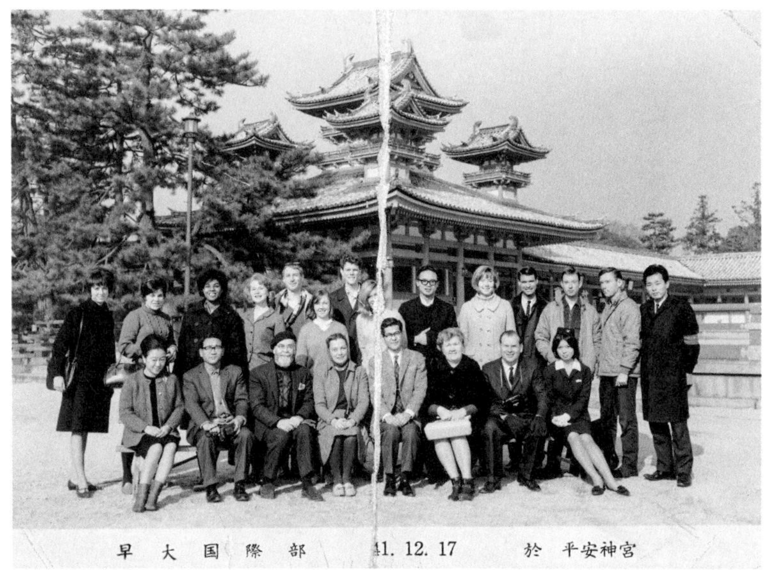

NENGUDI (TOP ROW, THIRD FROM LEFT) WITH WASEDA UNIVERSITY INTERNATIONAL CLUB AT HEIAN SHRINE, KYOTO, DECEMBER 17, 1966

→→ NENGUDI IN HER APARTMENT, EAST 118TH STREET, NEW YORK, CA. 1971–73

The suite begins in the stalemate between the brimming potential and grinning "fear of just sitting down and doing art." Levity floats in the comedic ventriloquy of divine providence, "I am the resurrection and the life," but is anchored by a "scary cat." In the following sheet, writing is reduced to marginal annotation or voice-over for the image which presents two superimposed tracings of the artist's hand, one with her fingers closed and one spread open: "finally got started." The shift from vision to touch provokes erotic jouissance and the incoherence of delineation; soon "frustration" ensues. The graphic line is endowed with the plastic solidity of sculpture in the perfectly balanced seesaw that concludes the suite, ultimately trading weight with sight.[16]

Drawing and writing alternate leading roles in a series of illustrated journal entries from 2008, each one reinventing relationships of causality between word and image. While in "Costume" (p. 227) the titular article of clothing roundly takes the center of the page only to be surrounded and left behind by ant-like ebullient writing, in "Science Fiction" (p. 223) a pointy-headed alien and its stack of weapons compose a recursive loop that overlay the poem with the relentless rhythm of a military soundtrack. As Nengudi comes to realize in "Julian Schnabel on Charlie Rose" (p. 224), thinking things, as opposed to making them, can act as both an art method and a theory of value. The later entry, "Rite Light" (May 16, 2010; pp. 232–33), conjures this mystical pledge by juxtaposing the blinding allure of expenditure ("wealth / beyond compare / aching to be used up / readily available / for unblinking eyes") with a female figure arching her back, on all fours and in lost profile, as if about to spring into the depths of the page.[17]

A voluptuous do-nothing attitude, the assurance of time, and the haptics of air erotically and politically charge a group of poems from the 1990s that redefine common conceptions of work and value.[18] While "Lilies of the Valley, Unite!" (fall 1998) triumphs in the regal refusal to work, "Then(n) am I the Queen Bea / Content to have my Grapes Peeled / Or not," the lines of "Assurances" (May 1993) thread

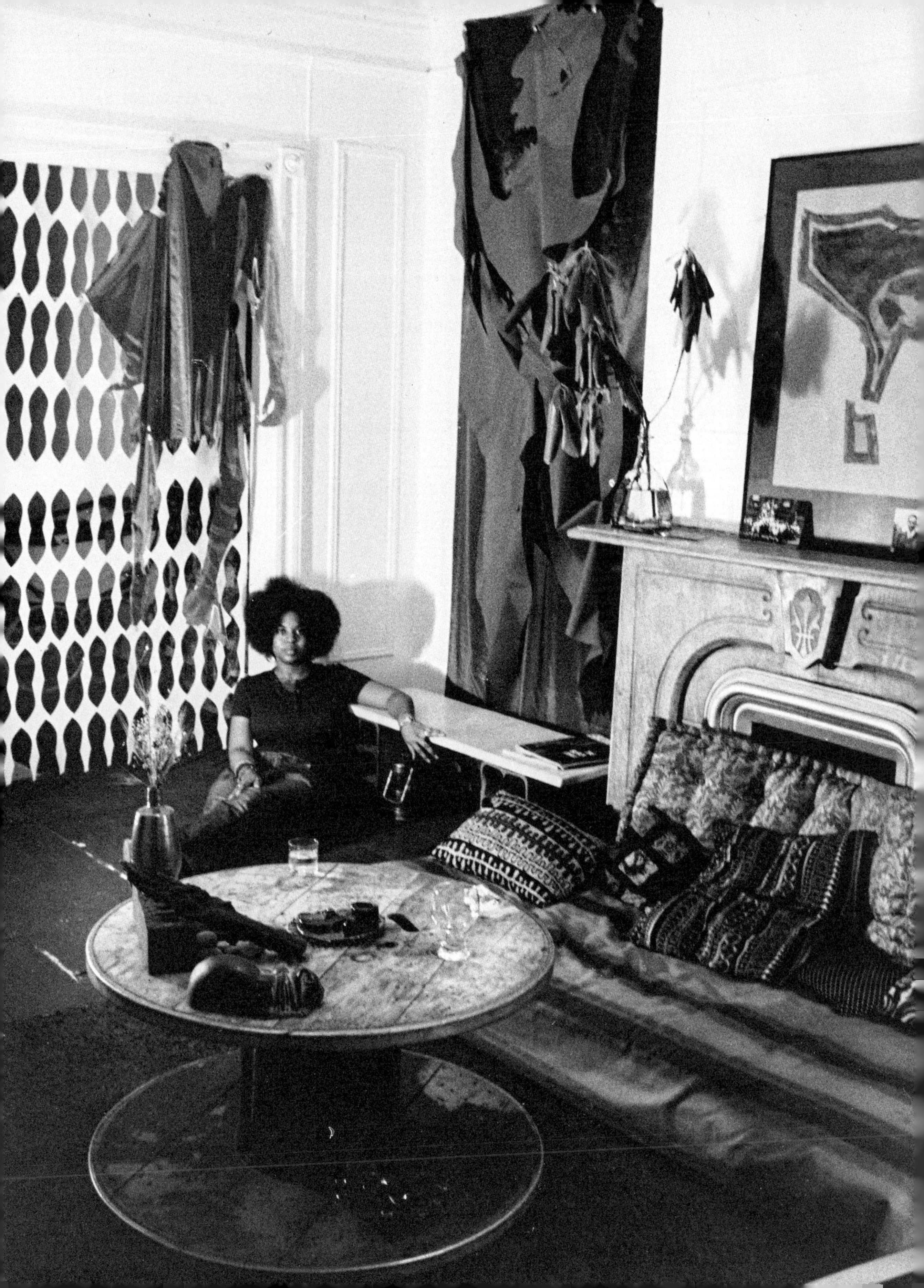

the temporal signature of recursive ritualized gestures across millennia.[19] Elsewhere, movement is communicated not by words but by breath as in "Populated Air" (1997), where she hums the reader out of danger: "Be careful, mind your way / This way— this way."[20]

Nengudi's scores for performance are coded propositions rather than instructions, intended to provoke interplay and break down the walls between performer and audience. With her artist lecture "Performance Truths" (1997; p. 189), for example, she writes herself out of a situation like a comedian would do, shattering power structures with her concisely anarchic act. In 1997, artist Kerry James Marshall invited Nengudi to deliver a lecture at the University of Illinois, Chicago. Midway through her talk, she circulated among the students three hypothetical scenarios: "A few of the things I just told you was a lie," "Some of what I just told you was a lie," and "Most of what I just told you was a lie." Her absurdist mistrust did not put her young audience at ease. In creating uncertainty, she launched a profound critique of the artist lecture as a form and system of value that fixes creativity into relations of influence and scaffolds practice out of provenance.[21]

Like the language-based scores of Fluxus, the prompts collected daily in *Ivy League Notebook* (2001; pp. 190–95) aren't finished until they are realized by a reader.[22] They are invitations that to different degrees shift perception of quotidian activities such as running a business, harboring feelings, or asking "what is black." The scores' essential incompleteness bridges the impasse between words and actions while rustling into art the incontrovertible matters of life itself—sustenance, love, and the cultural production of identity.

DRAWINGS

In Nengudi's drawings, style commences in a performative register, then shape-shifts into subject matter. Never interested in mere illustration, she invents reality by observing it. Increasingly, the page loses neutrality and becomes stage architecture within which her figures contend, as exemplified by three suites of drawings spanning a decade: *West African Sculptures* (1966; pp. 36–47), *Strathmore Sketchbook* (1976–77; pp. 58–67), and *Angst on Pink Paper* (1977; pp. 68–75).

Bodies rendered through the prism of abstraction, aesthetic decisions inflected by material and use, and improvisation within a set vocabulary are some of the traits on display in Nengudi's *West African Sculptures* made in conjunction with a term paper while a student at California State University, Los Angeles.[23] As such, they retain the enthusiasm of discovery while advancing a personal interpretation of the material. Rather than reproducing static art objects, Nengudi finds inspiration in their intended use as dwellings for spirits. In a sleight of hand, she transforms their taxonomic nomenclature into a casual first name, endowing the statuettes with character and individuality. "Bayaka," for example, looks frightened in a contrapuntal pose. His nose points up and eyes droop down, the arms converging close to the chest while the legs splay out and bend, his round face echoing his round belly. Realized in black ink and wetted in places to selectively smudge, blur, and expand the contours of the figures, the suite animates an archive of poses, gestures, and expressions, showing Nengudi's early interest in abstraction and recourse to improvisation as an analytical tool.

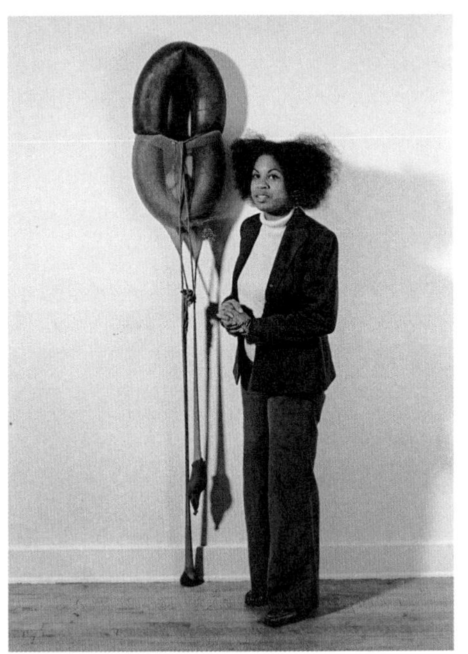

NENGUDI WITH *R.S.V.P. XI*, 2409 WEST SLAUSON AVENUE STUDIO, LOS ANGELES, 1977

Strathmore Sketchbook collects domestic portraits made when the household quiets down and gives way to sleep. Different modes of drawing, from the academic to the stylized, depict various family members and connote a range of moods. Lightly hatched, the house dog lies its muzzle on the bottom-right corner of the sheet, its resting body and legs hinted at by descending angles and curves. A pair of continuous line drawings offers close-up views of Nengudi's two-year-old child, mouth-breathing and rubbing his closed eyes with fists loosened by sleep. The external calm finds its counterpart in a sequence of cartoonish self-portraits that communicates the artist's internal disarray through drawn deformations of her own body. One such drawing attempts to inscribe her silhouette onto the syncopated profile of a West African sculpture, whose elegant stature she fails to match: The artist's arms receive and support her stretched breasts as they outweigh the balanced form that is supposed to contain her. Alien and sentient, her breasts take on an inflated life of their own in drawings that play with the edges of the page as both boundary and ground. In one of these, her nipples-turned-extruded-eyeballs lead the way; in another, she is dwarfed by balloon-like breasts that swell up into the foreground and take over the entire sheet. A third drawing expresses panic as her breasts deflate and wobble down to the bottom of the page.

The physical and emotional drama of deformation and adaptability is central to *Angst on Pink Paper*, a coeval suite of works in which a female figure—the artist's alter ego—grotesquely stretches, morphs, and idles within and against the literal confines of the sheet. Locating herself in the image and in relation to the slender architecture of the paper, the artist acts out her distress while testing her resilience vis-à-vis societal expectations.[24] Affective immediacy is conveyed by an economy of mark making, fast execution, and a combination of the graphic and the pictorial, including red pencil lines and brown brushstrokes that rub the weave out of the paper so that, in places, the visual ends and touch begins. The myriad travails of her condition as a black woman artist, mother, and wife are spatially distributed amid a metamorphic imaginary of available holes, domestic structures, coping mechanisms, and uncontainable body parts. Compositionally, the drawings rely on a system of oppositions. The gravity to which the figure and its parts are subjected is countered by the dynamic upward thrust of the living body, at once bulging and pulling her down—either stretching diagonally corner to corner or vertical and center as a load-bearing column. Rotate the sheet ninety degrees and Nengudi's alter ego is arrested in the shape of a volcano or a dwelling, her breasts anchoring her sloping sides and a conspicuous opening that could be a door or a vagina. Eating as an evasion strategy appears in the form of a gigantic sandwich that stretches edge to edge, a wide-open mouth encroaching upon it from behind. The guiding principle here is tension—emotional, material, and architectural.

By the mid-1970s, the tropes observed in Nengudi's works on paper are sublimated into her sculptures, where flexible materials like

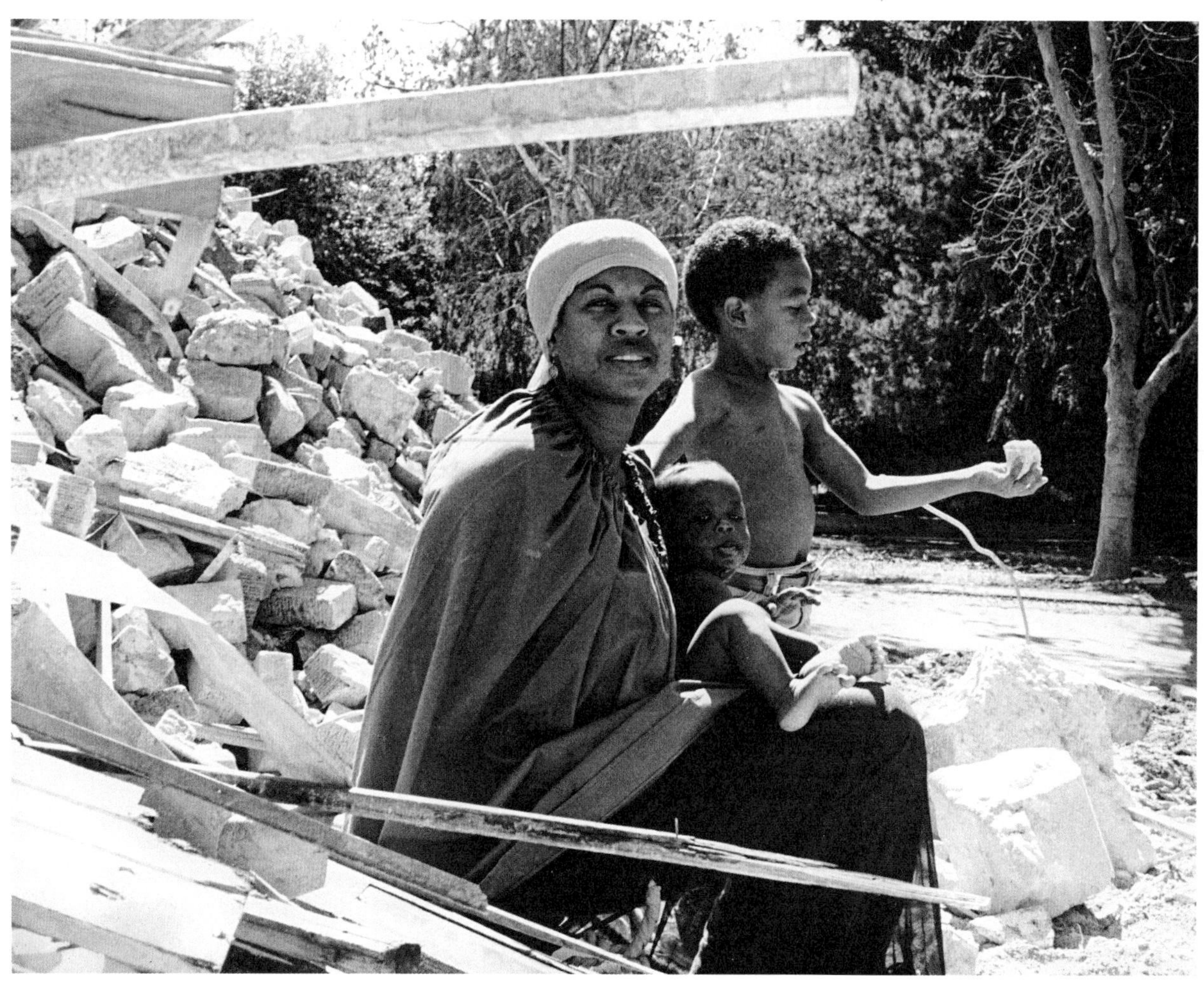

NENGUDI SETTING UP TO PERFORM *URBAN STUDY*, WEST ADAMS BOULEVARD, LOS ANGELES, 1980

nylon and vinyl are set in a relationship both with the sand and water they contain and the parameters of the space that contains them. Attachments, tensions, and resistances are as provisional as they are specific sculptural formations, as affirmed by the set of instructions for her ten-part work, *R.S.V.P. I* (1977). The *R.S.V.P.* sculptures, alternatively called the *Nylon Mesh Series*, debuted in New York and Los Angeles galleries in spring 1977, marking her first solo shows.[25] Taking advice from friends, she chose "nylon mesh" over "pantyhose" to prevent her polysemic works from being read univocally through the lens of gender.[26] Critic John Perreault's review of the New York show, the sole on record, attests to the limits of the gaze. "This is feminist art … and yet it is abstract," he writes, "her materials are pantyhose and sand. And yet the anthropomorphic is so stretched from wall to wall, from floor to ceiling, that the abstract and the personal and the sociological are perfectly wed."[27]

PERFORMANCES

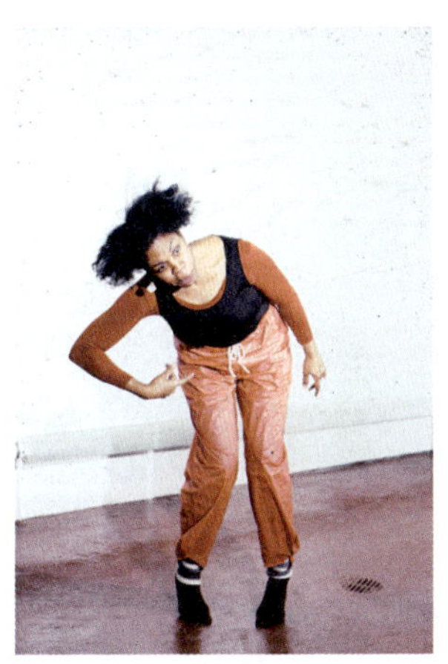

NENGUDI IN *AIR PROPO*, JUST ABOVE MIDTOWN GALLERY, NEW YORK, FEBRUARY 7, 1981

From the outset, the *R.S.V.P.* works set out to be both static compositions and changeable interfaces for contact improvisation. The combining of sculpture and dance is a method that Nengudi began to practice that same year in her studio performances—that is, performances staged for the camera rather than for the public. In those, she articulated a distinct object theater, where the boundaries between prop and performer become porous and blend into one while an internal rhythm paces her movements. Here, stasis is not inertia but vibrant transformation. These photographic sessions respond to her desire to test ideas without the pressure of a live audience and echo the dictum of her friend and collaborator Linda Goode Bryant, to "document, document, document."[28] A dialogue ensues with the photographic apparatus, whose defining features—time, light, and framing—she demonstrably leverages in her hybrid performances.

As if testing the medium by overstressing its most basic parameters, *Mesh Mirage* (1978; pp. 123–25) and *Masked Taping* (1978–79; pp. 126–29), two studio performances photographed by Adam Avila, present rock-solid stillness and its opposite, light-speed movement. She becomes an apotropaic mountain in *Mesh Mirage*, her body sartorially shrouded in craft paper and her head covered by pantyhose that has been cut to the crotch, with a slit for her nose and the legs telescoping her eyes. Calibrated lighting causes her tape-covered silhouette to blur, shimmer, and trail in the dark with each movement in *Masked Taping*, so that she is intermittently recognizable and amorphous.[29] While the exacting eye of Barbara McCullough, avant-garde filmmaker and Nengudi's friend, never imposes direction onto the performance, it certainly can be detected in works such as *Rapunzel* and *Urban Study* (both 1980; pp. 131 and 130).

The neorealist black-and-white aesthetics found, for example, in Charles Burnett's epoch-defining Los Angeles film *Killer of Sheep* (1977) are laid over these improvised tableaux.[30] Both *Rapunzel* and *Urban Study* respond to a situation unfolding on the streets of West Adams, where an old Catholic school, which had been the site of previous activities with Houston Conwill, David Hammons, Maren Hassinger, and Franklin Parker, was being torn down. The event inspired Nengudi to recode the standard of the Madonna and Child in *Urban Study*, substituting the canonical veil with a pantyhose hair wrap, which she then unfurled out of a window and spliced to extruded rebar covered with human hair (a remnant of one of Hammons's hair pieces) as a stand-in for Rapunzel's braids. Referencing the canon while subverting it, her staged appropriations mock the controlling male fantasy of women as virgins in distress.

The freedom one finds in being possessed, or how possession makes you free, is an experience that Nengudi first sought through masquerade and contiguity in her studio performances, often assimilating herself to the objects with which she interacts. These experiments grew equally from her multiple contact points with Afro-diasporic culture—from Sun Ra's capacity to endow the minor trinket with regal status to Katherine Dunham's studies on Haitian dance and how it expresses and embodies possession—and from her experience living in Japan—the framing of myth and slowing down of movement in Noh and Kabuki theater, the humbling architecture of tea ceremonies, and the extreme formality in the approach to routine daily tasks. For Nengudi: "When spirit is inside you, it allows you to let go, a freedom of letting spirit guide you and be free of yourself, free yourself. … I was watching a lot of films on possession, and I wanted to be that free."[31]

In both *Ceremony for Freeway Fets* (1978; pp. 105–15) and *Get-Up* (1980; pp. 141–45), Nengudi extends these explorations to manifest ritual in a public performance setting, probing the mutual transformation that can occur when bodies and sculptures interact. Presented at Paper Mill, the workroom of the Los Angeles Printmaking Society, *Get-Up* featured Conwill and Parker, who, "like prop men in traditional Japanese theater," were instructed to put sculptural forms and found objects onto fellow performers Hassinger and Yolanda Vidado.[32] In *Freeway Fets*, ceremony is also geography: Rather than staking a territory or gaining control over those in attendance, her sculptures afford a shared dimensionality for the ritual dissolve of power dynamics.[33] Nengudi delineated a section of land under the freeway overpass on Pico Boulevard in Los Angeles by strapping her multicolor nylon-and-sand works at the juncture where pillars and bridge meet, letting their globular appendages loose to sway

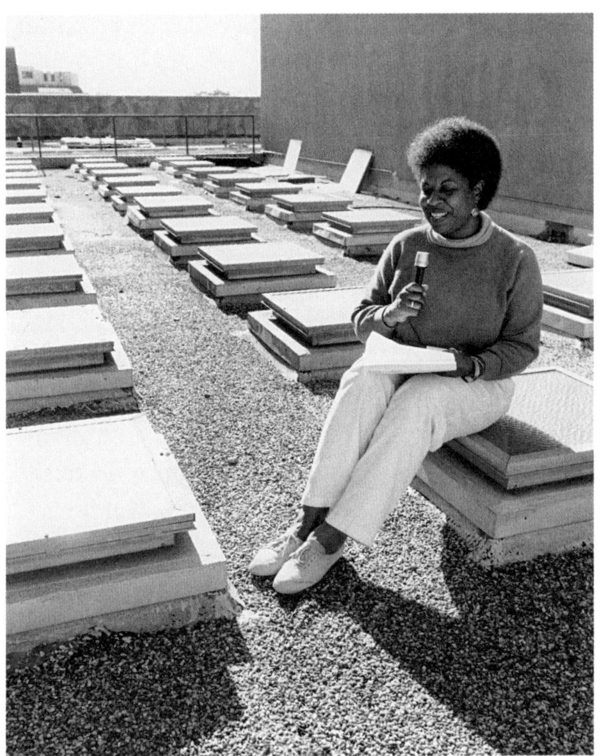

NENGUDI RECORDING *MOUTH TO MOUTH: CONVERSATIONS ON BEING—DOUBLE THINK BULEMIA*, CALIFORNIA STATE UNIVERSITY, LOS ANGELES, 1988

in the wind, gently brushing against the shafts. Within this enclosure, she staged a contemporary play; there was no script but a general underlying concept, unrehearsed and expressed collectively, which alluded to the tensions between men and women in the black community: Hammons and Hassinger impersonated male and female energies that Nengudi harmonized in her role.[34] For the cast and the band, she tailored paper costumes and pantyhose head coverings that partially or totally concealed their faces. "I felt I was someone else, practically possessed," she later recalled.[35]

We hear Nengudi's disembodied voice before we behold her slowly unraveling one such headgear in McCullough's *Shopping Bag Spirits and Freeway Fetishes* (1981; pp. 116–21), a work shot after the performance. In this collection of videotaped interviews, members of the collective Studio Z discuss the concept of ritual in art.[36] Unlike the colloquial delivery of her peers, Nengudi adopts an invocational speech register as she methodically removes nylons in yellow, blue, and brown hues to reveal her face. McCullough captures Nengudi's reflection in a mirror that frames her disguise in a room dense with other shapes and textures, then cuts to a frontal take as the recitation unfolds through and with the unfurling of the mask. Like a cloak, her words fall off her and onto her listeners: "Ritual means to me a ceremonious way of doing things," says Nengudi, "a form of doing it / something that has been done by other people before / generally in the same type of way … new experiences will happen to me / processed in my body / sent out through my hands / to communicate what I feel."

Following *Freeway Fets*, the male-female relationship is a nexus that she continued to explore through the trio form, as seen in *Alive: Kiss* (1980; pp. 136–39) and *Dance Card* (1986; p. 146–47).[37] Staged illicitly at the art gallery of California State University, Los Angeles, *Kiss* is a form of critique that showcases love even toward the exclusionary institution that they break into.[38] With their faces and bodies partially painted, Hassinger, Nengudi, and Parker pose as columns and floor and proceed to kiss the space between the architectural forms they mimic. Parker stands at the center with his arms raised, Hassinger and Nengudi hang from his hands and slowly pirouette, transported by the tune he sings.

The trio disbands as each performer moves freely, upright then crawling, not touching, eyes closed, smacking their lips, emphatically kissing the air. One of Nengudi's few scripted performances, *Dance Card* plays out an archetypal love triangle between a woman and two male suitors within the frame of exaggerated ballroom dancing reminiscent of the work of Rudy Perez, a choreographer with whom both Hassinger and Nengudi trained. The traditional configurations, as if sampled and collaged from popular media, make everything look artificial and picture-ready, as the sound of the camera shutter clicks audibly in the video recording against Butch Morris's cornet improvisation on tape.

Nengudi recalls that *Air Propo* (1981; pp. 148–57) and *Blind Dates* (1982; pp. 166–71), her performances with Just Above Midtown Gallery (JAM), differed from those in Los Angeles, where she improvised with a close-knit group with whom she shared a neighborhood and daily life.[39] At JAM, to work together first meant to create common ground, something thematized in *Blind Dates*, her collaboration with Blondell Cummings and Yasunao Tone about compromise and control.[40] The intermedia soiree resulted in a sequence of vignettes where each performer deployed their singular methodology while letting wires literally and metaphorically cross on stage. Exemplifying his decontrolled approach to performance and deployment of objects to interrupt set composition, Tone presented an early version of his *Molecular Music* (1982–85) while Cummings's own object theater—where objects are implied rather than actual—unfolded in her characteristic jagged movements and repeated actions. Nengudi's blues singing and paced motions culminated in a duet of sorts, a gyratory dance sequence where she was cloaked in a heavy paper costume, each move made concrete by her amplified breathing and crackling paper sounds. The most heightened spiritual aspects of breathing are the through line in *Air Propo*. Air circulates in and out of performers-as-wind-instruments, from Morris's circular-breathing cornet technique to Nengudi's and Cheryl Banks's nostrils, lungs, bodies, and back.

NENGUDI ACTIVATING *MOUNTAIN MOVING DAY*, COLORADO SPRINGS, CA. 2002-

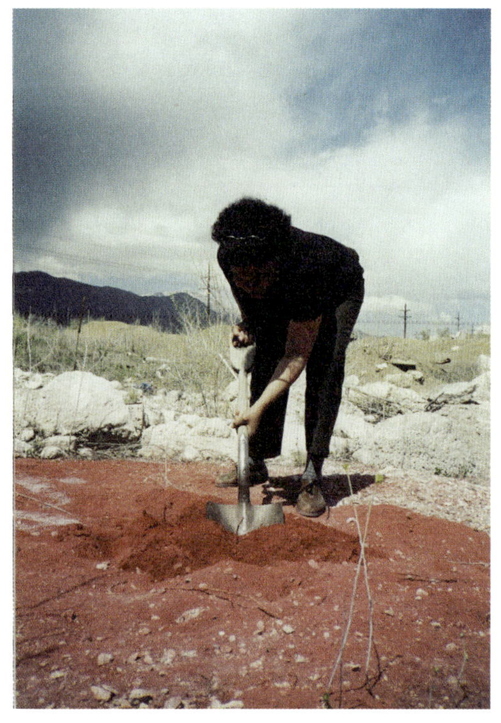

Collaboration in Nengudi's work extends to the living and the dead, and the words of turn-of-the-century feminist poet Yosano Akiko inspire *Mountain Moving Day* (ca. 2002– ; pp. 244–47), a ceremony to be performed yearly as a solo event or with any female-identifying partner. This is Land art according to Nengudi's method, where directional vectors of conquest become an

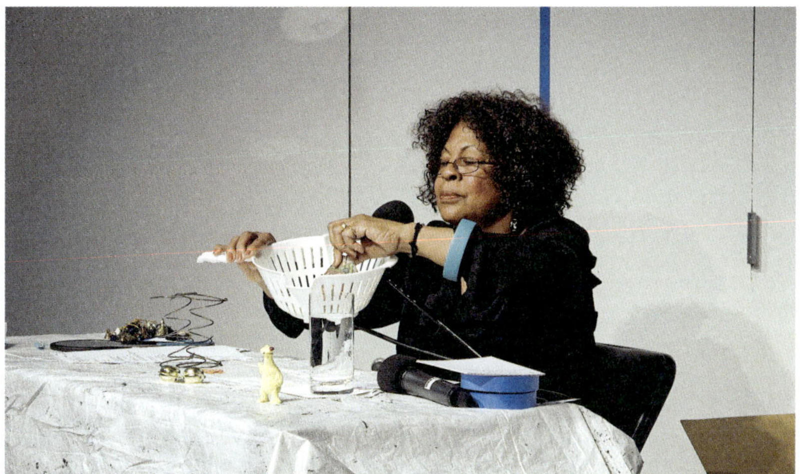

NENGUDI DISCUSSING JOAN JONAS'S WORK, ARTISTS ON ARTISTS LECTURE SERIES, DIA CHELSEA, NEW YORK, MAY 22, 2018

expansive internal process. Limitations of time and place, circumstances in her life, and thoughts that she wants to pursue continue to shape and inflect the artist's projects and aesthetic decisions to this day. In the early 2000s, while tending to her homebound mother in Colorado Springs, Nengudi began to employ the expressivity of her hands in domestic performances, such as in *Hands* and *Hands and Tape* (both 2001; pp. 240–41 and 236–39), that explore how basic gestures communicate and how ritual plays out in a quotidian setting. In these works Nengudi employs the fold—a formal operation where shape is a function of time turned onto itself—to exemplify the primacy of ritualized movement in reactivating the past. She considers the limits of aging in the measured range of her gestures, which are multidimensional rather than representational acts, much like Nengudi's oeuvre as a whole.

Profoundly concise and made from a deep-seated knowing, the works presented in *Populated Air* deploy registers from the comedic and the erotic to the surreptitious and the invocational to delineate boundlessness between permanence and transience, a space where the embodiment of relationships can be triumphantly visible or purely energetic.

Epigraph: Lily Bea Moor, "Populated Air" (1997), in this volume, p. 205.

In addition to the sources cited in this essay, the editors thank Senga Nengudi and those who provided information about her work through in-person and telephone discussions, most especially Thomas Erben, keyon gaskin, Linda Goode Bryant, Maren Hassinger, Suzanne Jackson, Barbara McCullough, Lorraine O'Grady, sidony o'neal, and Yasunao Tone.

1 Having consulted friends from Congo and Zimbabwe, the artist changed her name from Sue Irons to Senga Nengudi in 1974, meaning "auntie of the village that people come to for advice" and "woman who comes to power as a traditional healer." Senga Nengudi, "Senga Nengudi: Black Avant Garde Visual and Performance Artist," conducted by Bridget Cooks and Amanda Tewes in 2020, Oral History Center, Bancroft Library, University of California, Berkeley, 2022, under the auspices of the J. Paul Getty Trust, 2022, p. 8. In the 1990s, she adopted the monikers Lily Bea Moor for her poetry, Propecia Leigh for her photography, and Harriet Chin for her drawings.

2 On this topic, see in particular Kellie Jones, *South of Pico: African-American Artists in Los Angeles in the 1960s and 1970s* (Duke University Press, 2017); Daniel Widener, *Black Arts West: Culture and Struggle in Postwar Los Angeles* (Duke University Press, 2010); Thomas (T.) Jean Lax and Lilia Rocio Taboada, eds., *Just Above Midtown: Changing Spaces* (The Museum of Modern Art and The Studio Museum in Harlem, 2022).

3 Most notable is Nengudi's creative partnership with Maren Hassinger, which started in Los Angeles in the late 1970s and intensified during this time, when the two artists resided in different places but shared experiences of being caregivers, mothers, and wives while continuing to develop "techniques for staying whole and creative." Nengudi, "Maren and Me," African American Performance Art Archive, 2009, https://aapaa.org/artists/senga-nengudi/maren-and-me/.

4 Nengudi, conversation with the author, Colorado Springs, August 2022.

5 Nengudi, "Assurances" (May 1993), in this volume, p. 204.

6 Miss Sandra, "Boredom" (July 14, 1965), in this volume, p. 35.

7 "You can note Miss Sandra is a pre-persona." Nengudi, Zoom conversation with the editors, August 28, 2024. Tan Lin, "Warhol's Aura and the Language of Writing: A World of Likenesses," *Cabinet*, no. 4 (Fall 2001), https://www.cabinetmagazine.org/issues/4/lin.php.

8 Allan Kaprow and Jim Dine debuted their Happenings at the Pasadena Museum of Art. "With happenings you could do things that were kind of side interests you weren't fully talented in it, but you could incorporate that into your performance." Nengudi, conversation with the author, Colorado Springs, August 2022. "Noah Purifoy was one of her mentors." Barbara McCullough, telephone conversation with the editors, September 18, 2024.

9 *Mouth to Mouth: Conversations on Being—Double Think Bulemia* (December 15, 1988), in this volume, p. 172. *Bulemia* (1988) was also a room-size installation that Nengudi realized for the watershed exhibition, *Art as Verb: The Evolving Continuum*, organized by Leslie King-Hammond and Lowery Stokes Sims, Maryland Institute College of Arts, Baltimore, November 21, 1988–January 8, 1989.

10 Because of Abramson's sudden death, comedian Darryl Sivad voiced his lines. Part one of two programs, after its broadcast on December 15, 1988, NPR executives retracted their association due to what they had labeled sensitive content. The second, never-released program, *A Series from A to Z (Part A)*, is a three-part conversation with Sun Ra and Cecil Taylor, "On life, death and the fear of living. It exposes the emotional frailties of managing the death of a loved one; it touches the despair and cries for help from someone who is afraid to love; and offers an affirmation of life and the prescription for living." Senga Nengudi Papers, series 5, box 9, folder 15, Archives of American Art (AAA), Smithsonian Institution.

11 W. E. B. Du Bois, *The Souls of Black Folk* (1903; repr., Penguin Books, 1996), p. 8.

12 Renee Gladman, *My Lesbian Novel* (Dorothy, 2024), p. 7.

13 Nengudi, "Space Excursion" (June 22, 2004), in this volume, p. 221; Nengudi, "Time Travel" (June 22, 2004), in this volume, p. 220.

14 Nengudi, "Speeding Down the Throughway Boulevard" (1996), in this volume, p. 203.

15 Similarly, Nengudi has noted, "Lorna Simpson's piece, it's a grid of mouths, and what they're humming is, 'It's Easy to Remember (And So Hard to Forget).' This is kind of in our memory, but we kind of squash it down, because you can't function otherwise, but it's not forgotten. So if you ask any given person, they'll say, 'Oh yeah, George Floyd.' But then there was Emmett Till or—you know?" Nengudi, "Black Avant Garde Visual and Performance Artist," p. 98.

16 sidony o'neal and keyon gaskin, Zoom conversation with the author, November 5, 2024. Nengudi realized the seesaw sculpture for the first time in 2024 and directed o'neal and gaskin's contact improvisation performance on it, *See-see Riders*, organized by Allie Tepper, Reed College, Portland, February–March 2024.

17 "It is necessary to reserve the use of the word *expenditure* for the designation of unproductive forms, and not for the designation of all modes of consumption that serve as a means to the end of production." Georges Bataille, "The Notion of Expenditure," in *Visions of Excess: Selected Writings, 1927–1939* (University of Minnesota Press, 1985), p. 18.

18 Nengudi intended to collect these in a book titled *Assurances*, conversation with the author, Colorado Springs, August 2022.

19 Lily Bea Moor, "Lilies of the Valley, Unite!" (fall 1998), in this volume, pp. 209–11.

20 Moor, "Populated Air," p. 205.

21 "I hate doing lectures. I was circling about and midway into my talk, I sent each one of these around. This was pre-Trump. It shook people up so much, almost to their core. Once you say something like that, people don't trust you. They don't know what to trust." Nengudi, Zoom conversation with the editors, July 2024.

22 This notebook, like many other daily works in this book, was realized in correspondence with Maren Hassinger. Hassinger and Nengudi, conversation with the author, Dia Beacon, New York, February 14, 2023.

23 Sue Irons, "Sculpture of the Primitive Peoples of the Western Congo and Gabon," unpublished paper submitted in April 1966 for the class Primitive Art History. Nengudi remembers that her instructor accused her of plagiarism. Nengudi, conversation with the author, Colorado Springs, August 2022.

24 "Oh these, these are my angst on paper . . . about images, body images, and my angst, you might say. The pink is intentional, the colors are intentional, all of that." Nengudi, Zoom conversation with the editors, August 29, 2024.

25 *Senga Nengudi: Répondez S'il Vous Plaît*, Just Above Midtown Gallery, New York, March 8–26, 1977. *Senga Nengudi: Nylon Mesh Series*, Pearl C. Woods Gallery, Los Angeles, May 13–29, 1977.

26 Josine Ianco-Starrels, her friend and then-director of the Municipal Art Gallery at Los Angeles's Barnsdall Art Park where Nengudi and her crew presented projects, allusively advised: "You can't call it pantyhose, you have to call it nylon mesh, because people [will devalue it] . . ." Nengudi, "Black Avant Garde Visual and Performance Artist," p. 93.

27 John Perreault, "Stretching It: Senga Nengudi at Just Above Midtown," *Soho Weekly News*, March 24, 1977, p. 22.

28 Linda Goode Bryant, conversation with the author, Dia Beacon, New York, February 14, 2023.

29 Entrusted to Goode Bryant, these enigmatic images infiltrated downtown New York and were printed on Just Above Midtown Gallery invitation cards, book covers, playbills, and newspaper ads into the following decade.

30 McCullough, telephone conversation with the editors, September 11, 2024.

31 Nengudi, telephone conversation with the editors, September 19, 2024.

32 Nengudi, "Get-Up," Senga Nengudi Papers, series 5, box 9, folder 30, AAA. A member of the Printmaking Society, Houston Conwill secured the space. The performance was accompanied by improvised music by oft-collaborator Roberto Miranda with Billy Hinton and Sabir Mateen.

33 "Ceremony is the continual disruption of the formation of the structural opposition that creates an us and a them or the geo-epistemology of the line." Tiffany Lethabo King, *The Black Shoals: Offshore Formations of Black and Native Studies* (Duke University Press, 2019), p. 204.

34 "Some columns represented female energy, the others male energy. On one column I inscribed the names of our children, on another the name of our ancestors, relatives, and personal friends, some of whom has succumbed to the dis-ease of being black in America." Nengudi, "Freeway Fets," Senga Nengudi Papers, series 5, box 9, folder 30, AAA.

35 Nengudi, telephone conversation with the editors, September 19, 2024.

36 McCullough, *Shopping Bag Spirits and Freeway Fetishes: Reflections on Ritual Space* (1981), in this volume, pp. 116–21. From 1976 through the end of the decade, Studio Z included Conwill, Kathy Cyrus, Ron Davis, Greg Edwards, David Hammons, Duval Lewis, McCullough, Franklin Parker, Joe Ray, RoHo, and Roderick "Kwaku" Young. The group used the 2409 West Slauson Avenue studio that Hammons and Nengudi shared as a venue for their work and to host concerts of their peers.

37 First performed in 1986 at the Contemporary Arts Forum, Santa Barbara, under the site-specific sculpture *Blanket of Branches* (1986) by Hassinger, *Dance Card* was reprised and photographed in McCullough's apartment.

38 Of her collaborative work in these years, Nengudi has said: "There's the fighting of the mainstream trying to keep you in a little ball, and then there's the fighting of your own community saying, 'You have to do it this way. The world is looking at us,' and so it puts a lot of restrictions on you. So we just didn't want it to go further, and still explore blackness, but in a very different way." Nengudi, "Black Avant Garde Visual and Performance Artist," p. 97.

39 Nengudi, Zoom conversation with the editors, August 2024.

40 For a video recording of *Blind Dates*, see: https://vimeo.com/82061010.

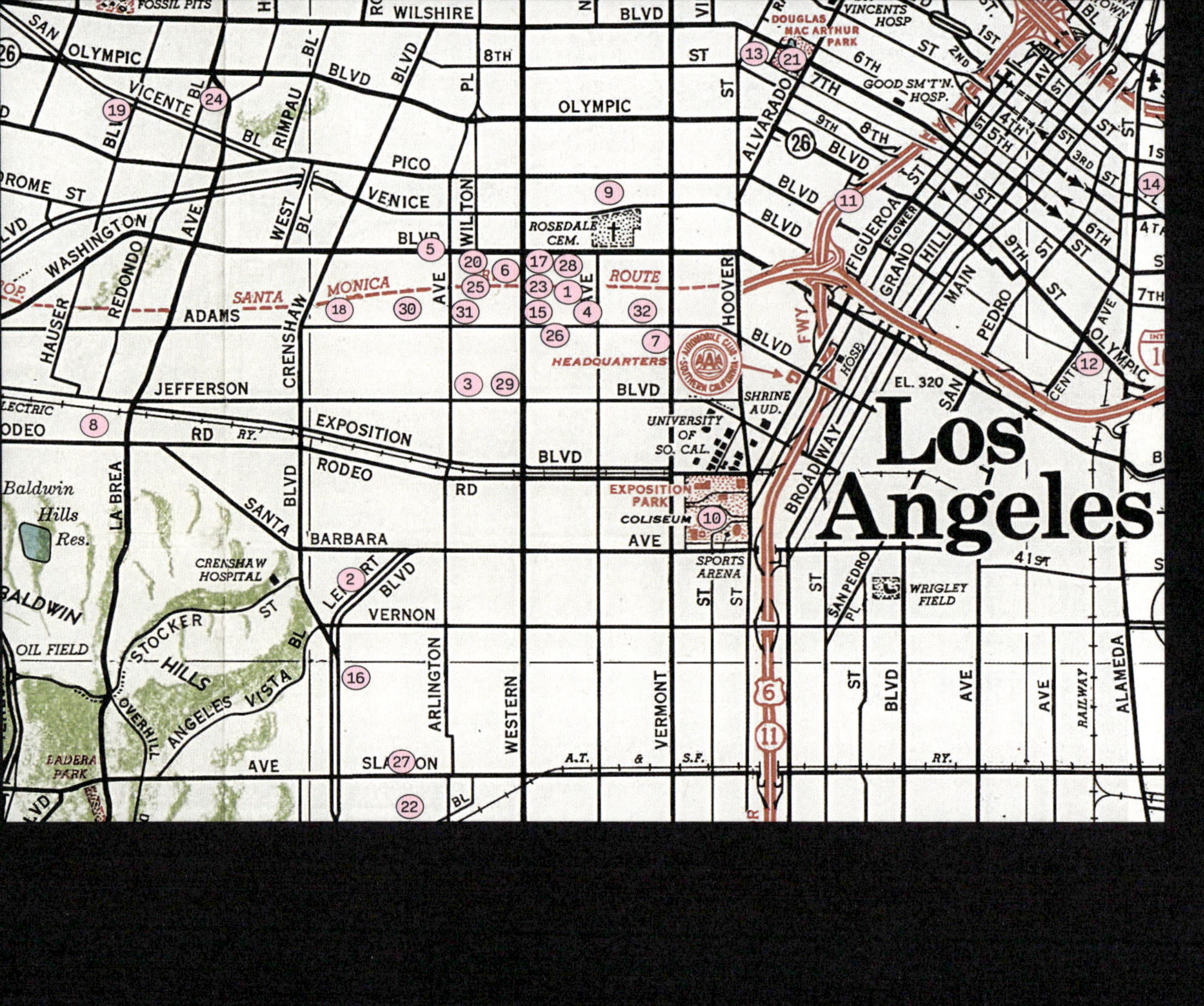

Los Angeles
WILSHIRE
BLVD
OLYMPIC
SAN VICENTE BL
RIMPAU BL
8TH PL
PICO
VENICE BLVD
WASHINGTON
REDONDO
HAUSER
WEST BL
CRENSHAW
WILTON
ROSEDALE CEM.
SANTA MONICA ROUTE
ADAMS
HOOVER
HEADQUARTERS
JEFFERSON BLVD
EXPOSITION BLVD
RODEO RD
UNIVERSITY OF SO. CAL.
SHRINE AUD.
EXPOSITION PARK
COLISEUM
SPORTS ARENA
LA BREA
Baldwin Hills Res.
BALDWIN
OIL FIELD
CRENSHAW HOSPITAL
STOCKER ST
HILLS
ANGELES VISTA BL
OVERHILL
LADERA PARK
SANTA BARBARA AVE
LEIMERT BLVD
VERNON
ARLINGTON
WESTERN
VERMONT
SLAUSON
A.T. & S.F. RY.
ALVARADO
DOUGLAS MAC ARTHUR PARK
VINCENTS HOSP
GOOD SM'T'N. HOSP.
FIGUEROA
FLOWER
GRAND
HILL
MAIN
SAN PEDRO
BROADWAY
HARBOR FWY
EL. 320
WRIGLEY FIELD
CENTRAL AVE
ALAMEDA
41 ST

1. BARBARA MCCULLOUGH'S HOMEBASE
SITE OF THE OPENED I, INC., ARTS NONPROFIT
1832-1834 WEST 24TH STREET

2. BROCKMAN GALLERY
4334 DEGNAN BOULEVARD

3. BUDDHIST CENTER
2500 CIMARRON STREET
A BUDDHIST PRIEST PLAYED A DRUM TO BLESS OUR NEIGHBORHOOD ON A DAILY BASIS

4. BUTCH MORRIS'S REHEARSAL SPACE
1830 WEST 24TH STREET

5. CATHOLIC SCHOOL
ARLINGTON AVENUE & WASHINGTON BOULEVARD
SITE OF *RAPUNZEL* AND *URBAN STUDY* (BOTH 1980)

6. CHABELITA
2001 SOUTH WESTERN AVENUE
FORMER TACO AND BURRITO PLACE ACROSS FROM PEARL C. WOODS GALLERY

7. DAVID HAMMONS'S OPEN-AIR STUDIO
ADAMS BOULEVARD & VERMONT AVENUE
SITE OF HIS INTERVIEW FOR *SHOPPING BAG SPIRITS AND FREEWAY FETISHES: REFLECTIONS ON RITUAL SPACE* (1981), A DOCUMENTARY BY BARBARA MCCULLOUGH

8. DORSEY HIGH SCHOOL
3537 FARMDALE AVENUE
ALONZO AND DALE DAVIS, BOB KARDASHIAN, GREG PITTS, AND I ALL ATTENDED THIS HIGH SCHOOL. KARDASHIAN WAS STUDENT BODY PRESIDENT IN MY SOPHOMORE YEAR

9. ERIC DOLPHY'S PARENTS' HOME
ACROSS THE STREET FROM NORMANDIE PLAYGROUND

10. EXHIBITION PARK
700 EXPOSITION PARK DRIVE

11. *CEREMONY FOR FREEWAY FETS* PERFORMANCE SITE
UNDER THE FREEWAY AT PICO BOULEVARD & FIGUEROA STREET

12. GALLERY 1015
1015 CENTRAL AVENUE

13. GALLERY 32
672 SOUTH LA FAYETTE PARK PLACE
SUZANNE JACKSON'S GALLERY

14. *GET-UP* PERFORMANCE SITE
800 NORTH TRACTION AVENUE
THE PAPER MILL, LOS ANGELES PRINTMAKING SOCIETY

15. GOLDEN STATE MUTUAL LIFE INSURANCE COMPANY BUILDING
1999 WEST ADAMS BOULEVARD
DESIGNED BY PAUL WILLIAMS AND HAD THE LARGEST AFRICAN AMERICAN ART COLLECTION AT ONE POINT

16. HORACE TAPSCOTT'S REHEARSAL SPACE
4901 11TH AVENUE
UNION OF GOD MUSICIANS AND ARTISTS ASCENSION HOUSE AND SITE OF THE PAN AFRIKAN PEOPLES ARKESTRA

17. JOHNNY OTIS'S HOUSE
2077 SOUTH HARVARD BOULEVARD

18. JOHNNY'S PASTRAMI
4327 WEST ADAMS BOULEVARD

19. MAREN HASSINGER'S HOUSE/STUDIO
5617 SAN VICENTE BOULEVARD

20. MARVIN GAYE'S PARENTS' HOUSE
2101 SOUTH GRAMERCY PLACE
SITE OF GAYE'S DEATH ON APRIL 1, 1984

21. MACARTHUR PARK
WILSHIRE BOULEVARD & ALVARADO STREET

22. NELLIE LUTCHER'S HOUSE

23. PEARL C. WOODS GALLERY
WESTERN AVENUE AT SANTA MONICA FREEWAY
GREG PITTS RAN THIS GALLERY IN THE ACTIVITY ROOM OF THE COMMUNITY BUILDING OF THE TRIANGULAR CHURCH OF RELIGIOUS SCIENCE, THE FIRST BLACK INTERDENOMINATIONAL CHURCH IN LOS ANGELES, FOUNDED IN 1932 BY HIS GRANDMOTHER PEARL C. WOODS. AT ONE TIME THE CHURCH HAD OVER 1000 MEMBERS, AUGMENTED BY JAZZ IMPRESARIO FATS WALLER AND OTHER CELEBRITIES

24. POETS' HOMEBASE
SAN VICENTE BOULEVARD & LA BREA AVENUE
SITE OF INTERVIEWS WITH KAMAU DAÁOOD, K. CURTIS LYLE, AND KENNETH SEVERIN FOR *SHOPPING BAG SPIRITS* AND *FREEWAY FETISHES*

25. SENGA'S HOUSE
2158 WEST 24TH STREET
PREVIOUS OWNER HOSTED LANGSTON HUGHES WHILE HUGHES WAS GIVING A TALK AT UCLA

26. SENGA'S STUDIO ON WEST ADAMS
LASALLE STREET & WEST ADAMS BOULEVARD

27. STUDIO Z
HAMMONS'S STUDIO (ENTIRE DANCE HALL ON TOP FLOOR)
ROHO'S STUDIO (GROUND FLOOR)
2409 WEST SLAUSON AVENUE
PERFORMANCES BY THE ART ENSEMBLE OF CHICAGO, JULIUS HEMPHILL, AND OLIVER LAKE WERE ALSO HOSTED HERE

28. SUZANNE JACKSON'S HOUSE
1649 SOUTH HOBART BOULEVARD

29. THE MILLS BROTHERS' HOUSE
JEFFERSON BOULEVARD & WESTERN AVENUE

30. THE WILFANDEL CLUB
3425 WEST ADAMS BOULEVARD
IN 1945 A GROUP OF 50 LIKE-MINDED BLACK WOMEN CAME TOGETHER TO CREATE THIS HISTORIC CLUBHOUSE AS A COMMUNITY SPACE FOR BLACK CELEBRATION AND CULTURAL LIFE. THE CLUB OFTEN HOSTED NOTABLE BLACK ARTISTS AND WRITERS; I ONCE HEARD JAMES BALDWIN SPEAK HERE

31. UCLA WILLIAM ANDREW CLARK MEMORIAL LIBRARY
2520 CIMARRON STREET
SITE OF INSPIRATION AND PRIVATE IMPROVISATIONS

32. ULYSSES JENKINS'S HOMEBASE
VERMONT AVENUE & WEST ADAMS BOULEVARD
SITE OF OTHERVISIONS STUDIO

populated air

THERE IS SUCH A THING AS BOREDOM

IT CAN BE FELT IN THE MOST EXHILRATING MOMENTS

WHY DOES BOREDOM EXIST - TO BE CONQUERED

BOREDOM IS THE FEELING OF IN BETWEENESS

OF BEING SLEEPY BUT NOT REALLY SLEEPY

IT IS THE FEELING OF WANTING TO BE SOMEWHERE ELSE,

BUT WHEN YOU GET THERE WANTING TO BE SOMEWHERE ELSE AGAIN

BOREDOM IS THE INSANE MAN'S EXCUSE FOR LIVING AND THE

SAN MAN'S EXCUSE FOR DYING

- Miss Sandra

Miss Sandra

7/14/65

1/100

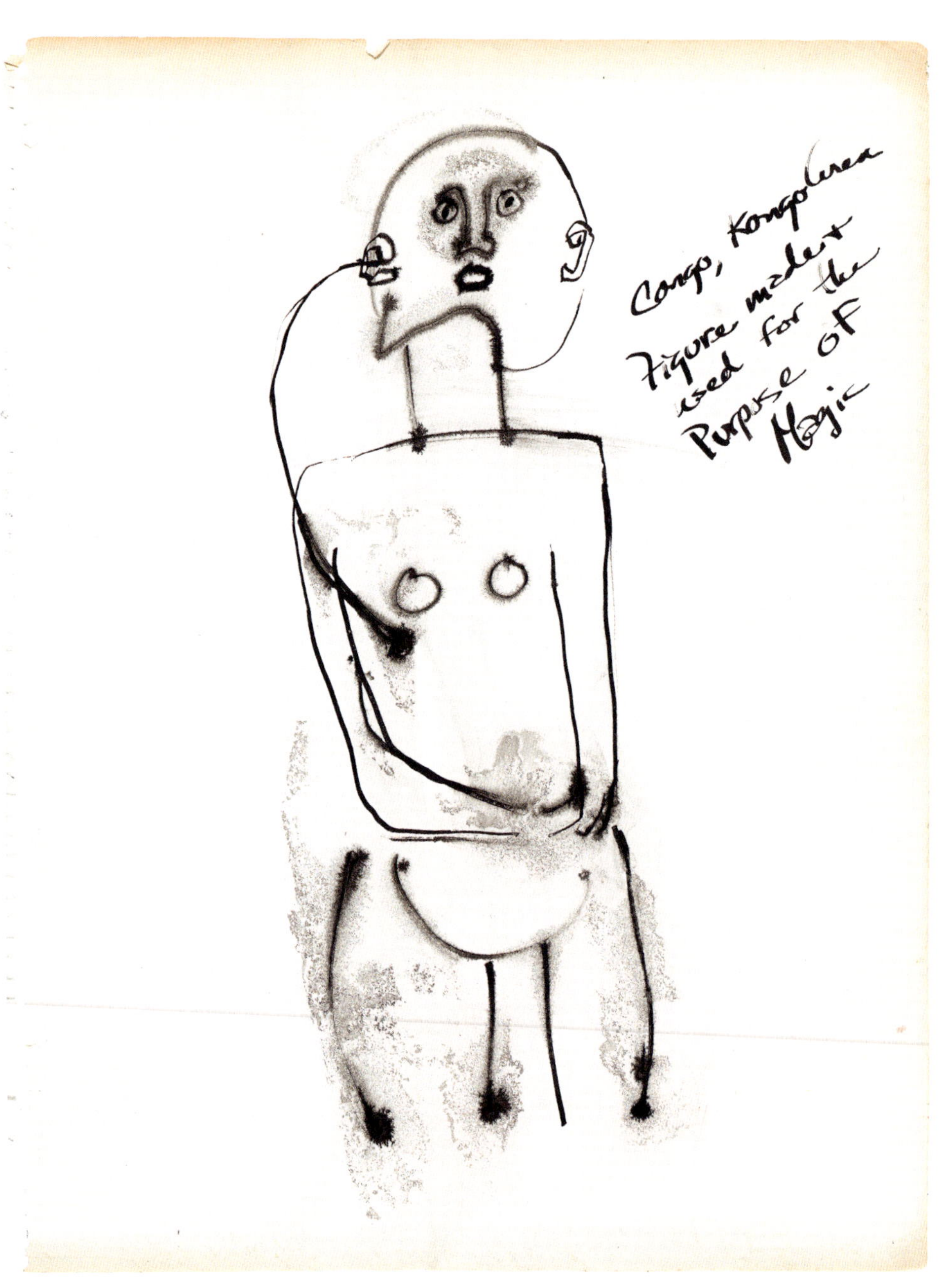

SUE IRONS, *WEST AFRICAN SCULPTURES*, 1966
INK ON PAPER, 12 PARTS:
12 × 9 INCHES (30.5 × 22.9 CM) EACH

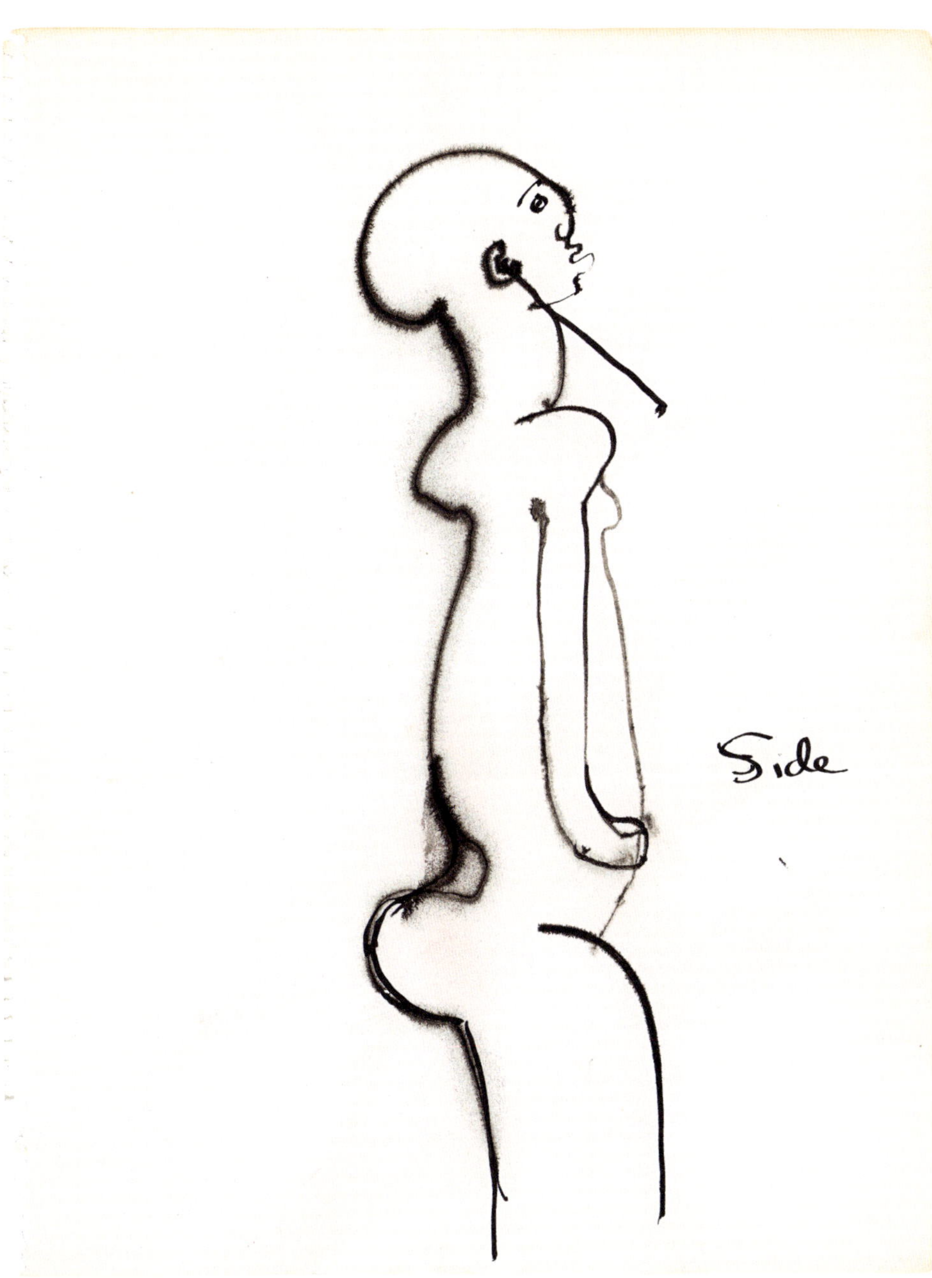
Side

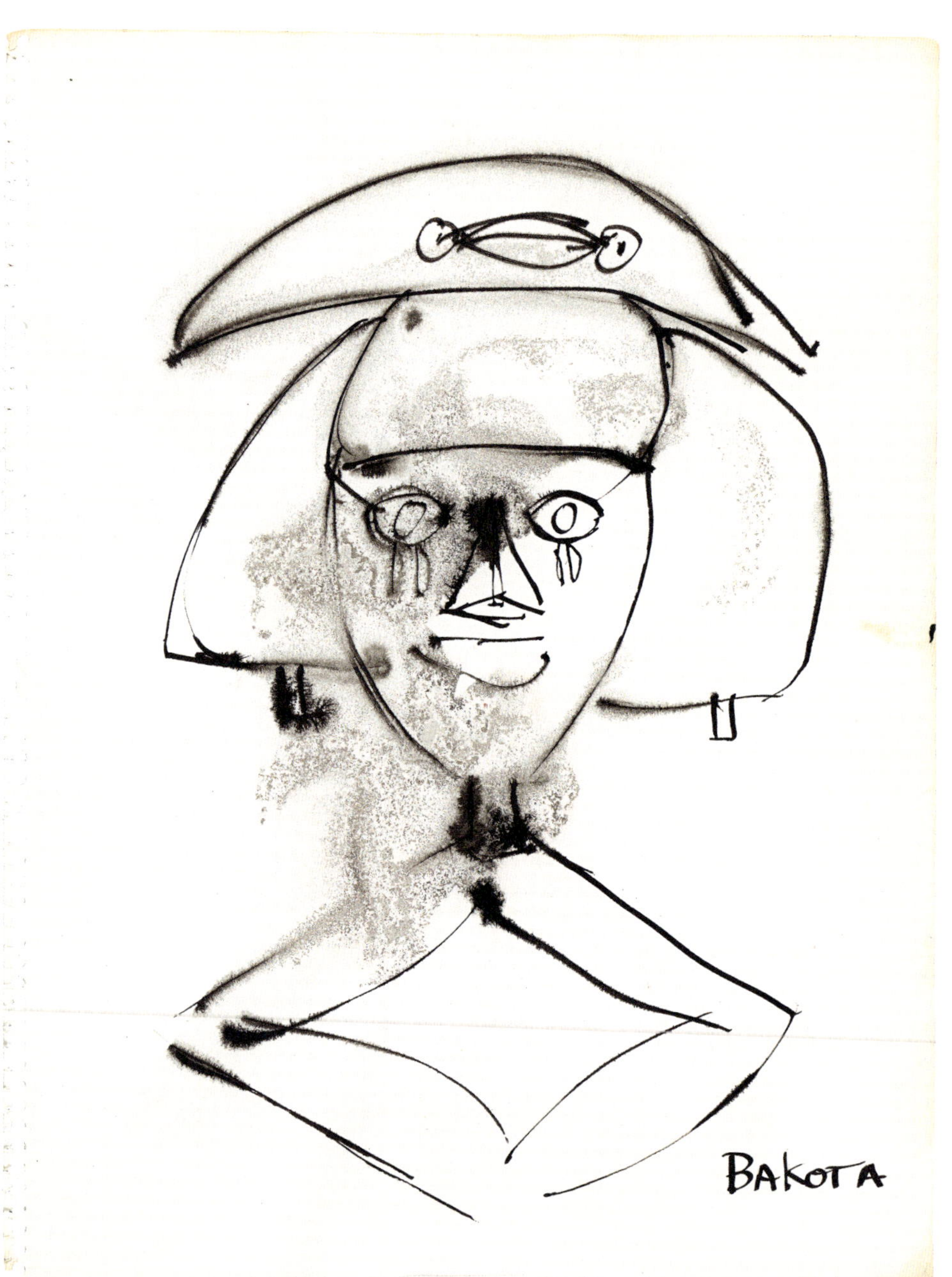
BAKOTA

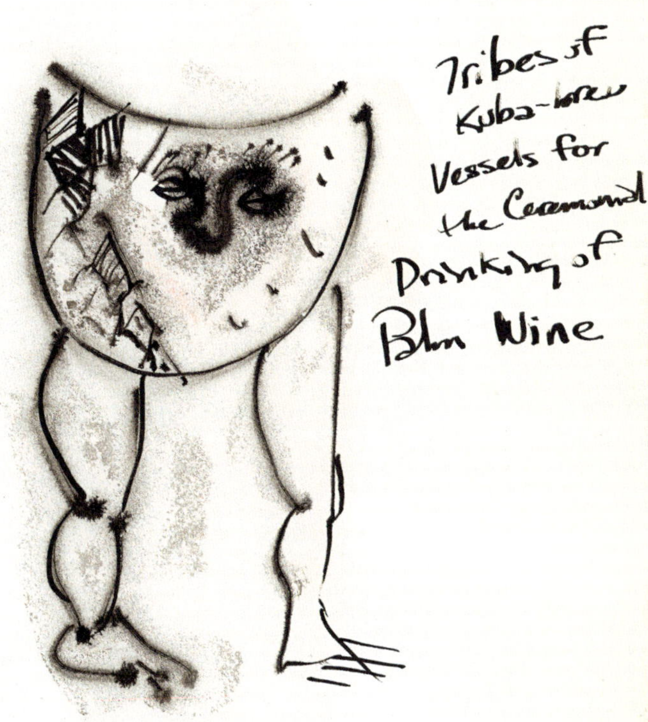
Tribes of
Kuba-
Vessels for
the Ceremonial
Drinking of
Palm Wine

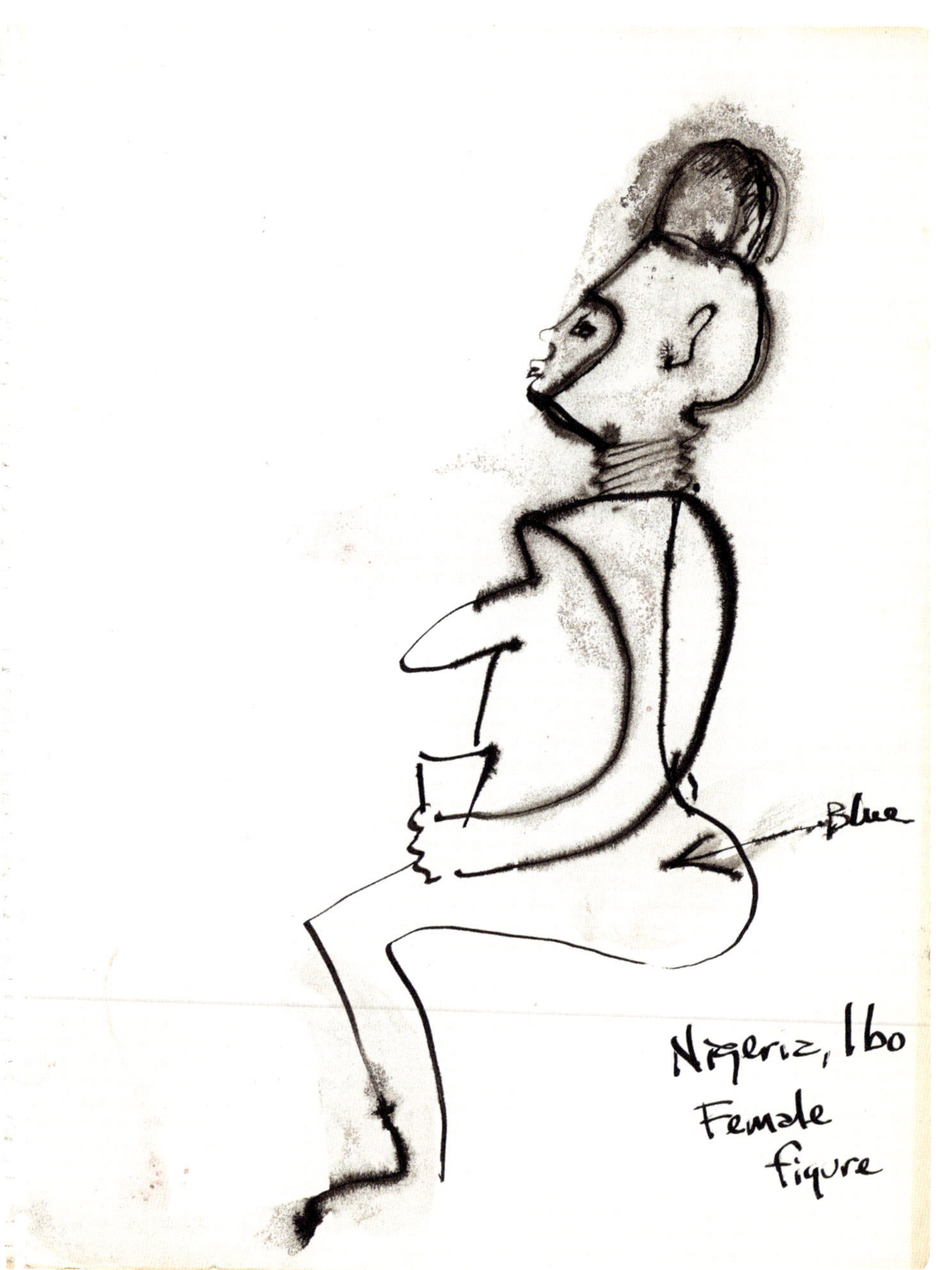
Blue
Nigeria, Ibo
Female
figure

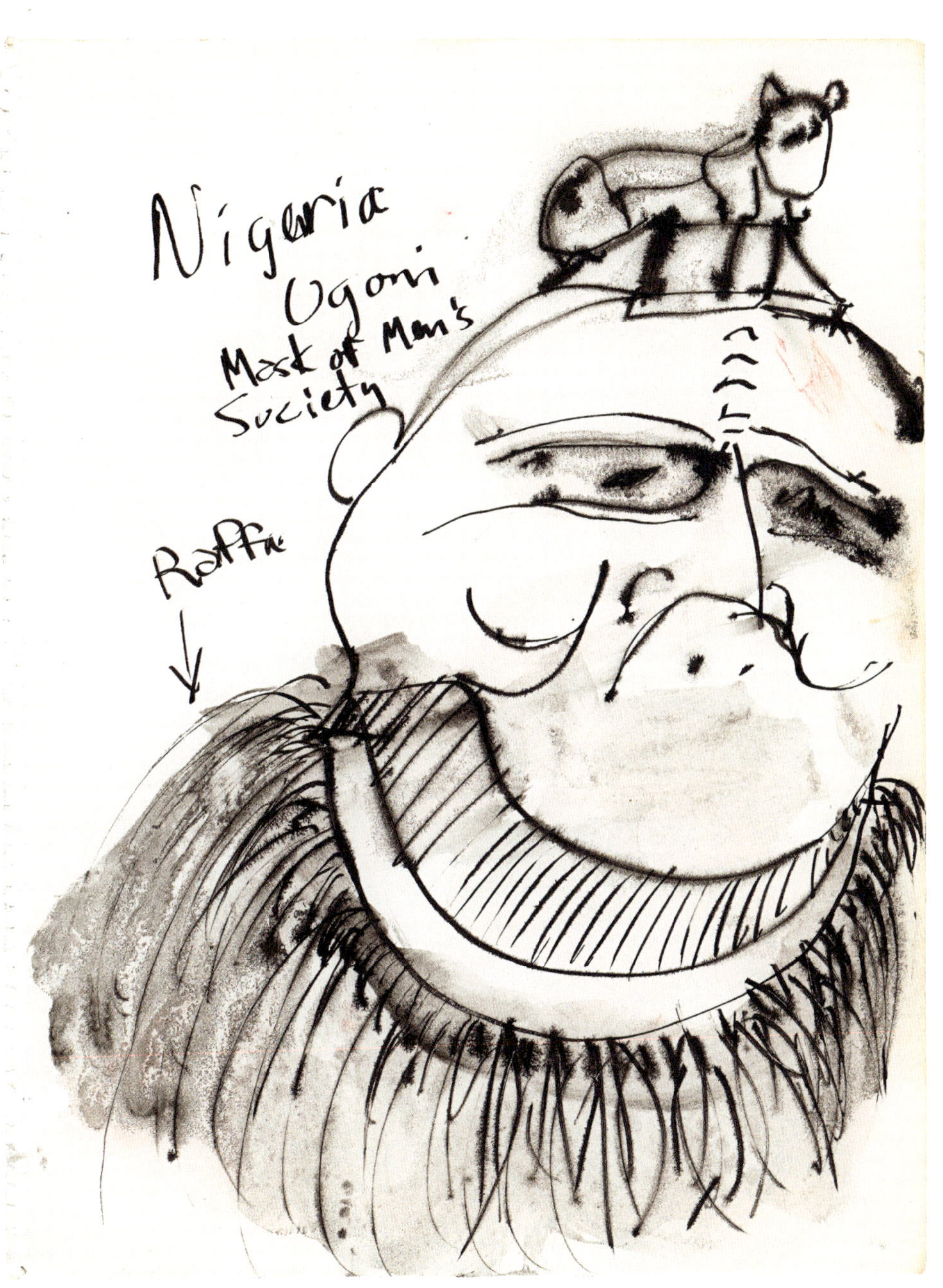
Nigeria
Ogoni
Mask of Man's
Society
Raffia

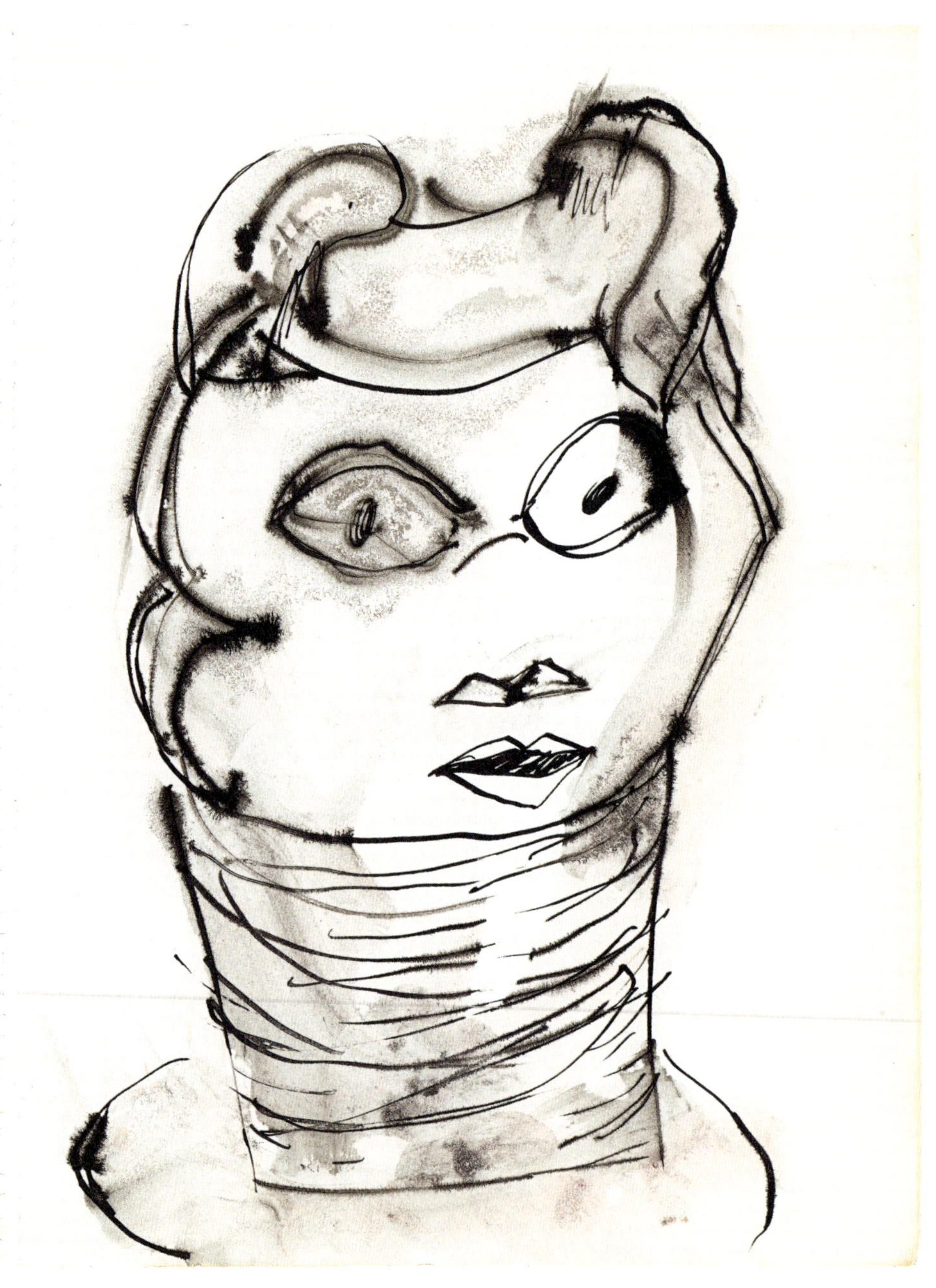

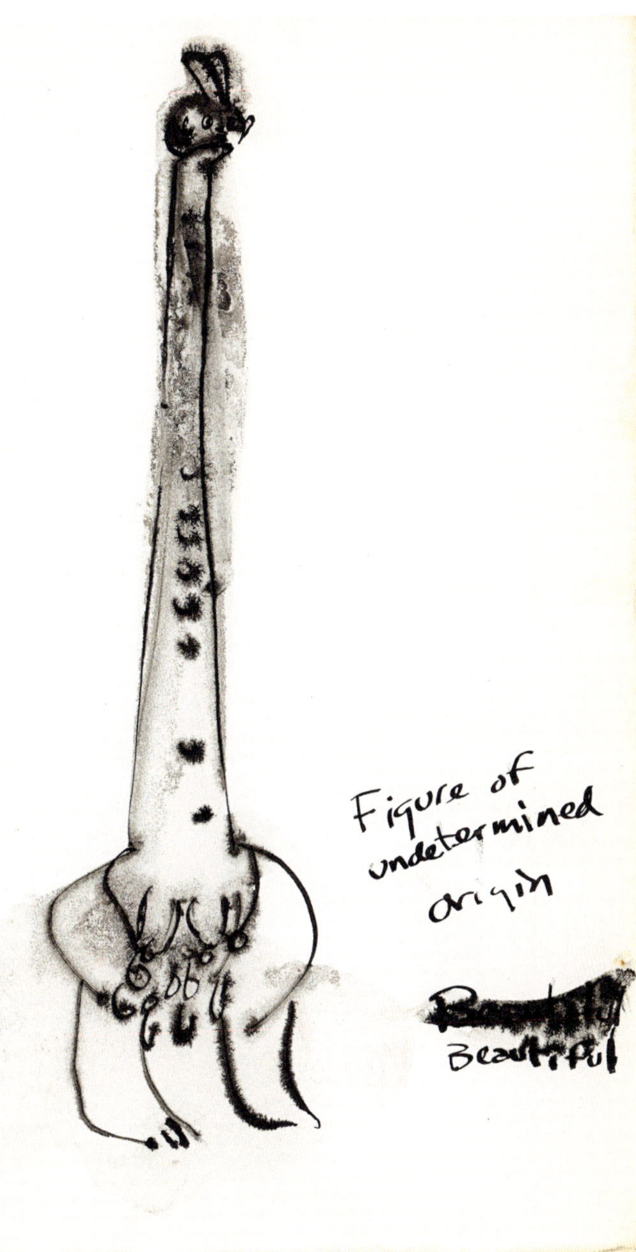
Figure of
undetermined
origin
~~Beautiful~~
Beautiful

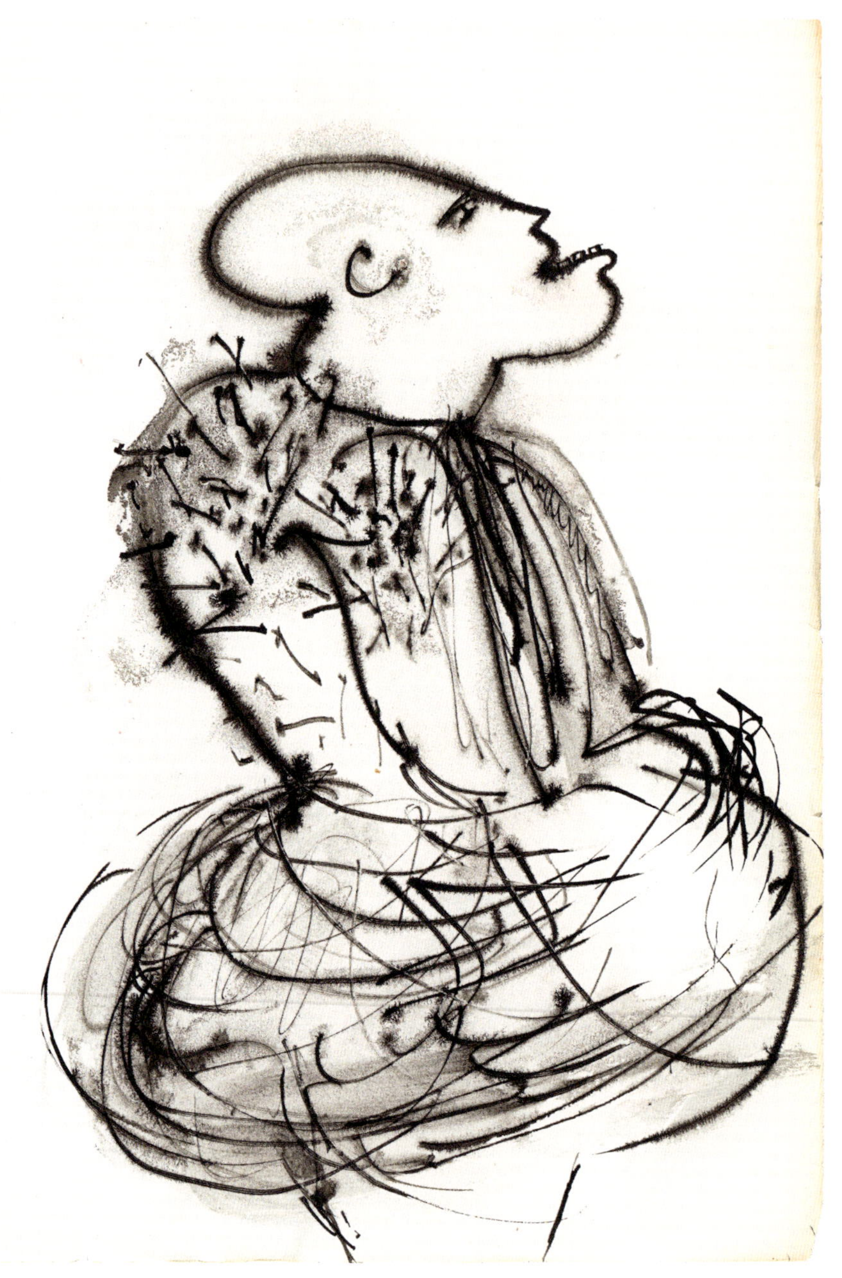

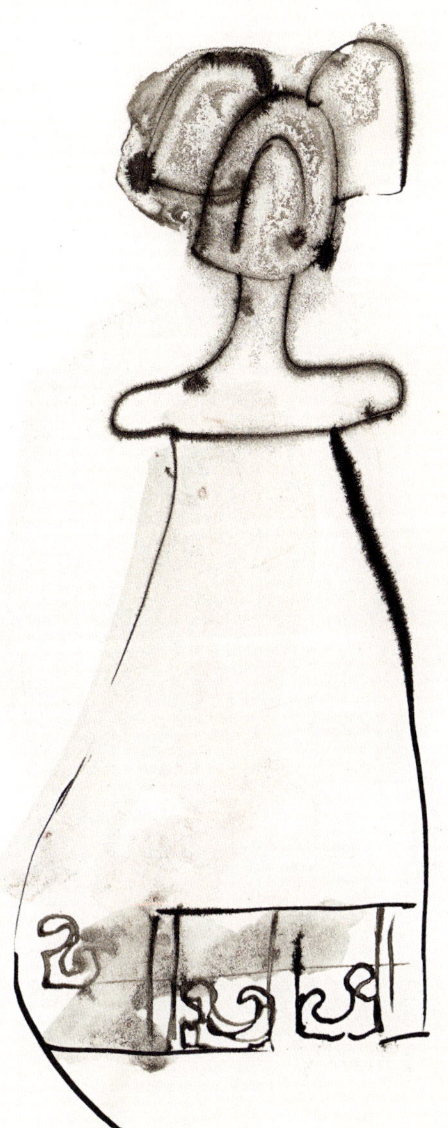

New Guinea
Massim
area
Club

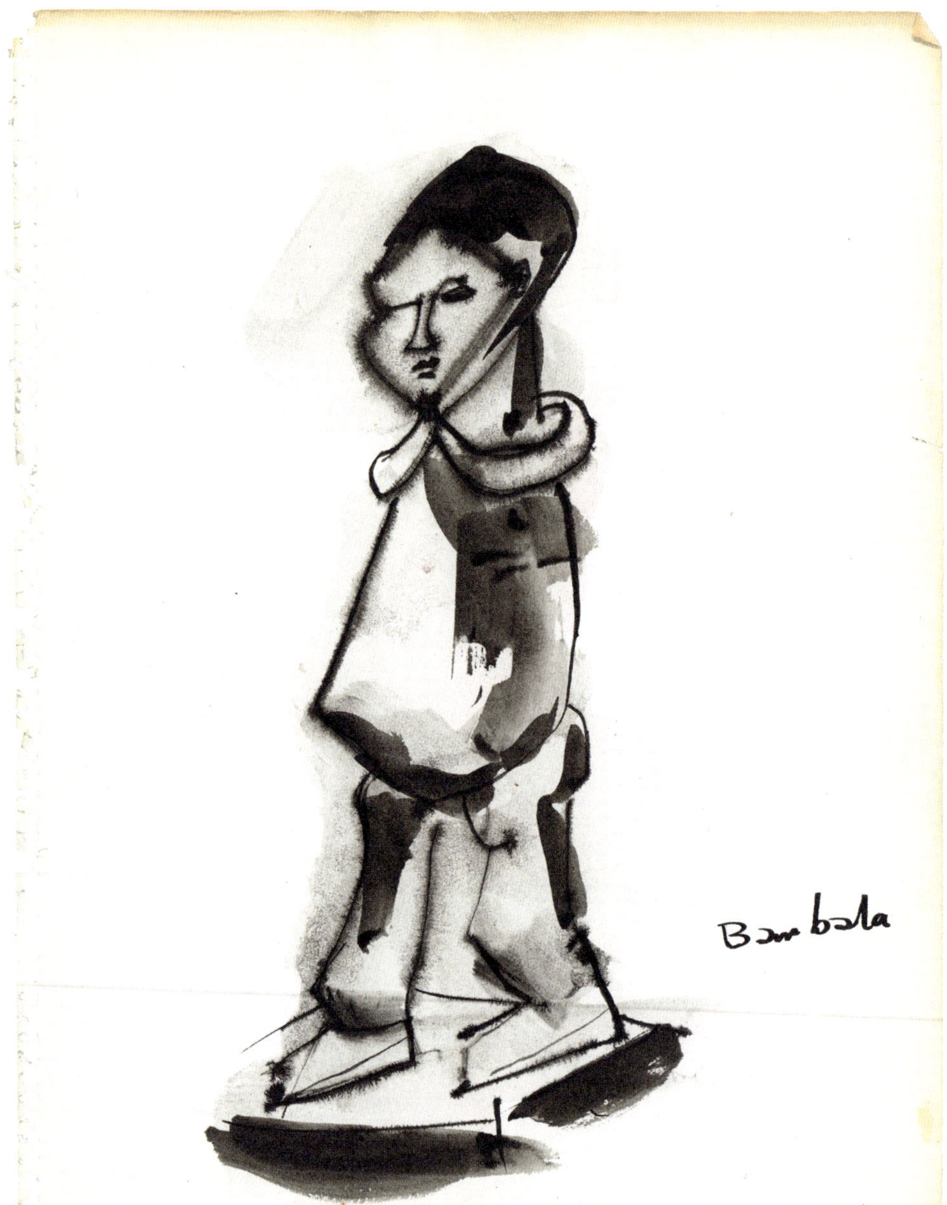
Bambala

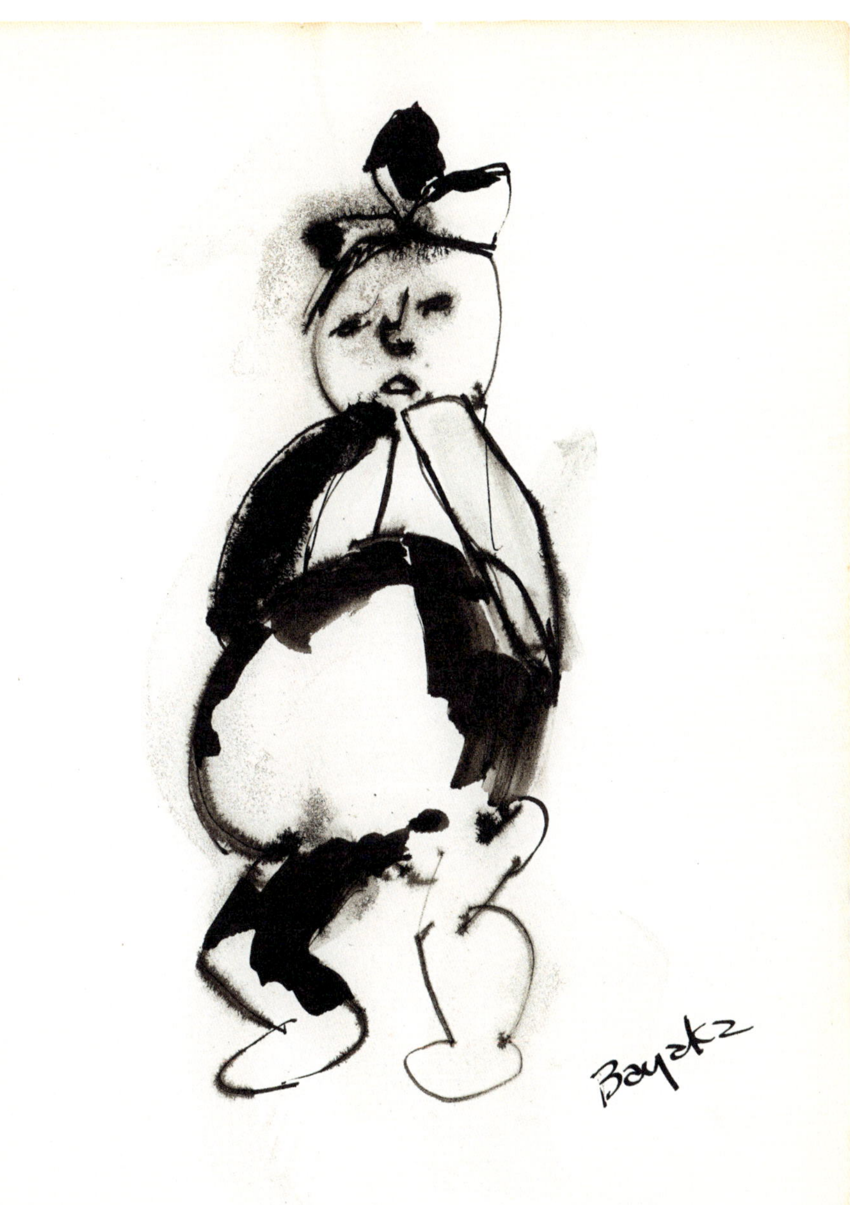

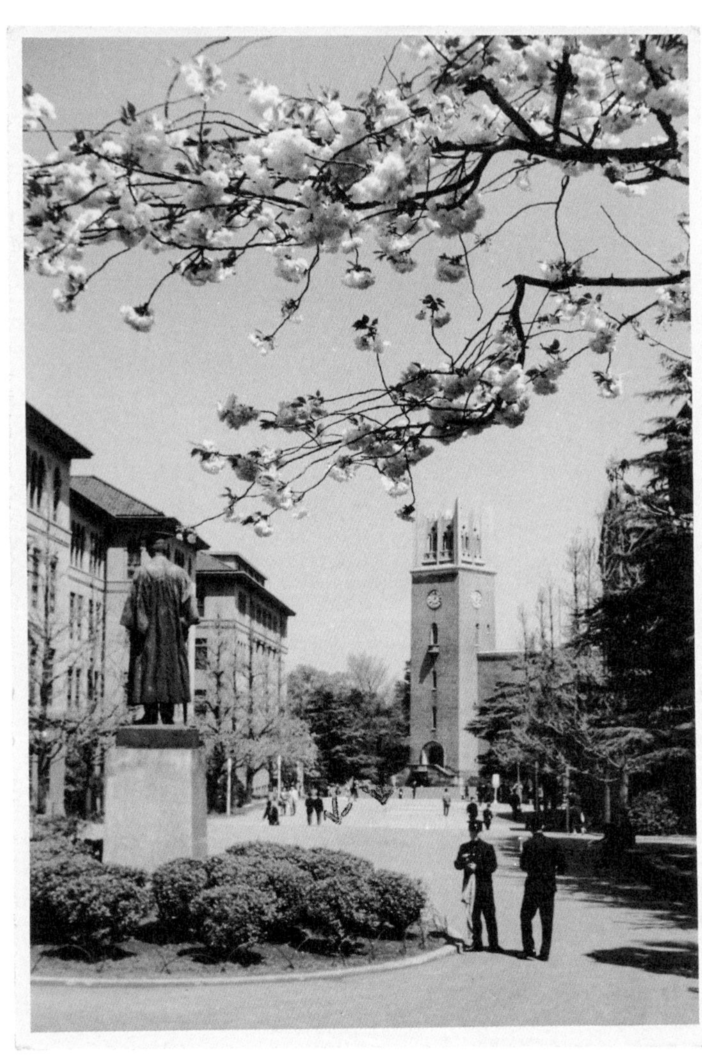

WASEDA UNIVERSITY, 1967
PEN ON POSTCARD, 6 × 4 INCHES (15.2 × 10.2 CM)

The arrows you see on this
photo were made by me.
Arrow one points to where the
students stage their more
violent demonstration.
Arrow two points to the other
area reserved for that purpose.
But usually when they
are held there they are of
a less violent nature.
And of course 99% of
the demonstrations are against
American Imperialism and
Viet Nam.
I've yet to meet a person
for the war. Or for any
form or kind of war period.
Oh yes. This is a cleaned
up photo of the campus. It
really has more character and
characters than shown here.

The arrows you see on this photo were made by me. Arrow one points to where the students stage their more violent demonstration. Arrow two points to the other area reserved for that purpose. But usually when they are held there they are of a less violent nature. And of course 99% of the demonstrations are against American Imperialism and Vietnam. I've yet to meet a person for the war. Or for any form or kind of war period. Oh yes. This is a cleaned up photo of the campus. It really has more character and characters than shown here.

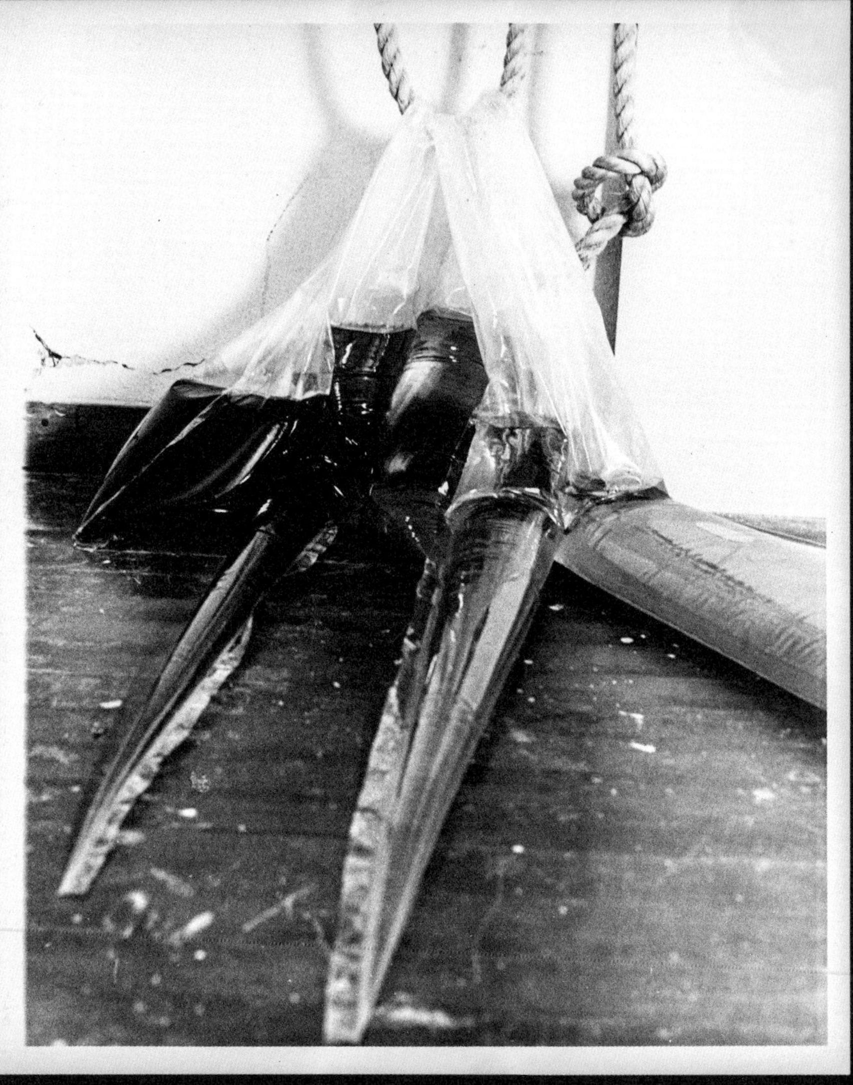

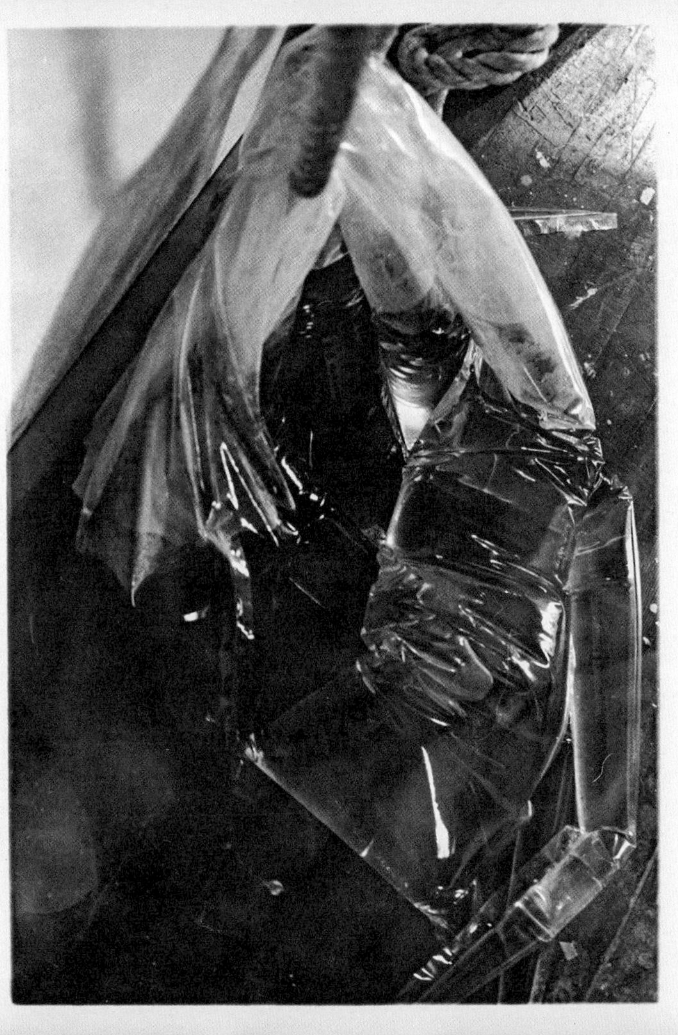

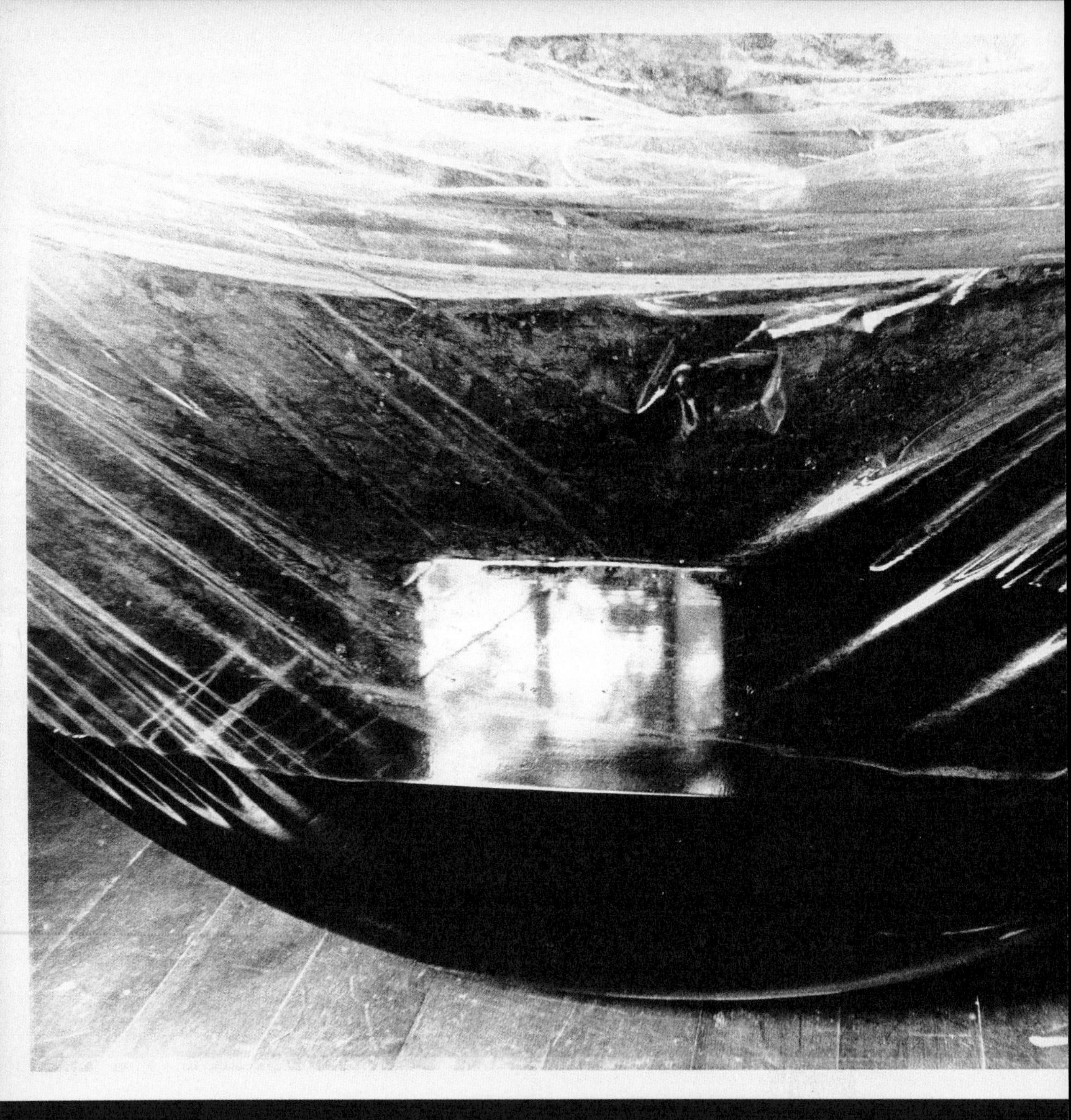

PHOTOGRAPHS OF *WATER COMPOSITION III*,
HOME STUDIO, PASADENA, 1970

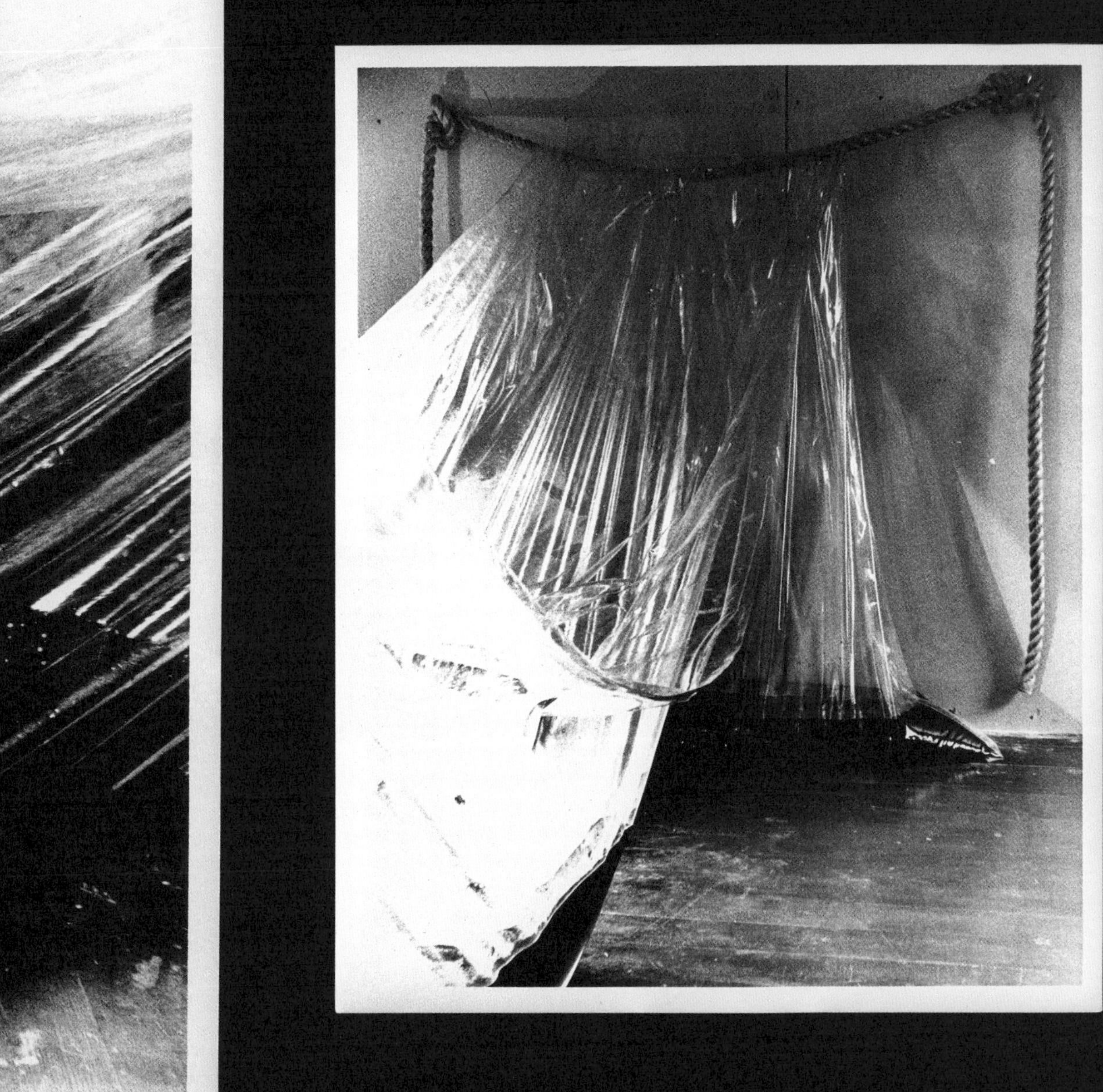

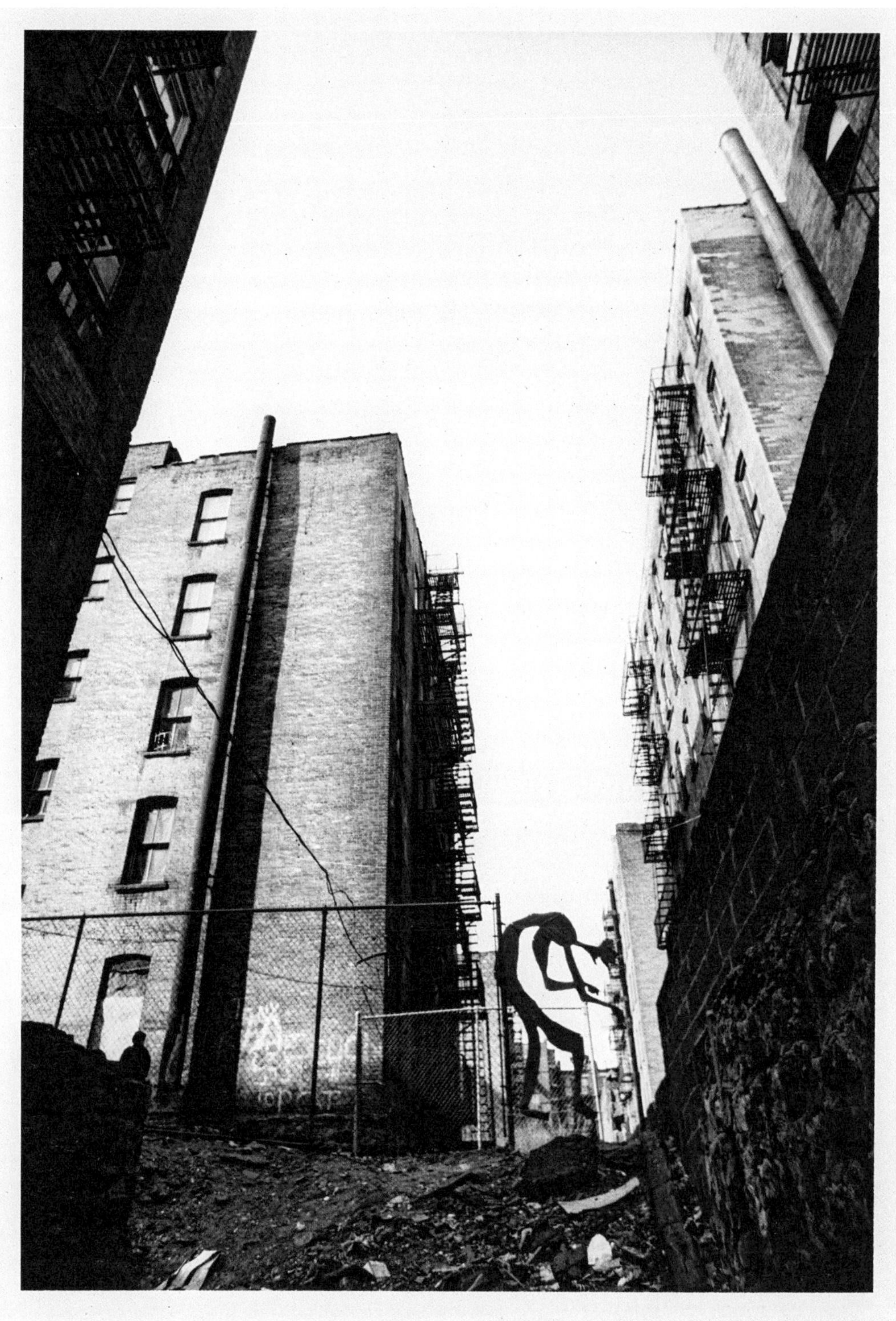

DOWN (PURPLE), 1972
GELATIN SILVER PRINT, 10 × 8 INCHES (25.4 × 20.3 CM)

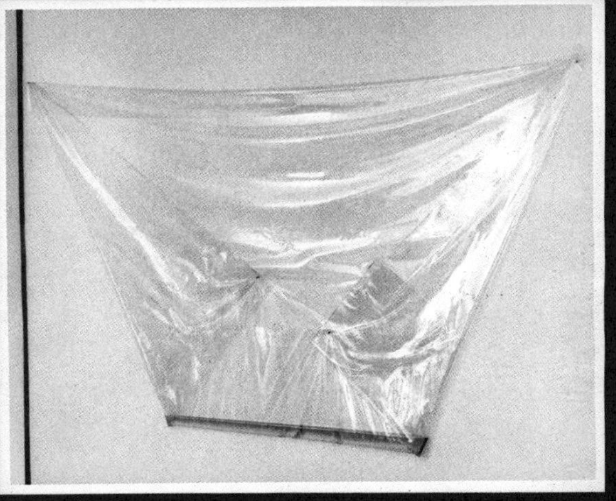

UNTITLED 3

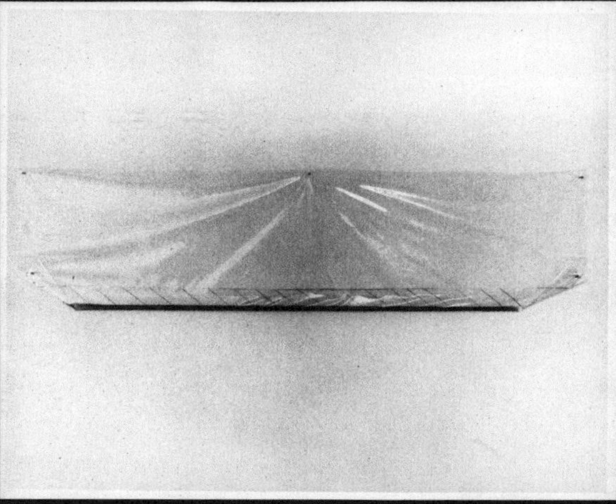

UNTITLED 2

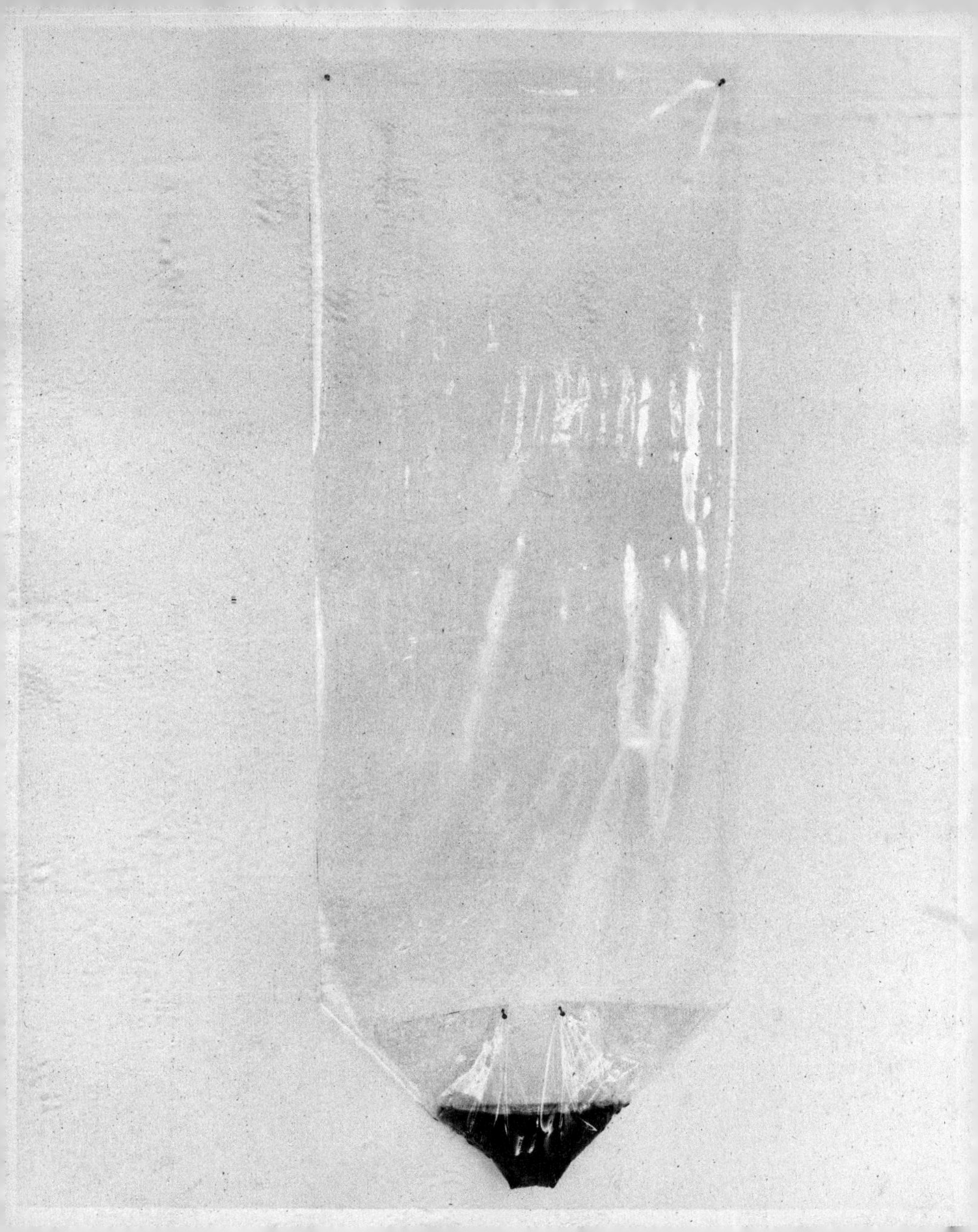

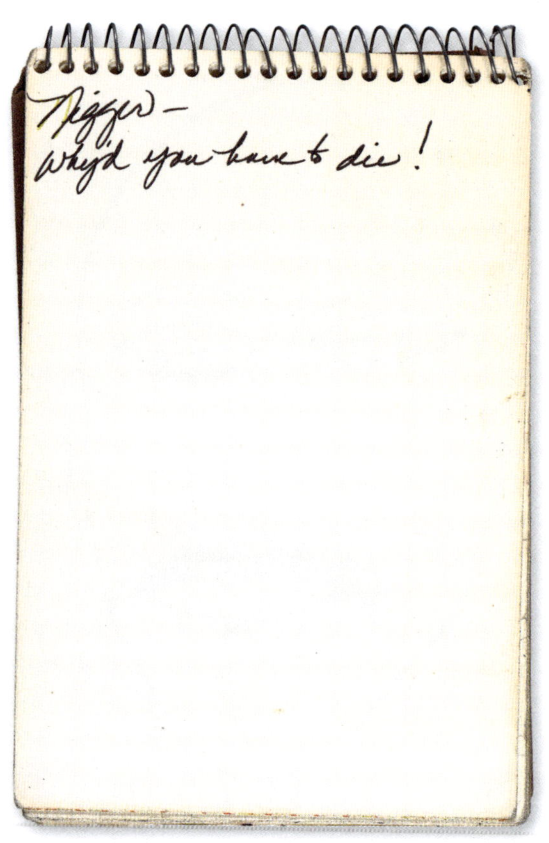

STRATHMORE SKETCHBOOK, 1976–77
PEN AND PENCIL ON PAPER,
12 PARTS: 6 × 4 INCHES (15.2 × 10.2 CM) EACH

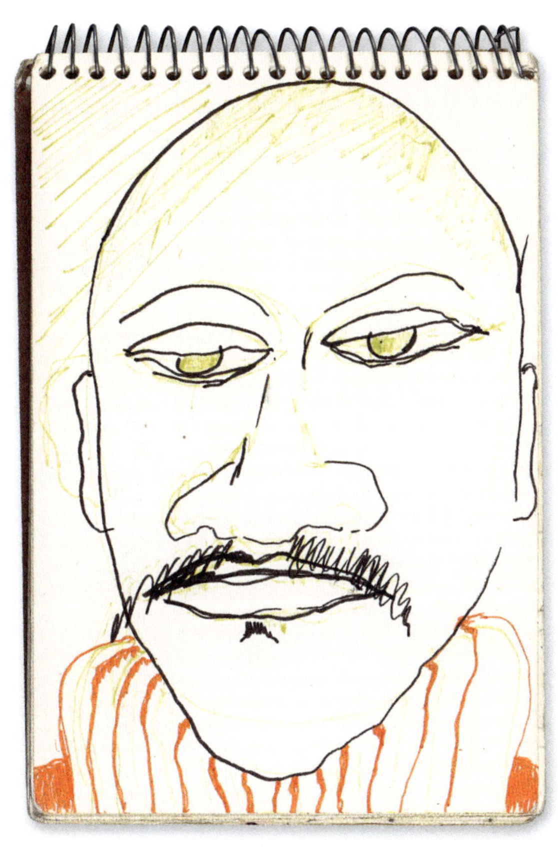

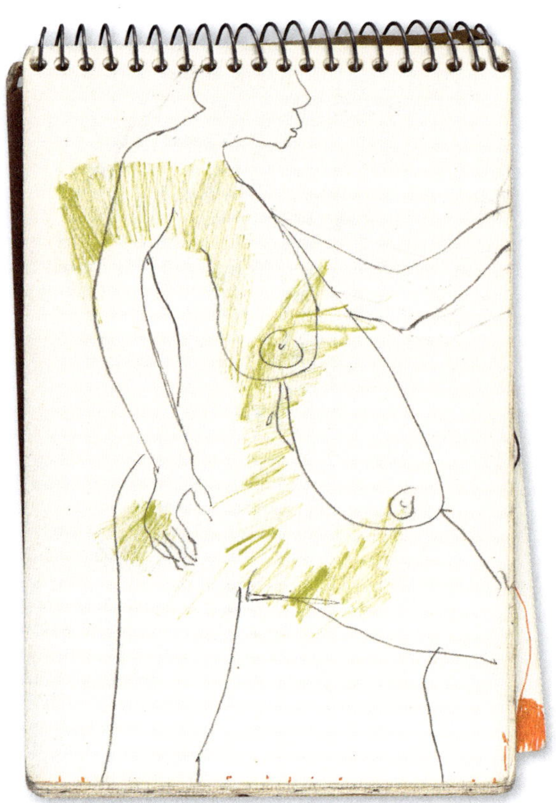

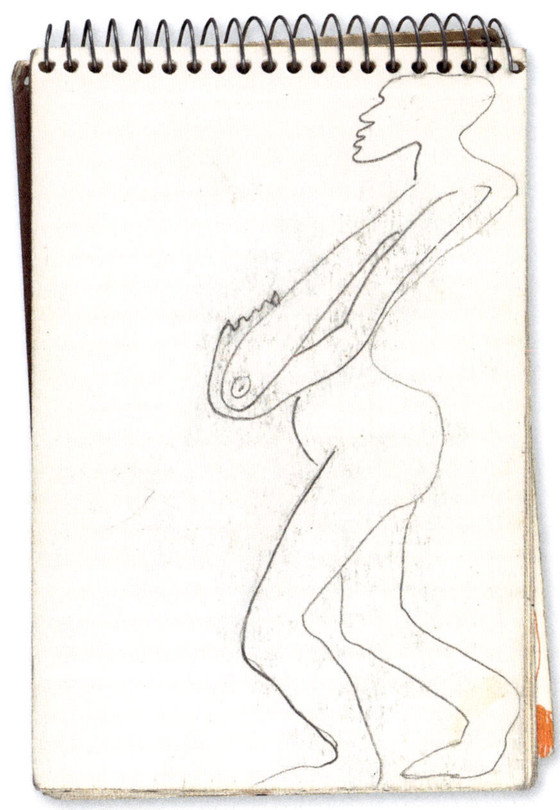

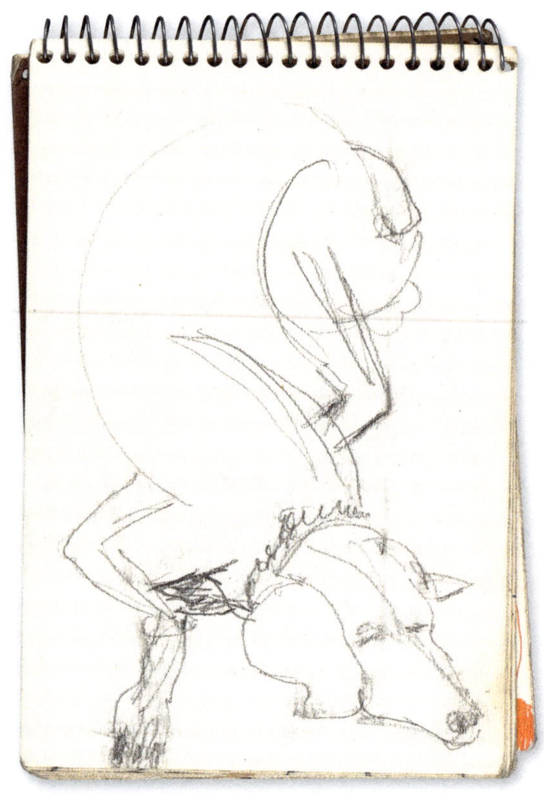

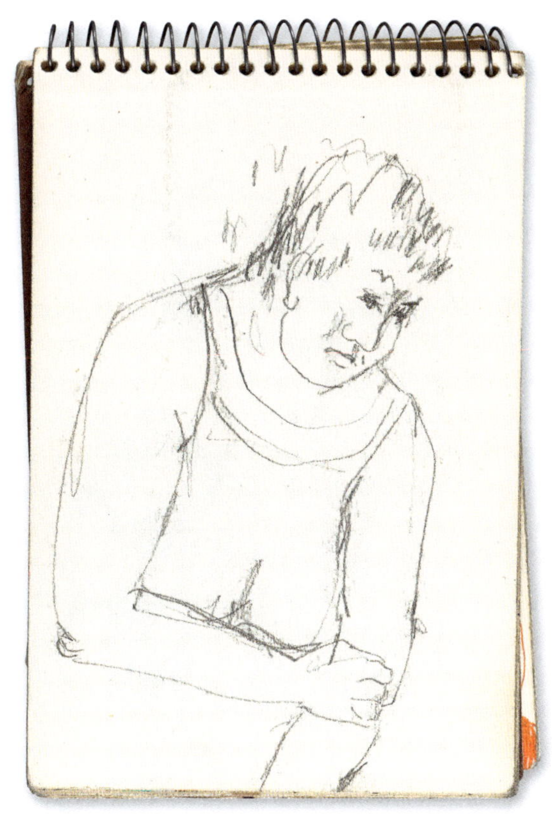

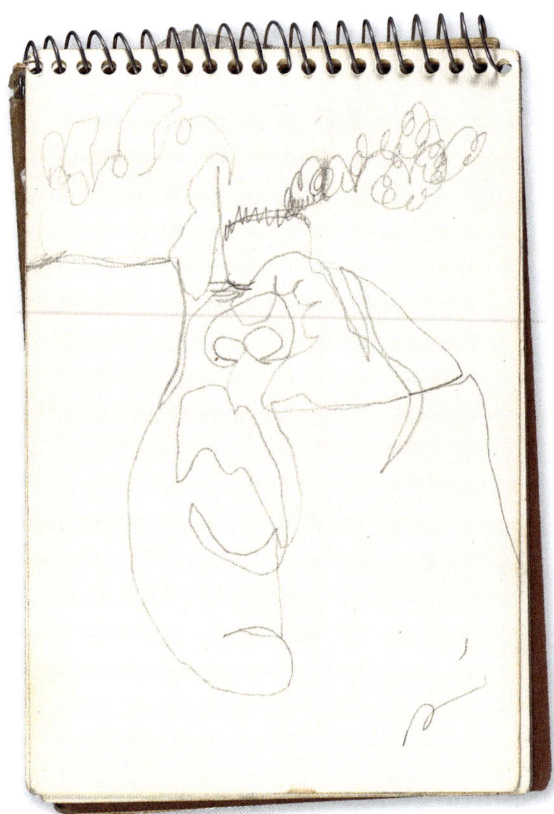

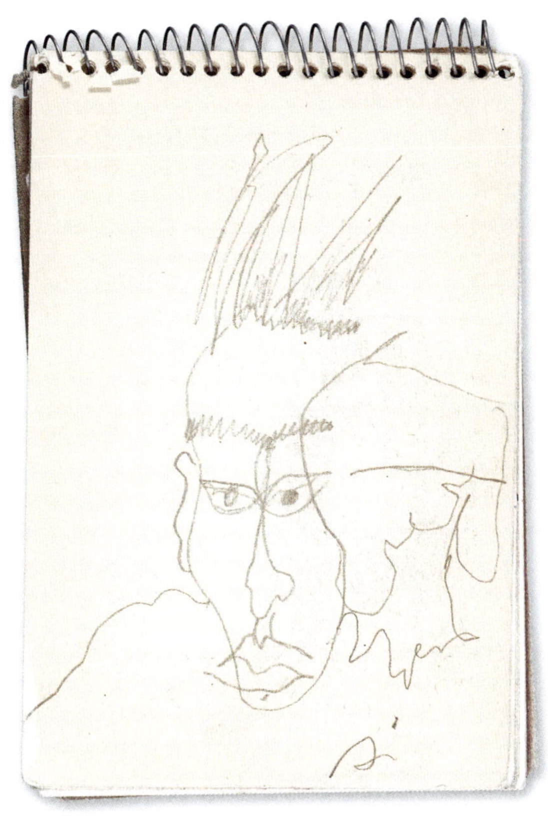

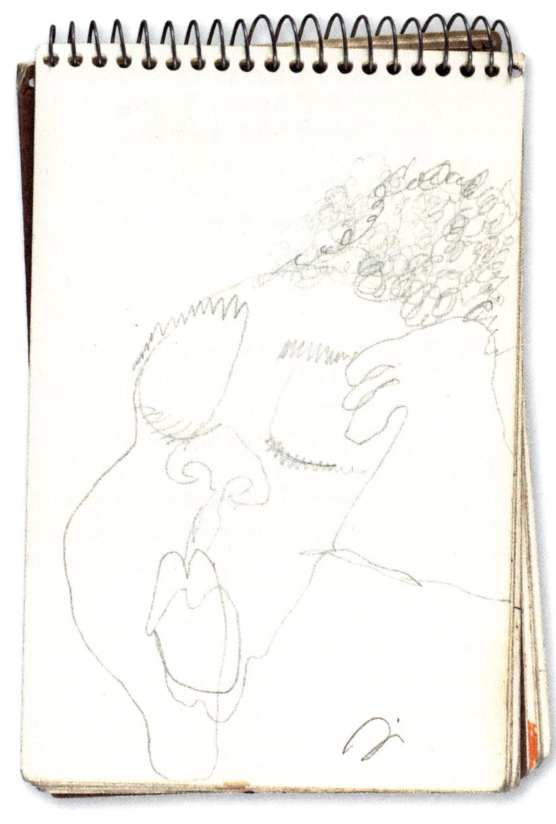

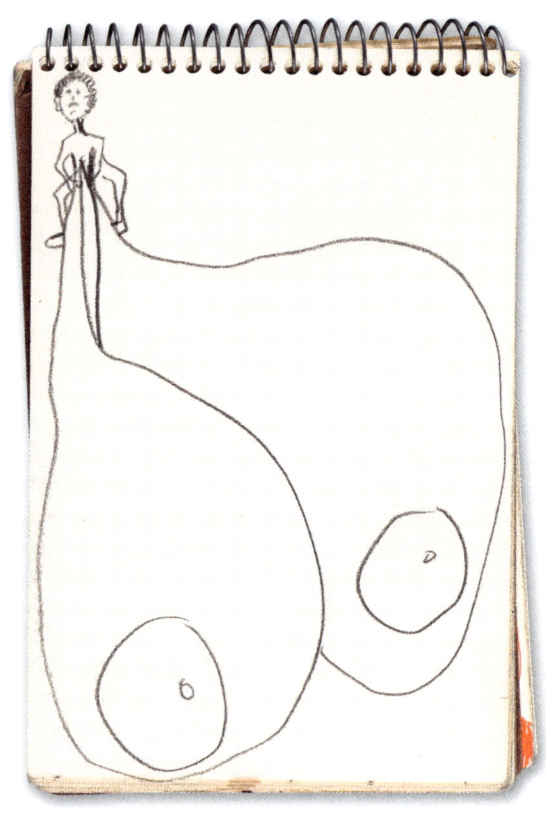

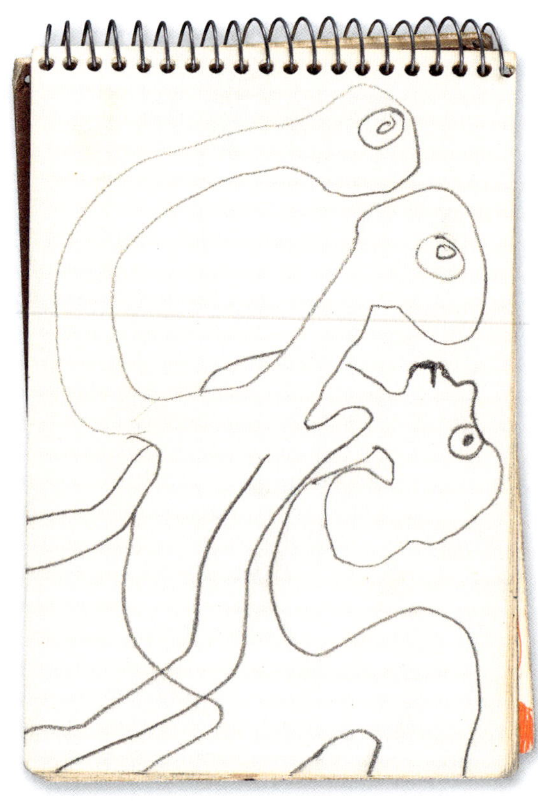

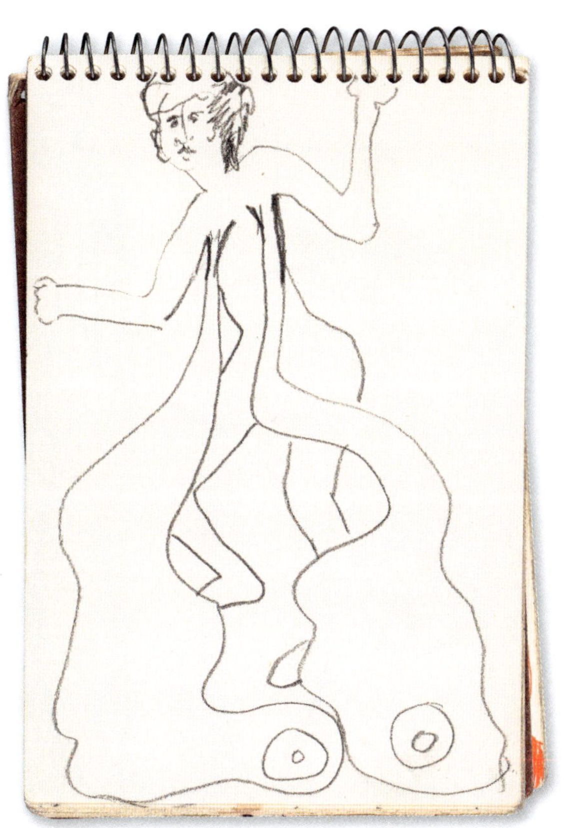

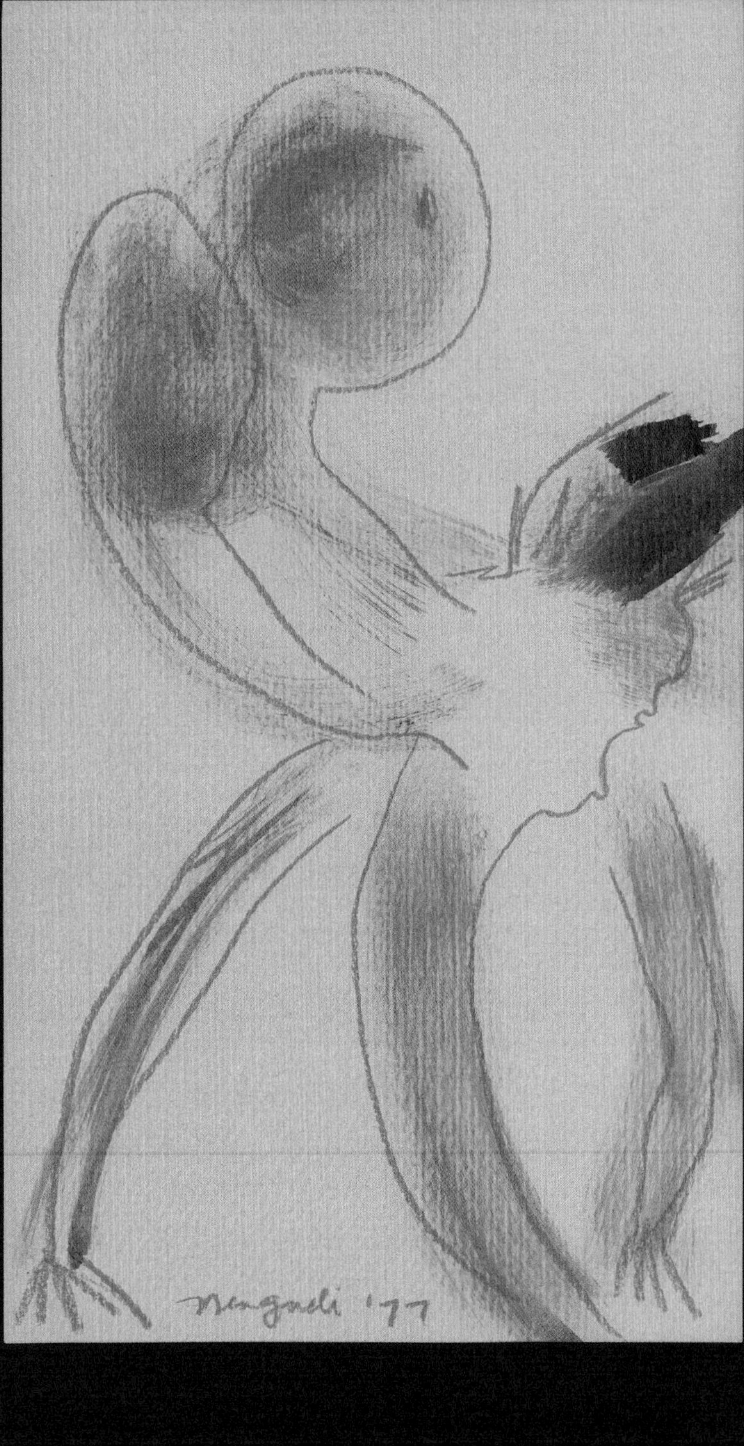

ANGST ON PINK PAPER, 1977
COLORED PENCIL AND GOUACHE ON PAPER,
7 PARTS: 11 × 6 INCHES (27.9 × 15.2 CM) EACH

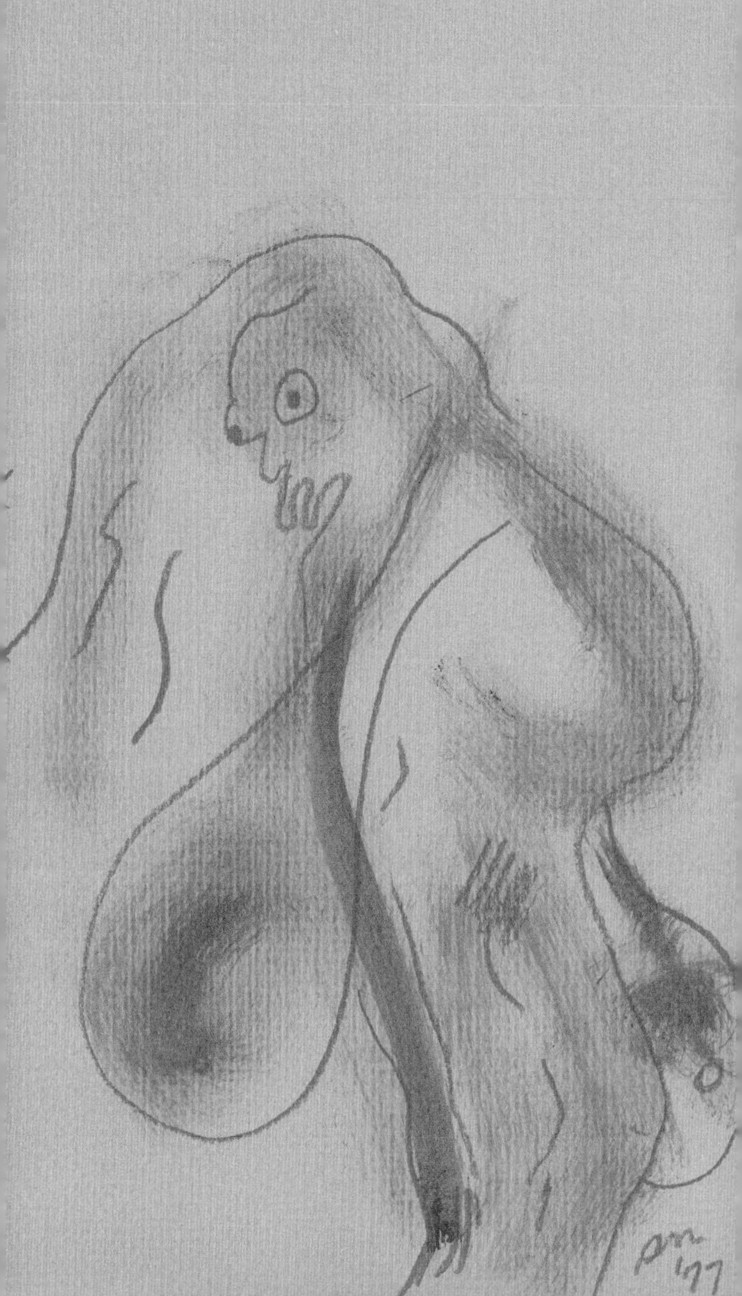

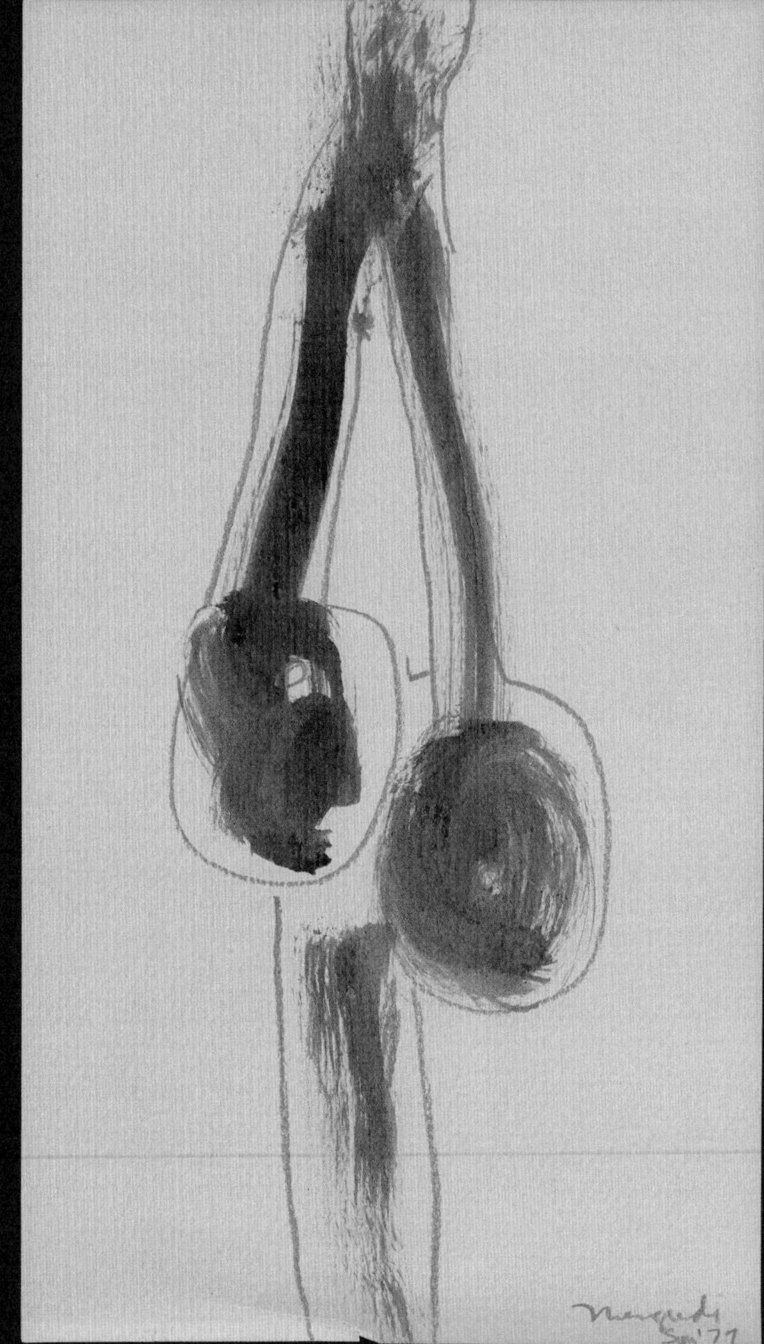

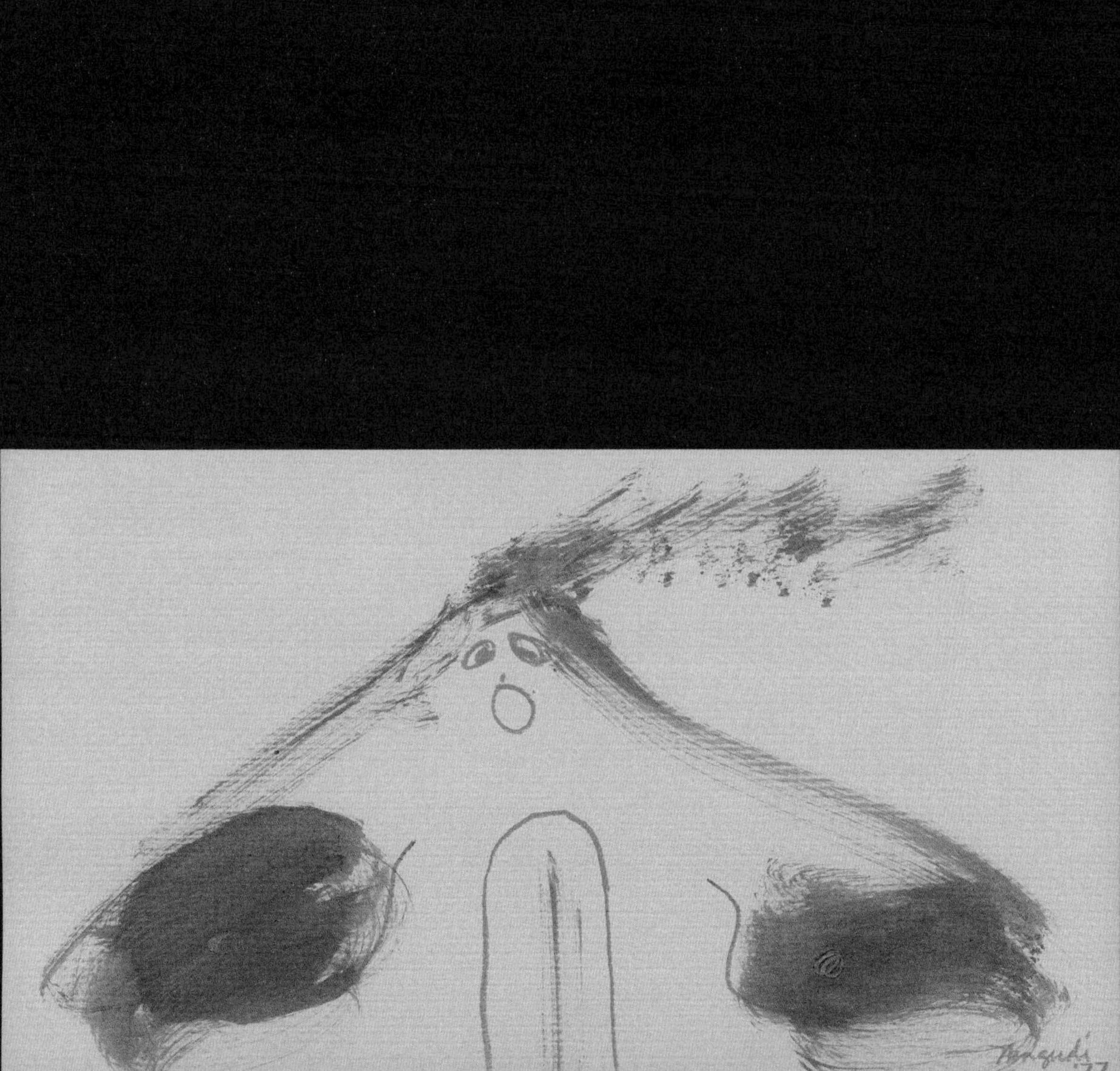

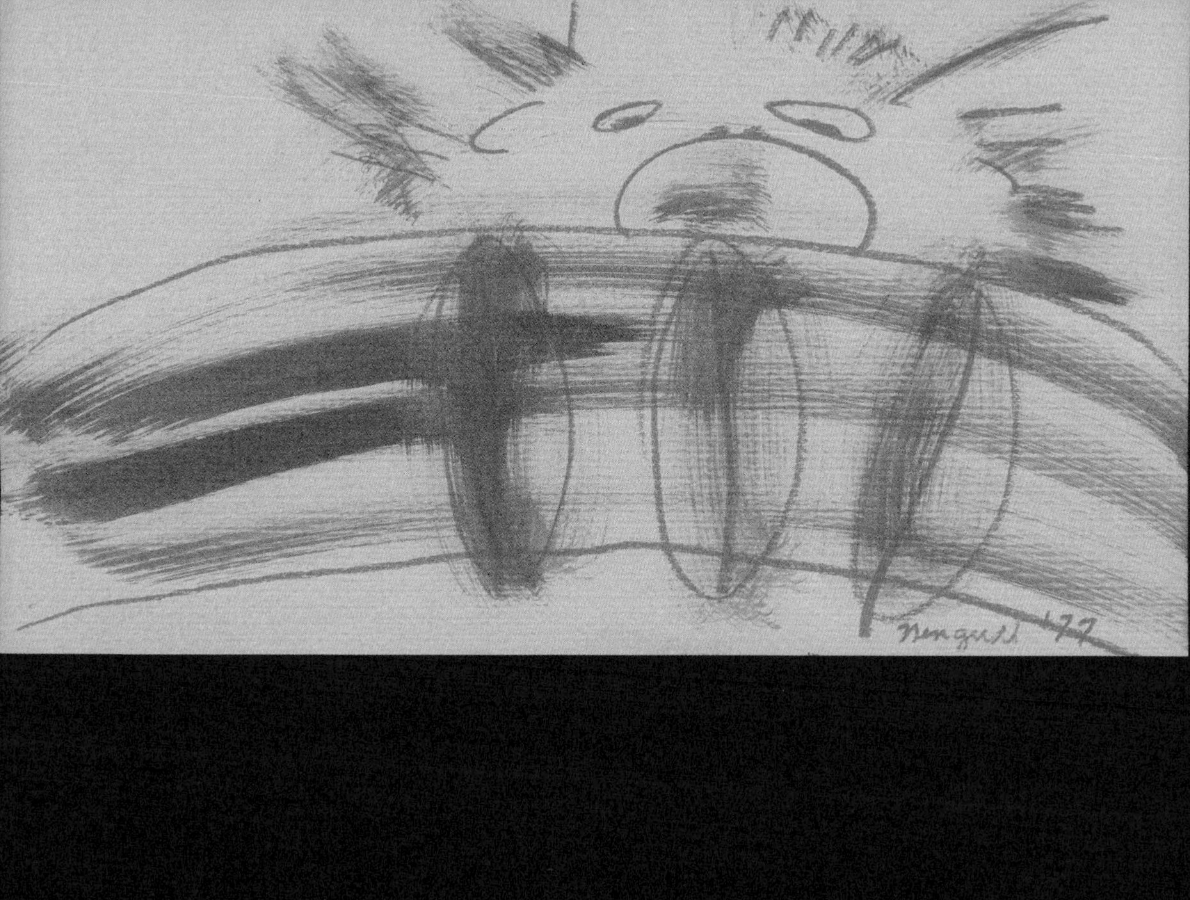

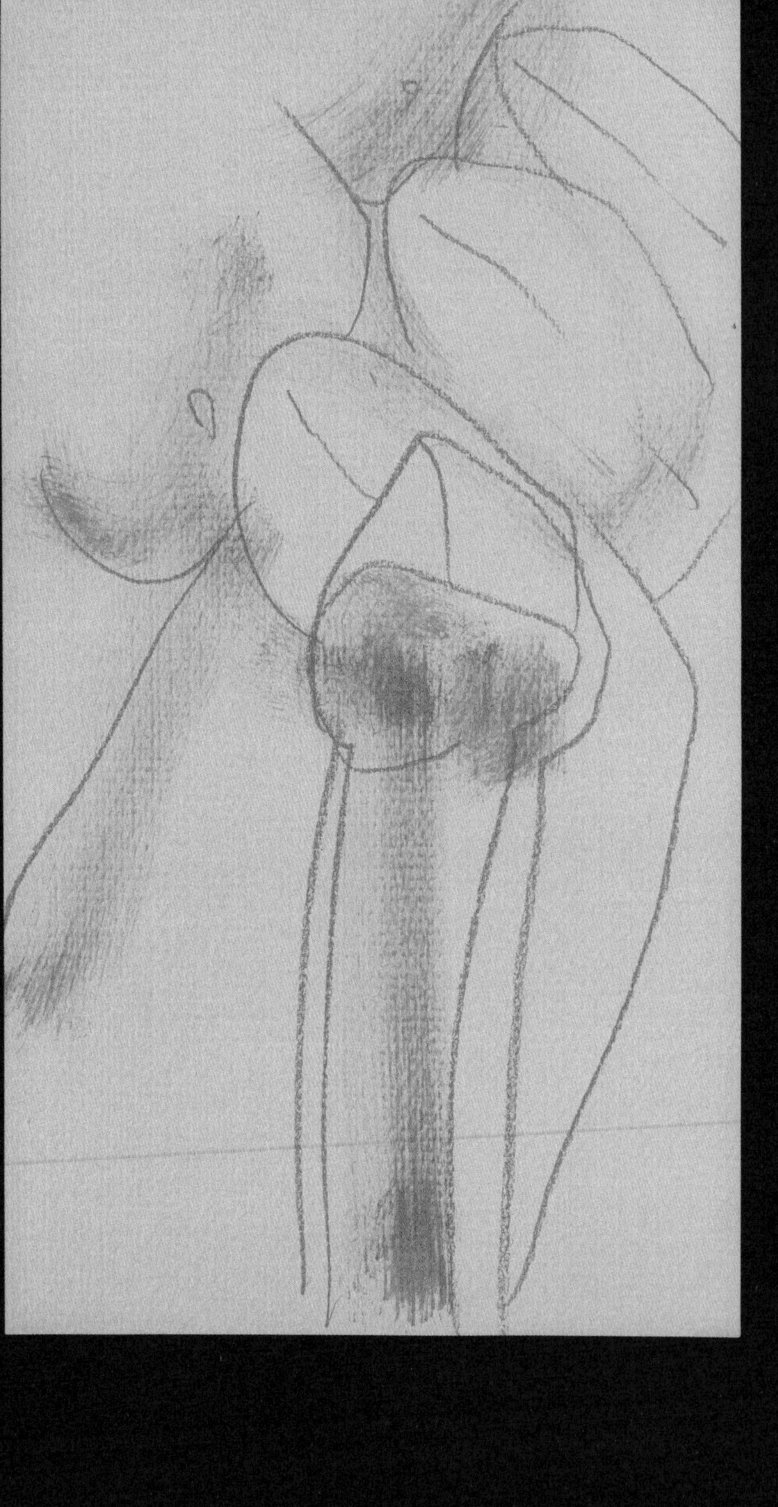

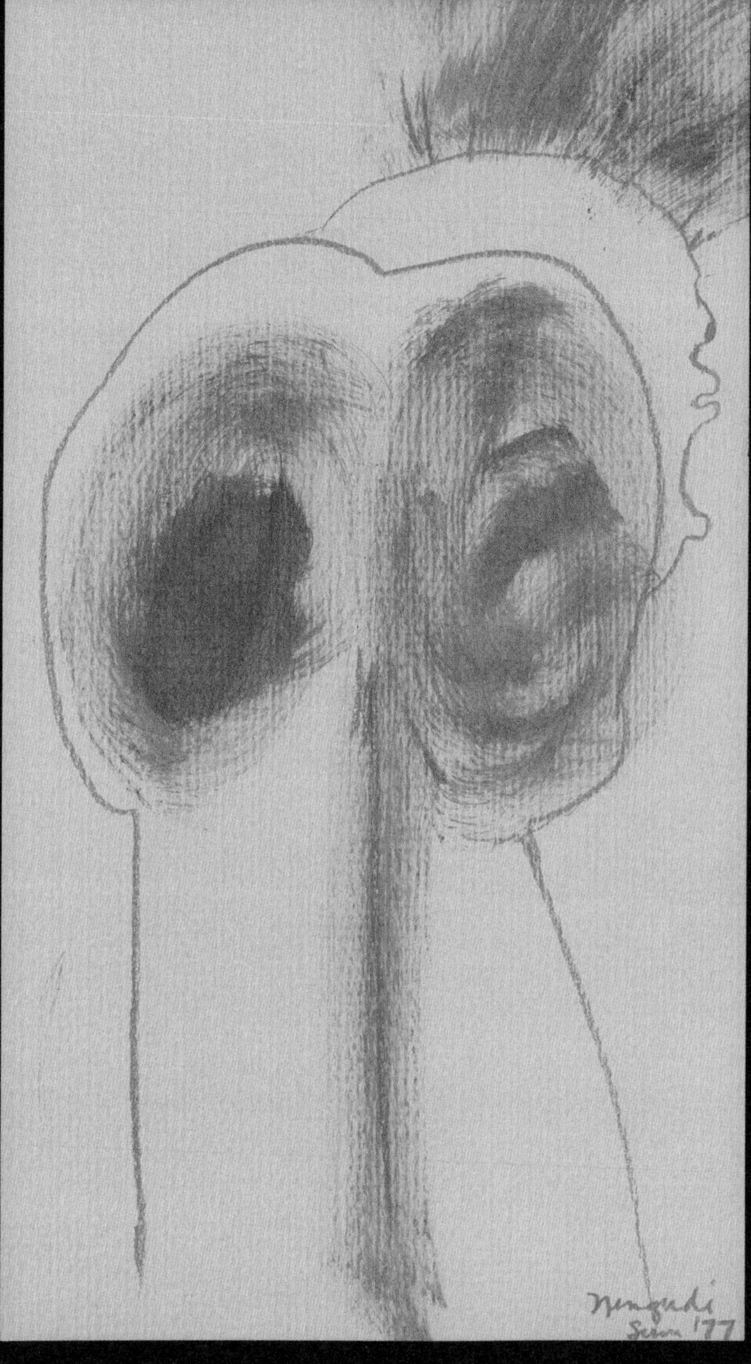

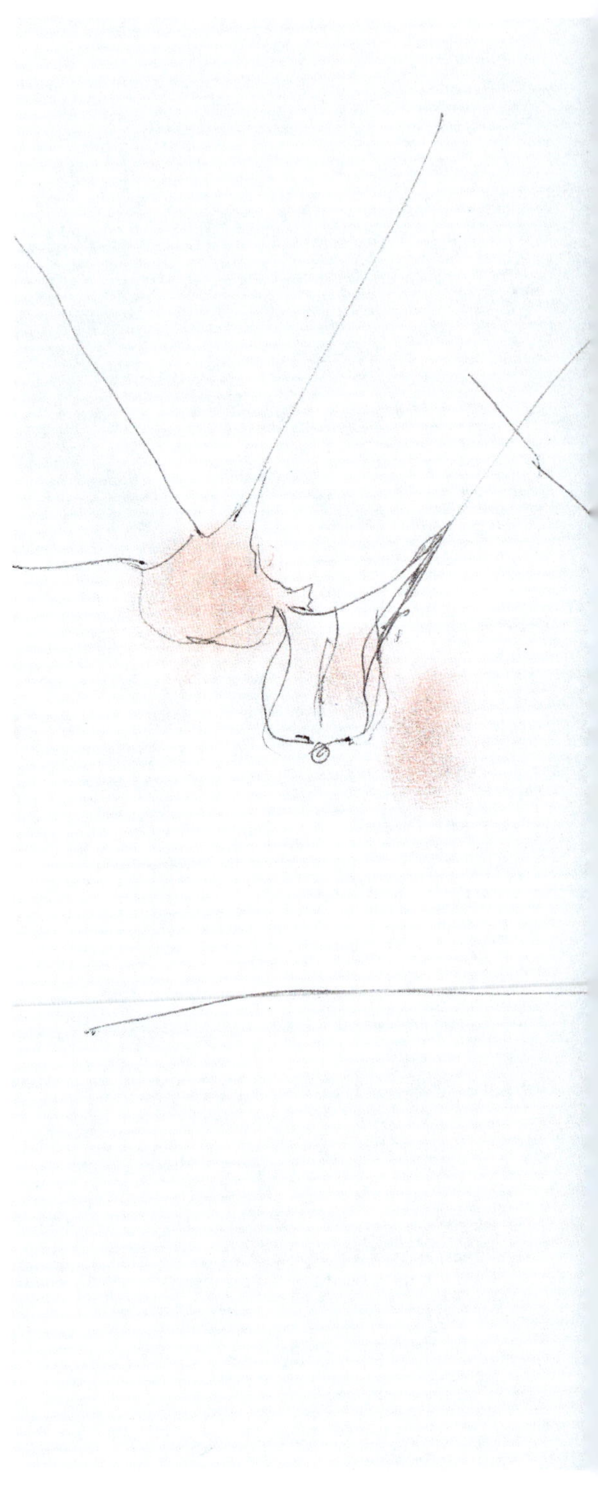

SKETCHES FOR *R.S.V.P. I*, 1977

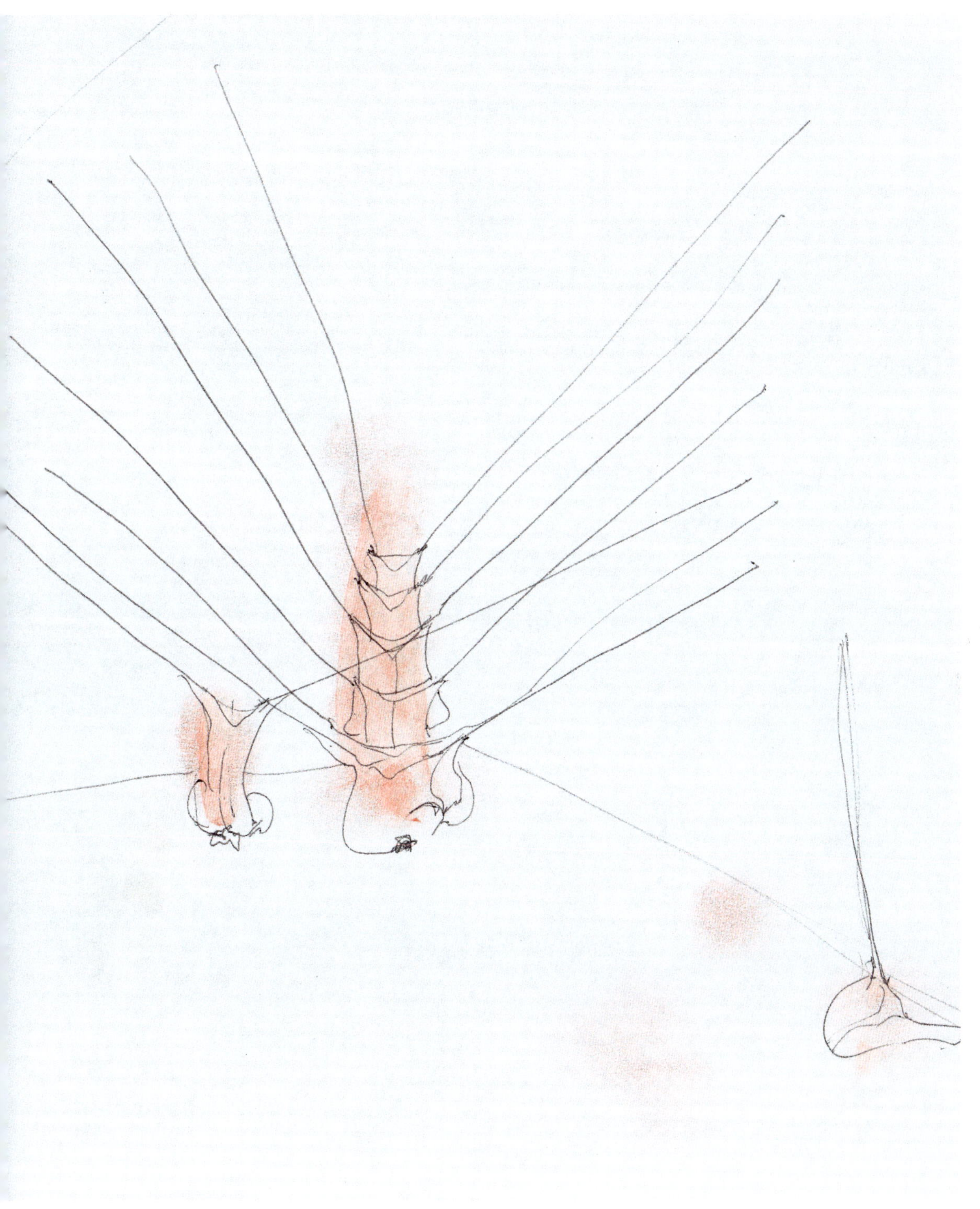

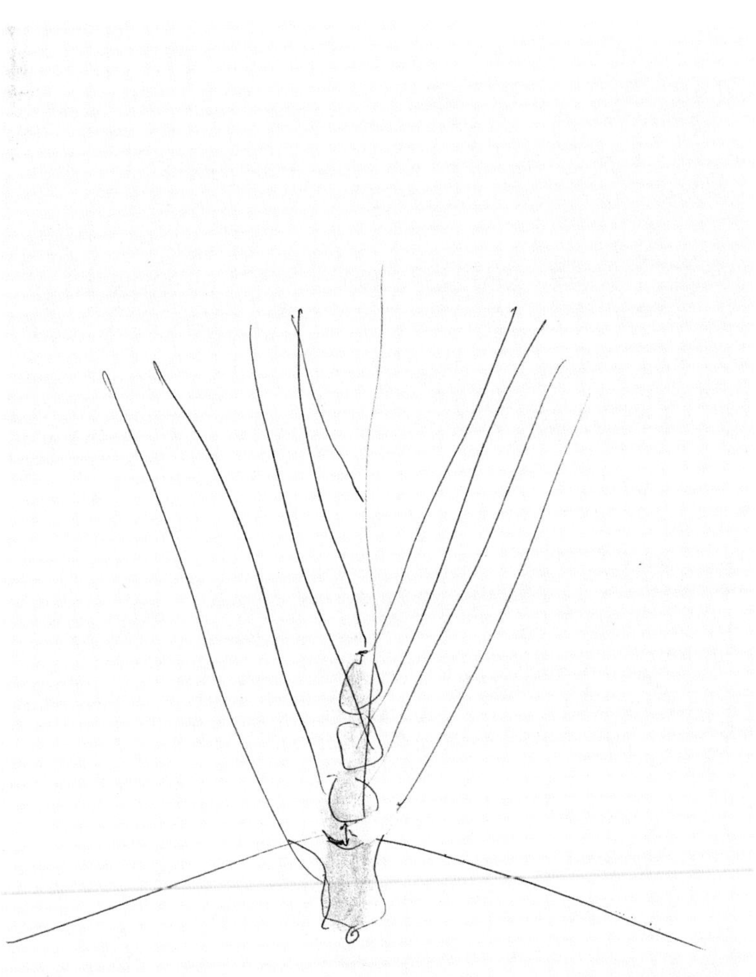

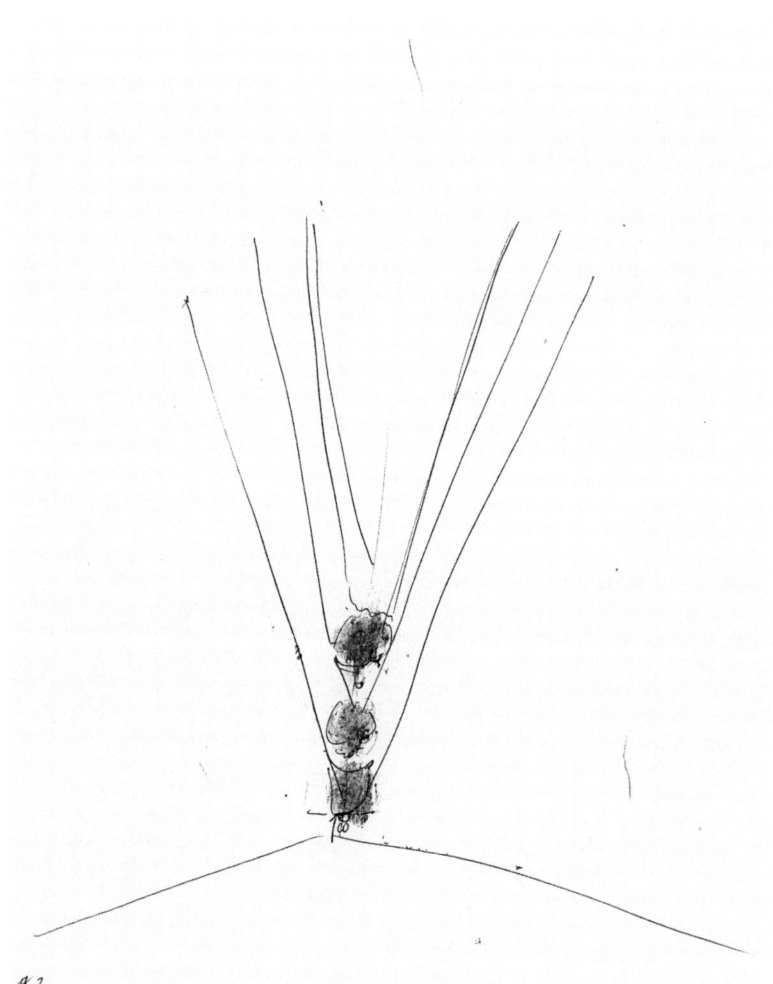
#3

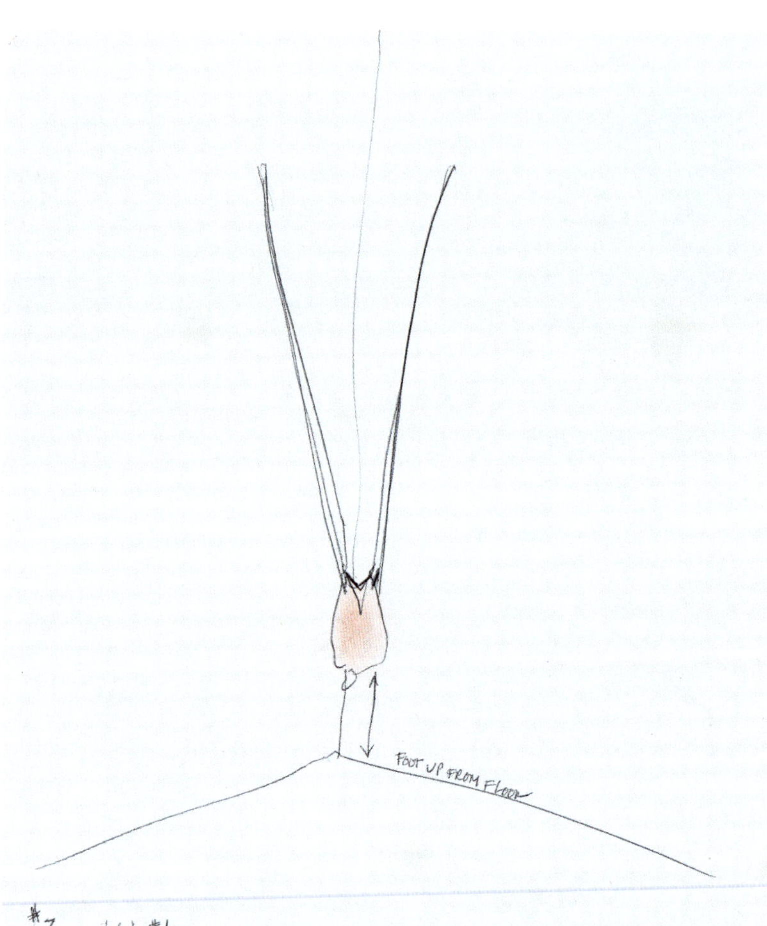

#7 or switch to #1

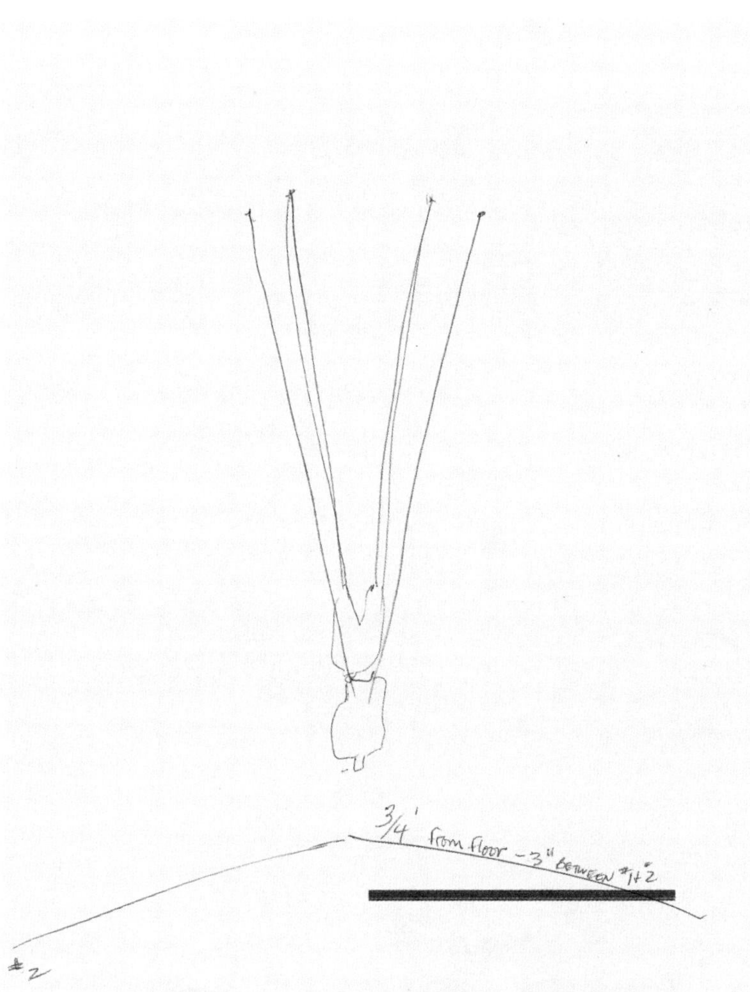
3/4' from floor – 3" BETWEEN #1 + 2
#2

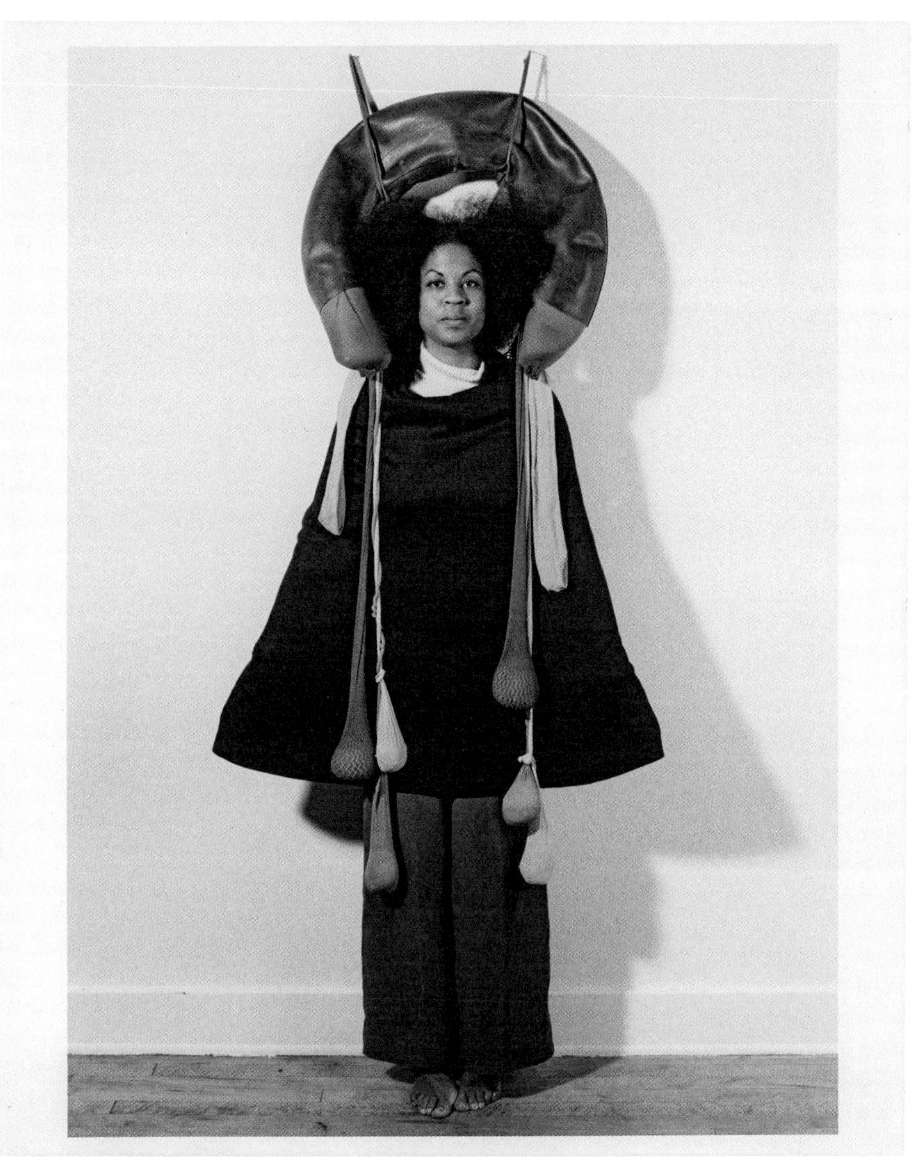

INSIDE/OUTSIDE, 1977
GELATIN SILVER PRINT,
10 × 8 INCHES (25.4 × 20.3 CM)
PHOTO: KEN PETERSON

NENGUDI SETTING UP TO PERFORM WITH *R.S.V.P. X*, 2409 WEST SLAUSON AVENUE STUDIO, LOS ANGELES, 1977

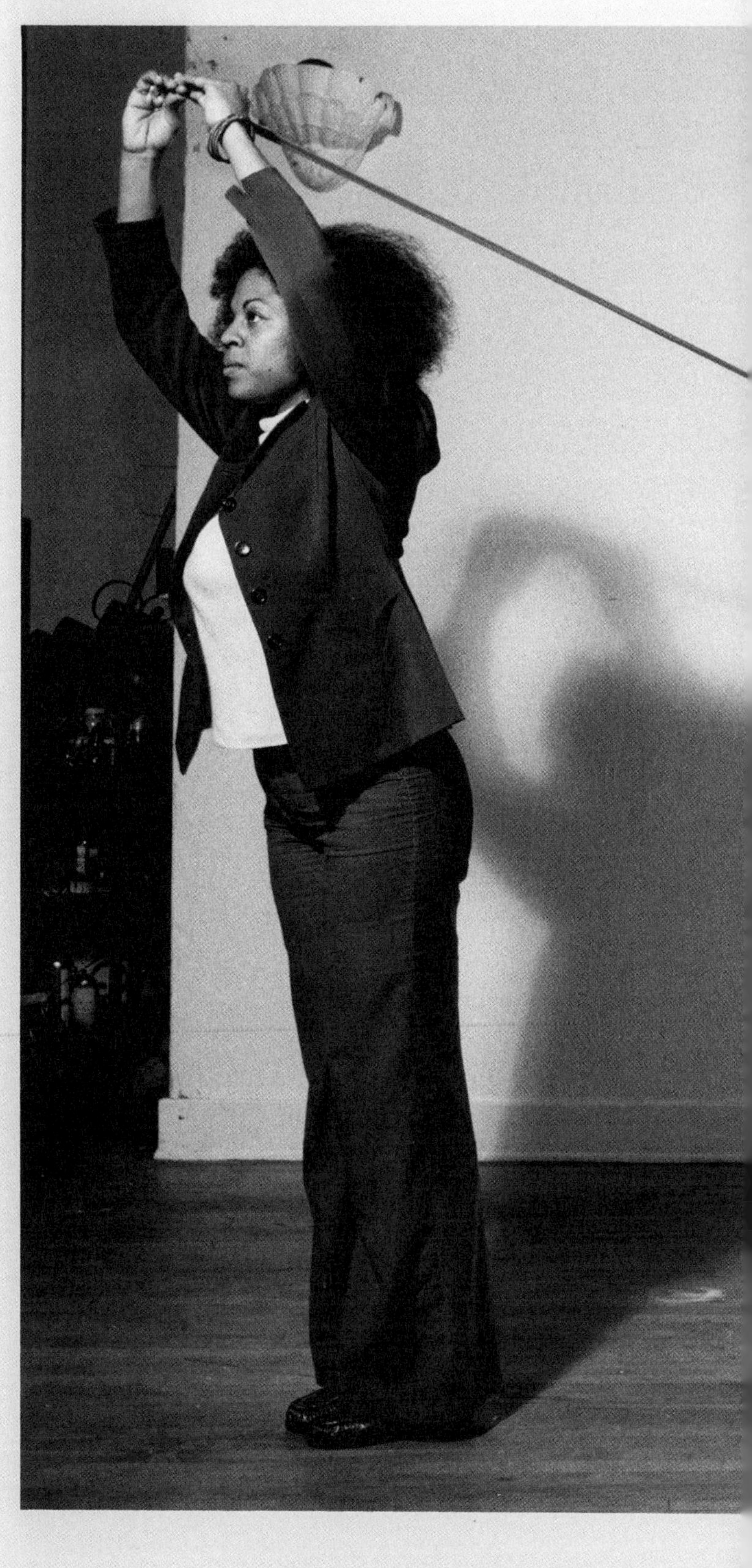

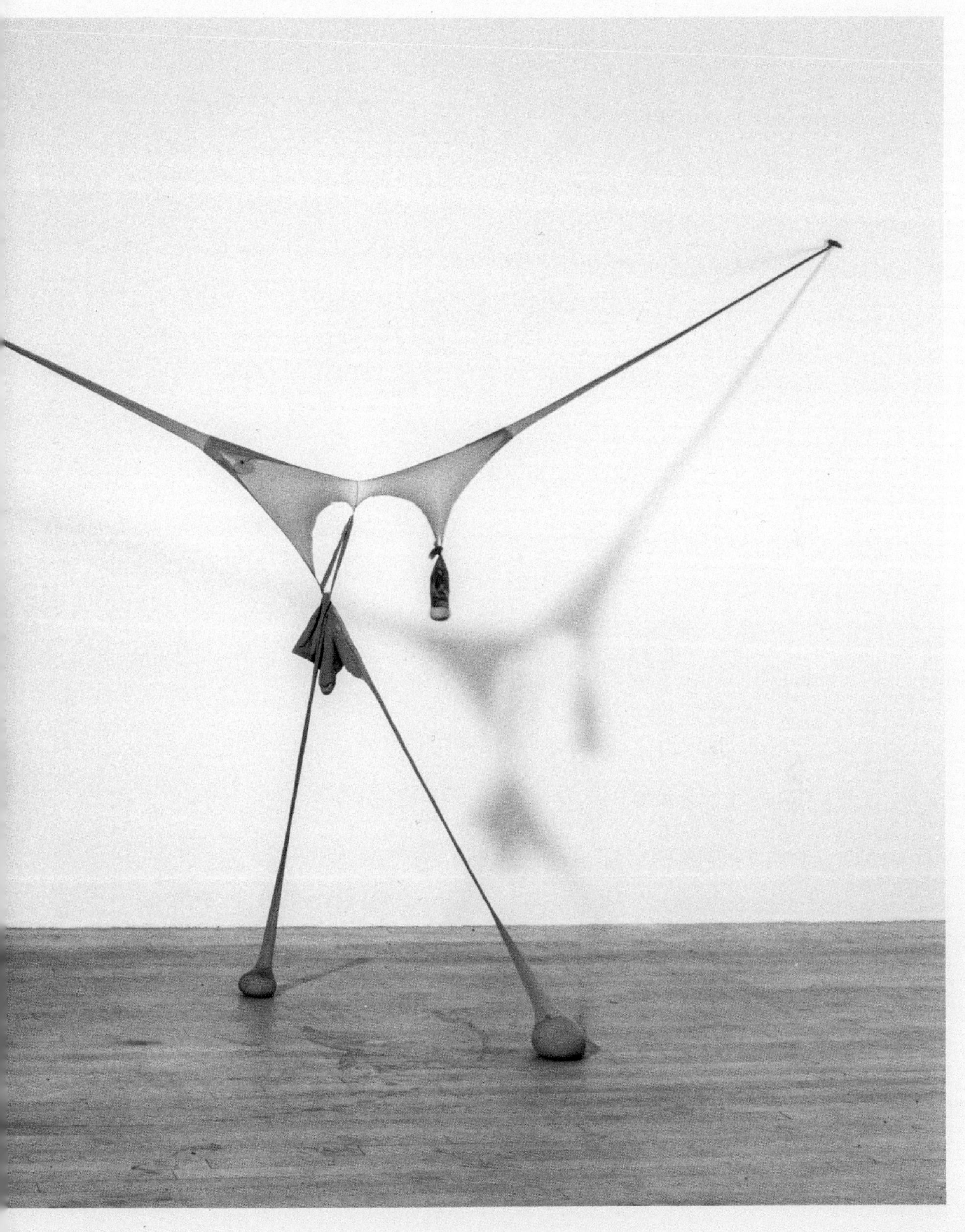

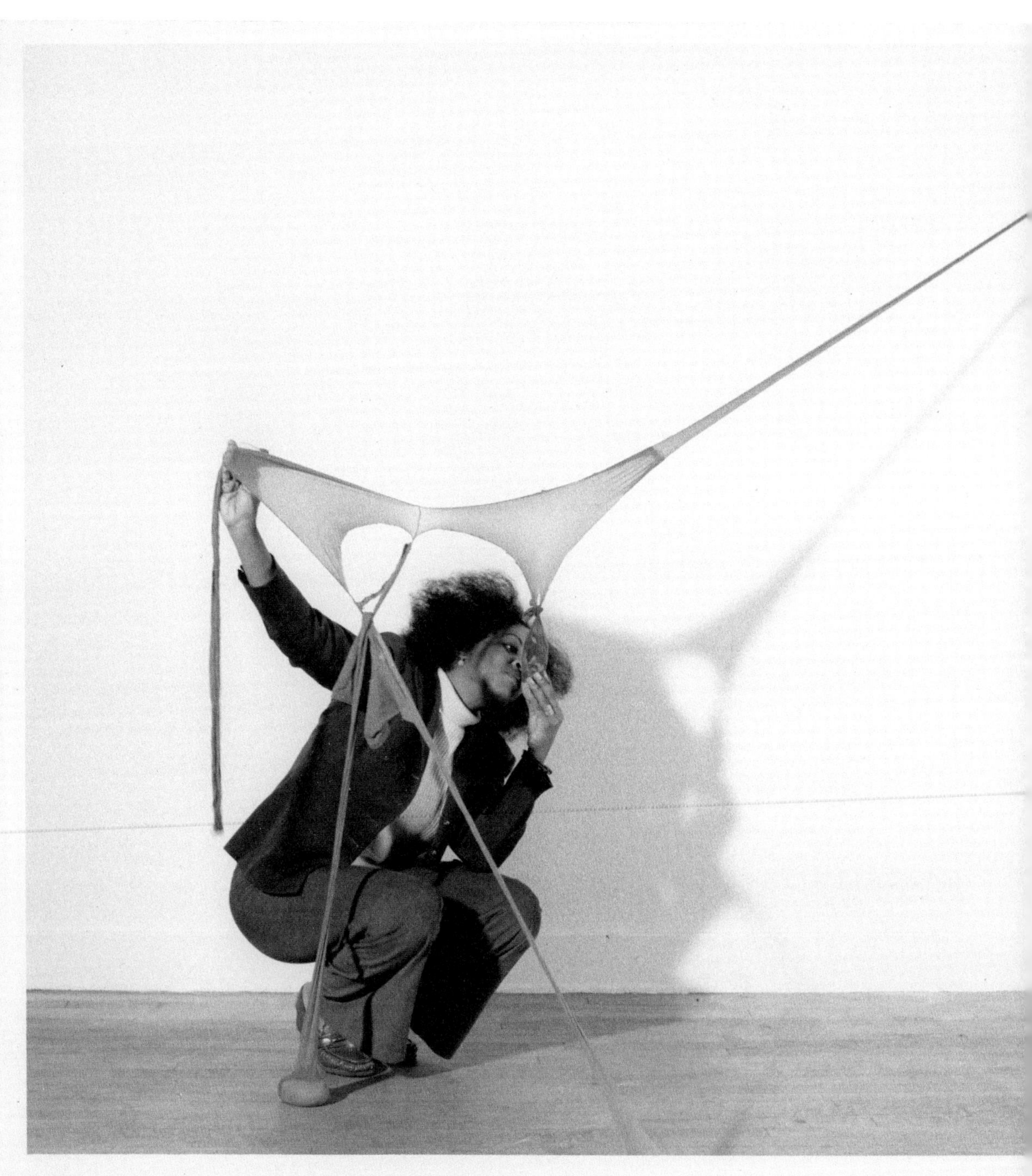

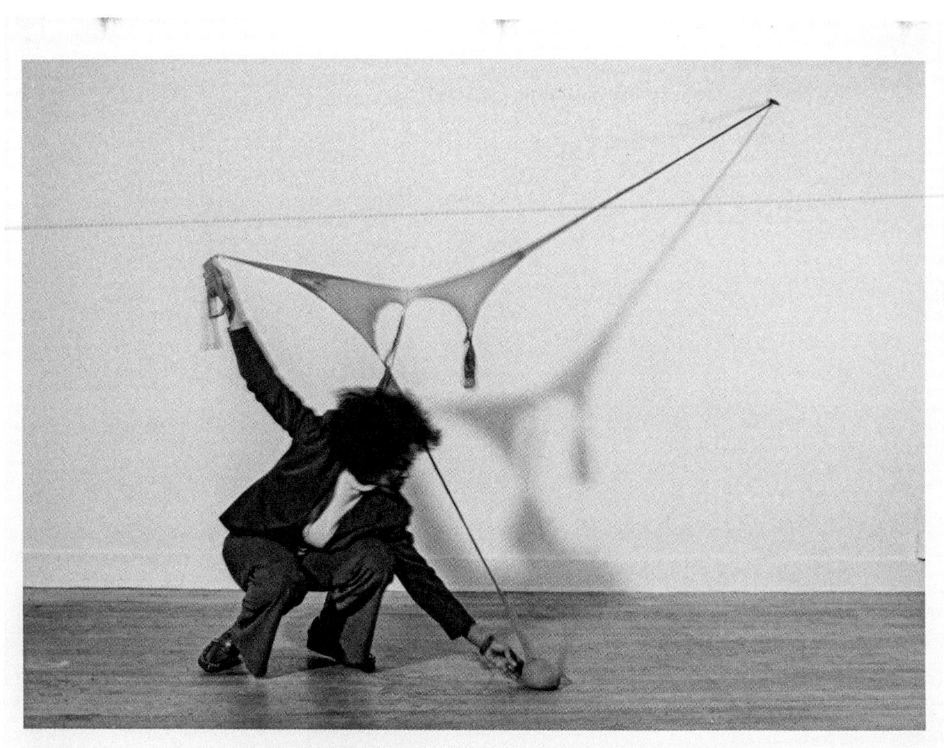

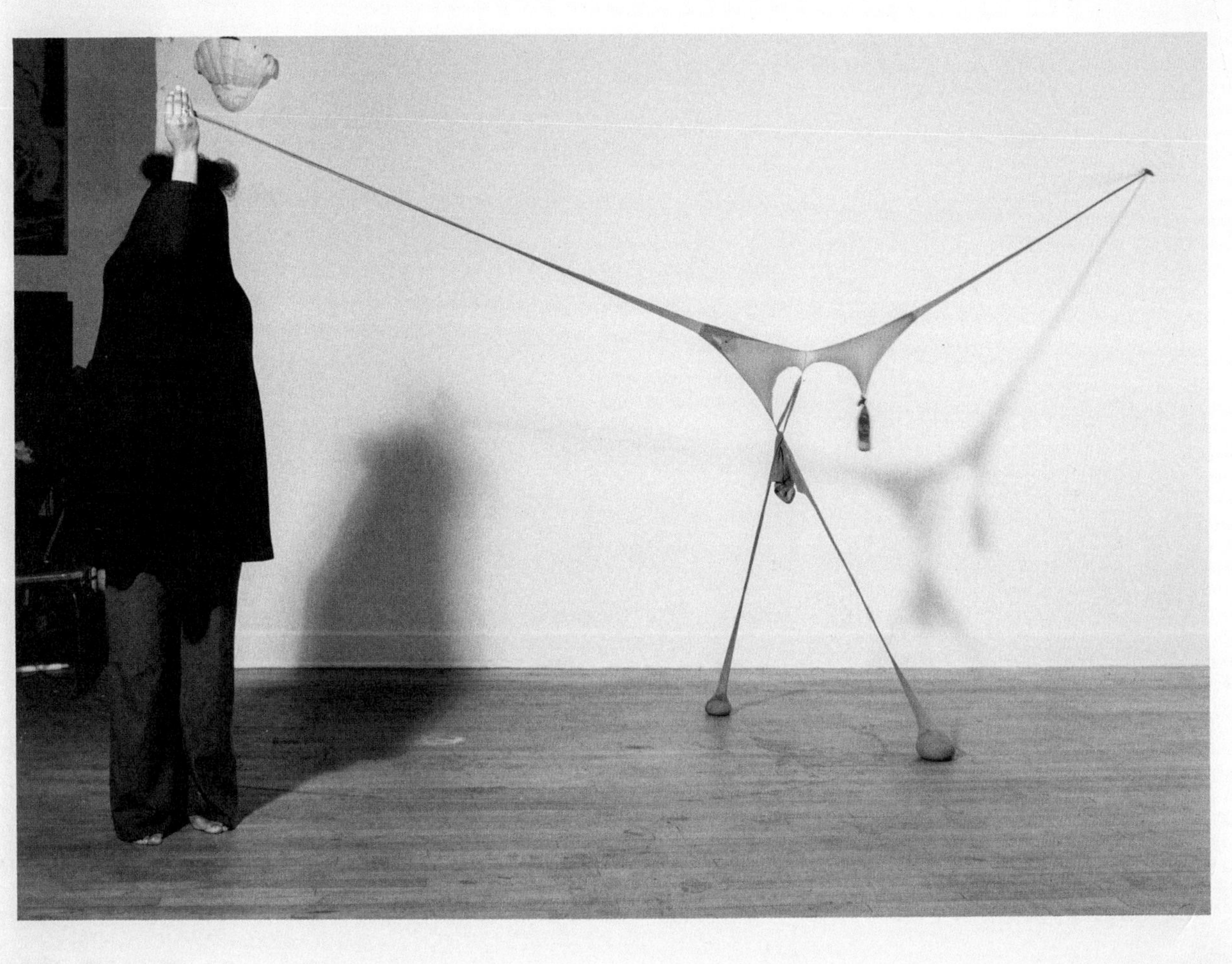

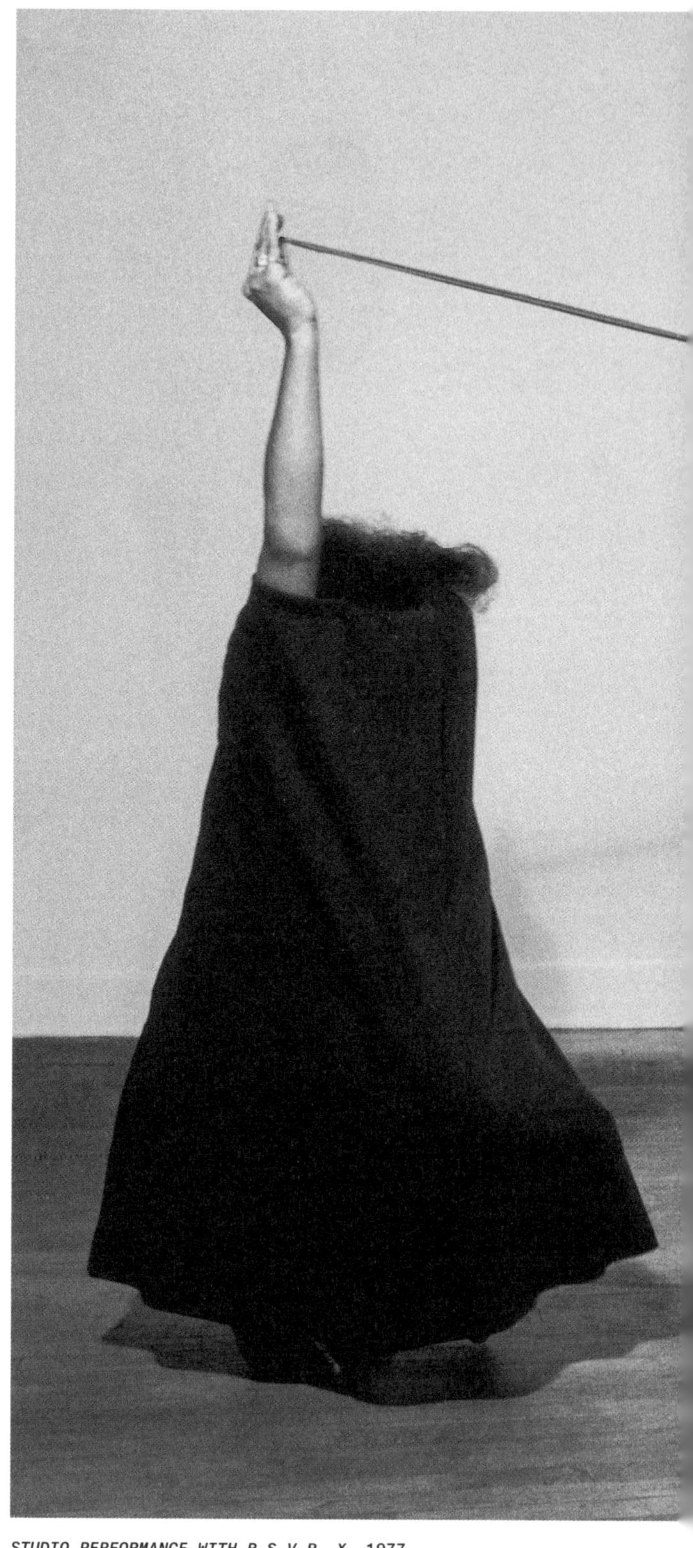

STUDIO PERFORMANCE WITH R.S.V.P. X, 1977
GELATIN SILVER PRINT,
30 × 40 INCHES (76.2 × 101.6 CM)
PHOTO: KEN PETERSON

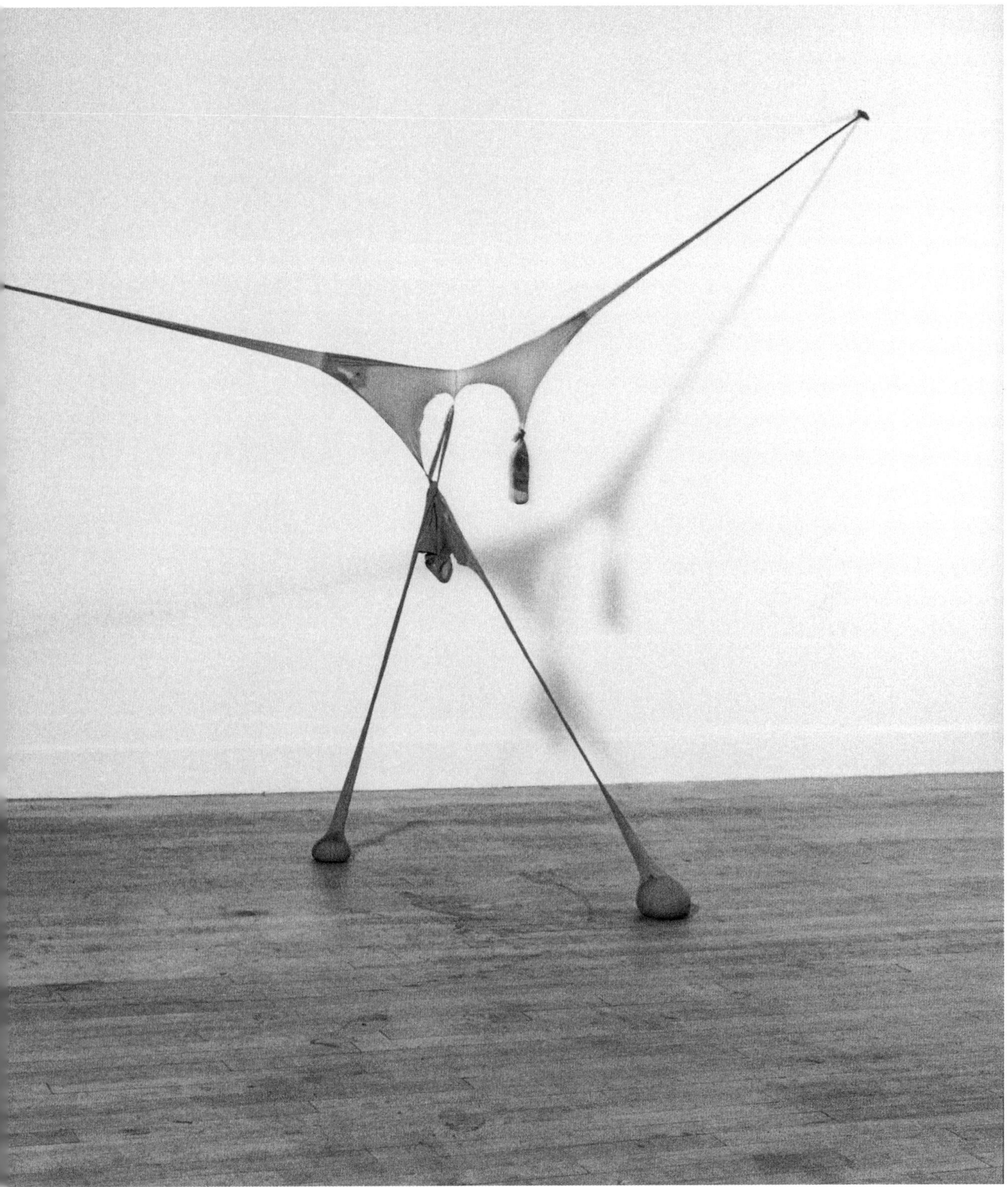

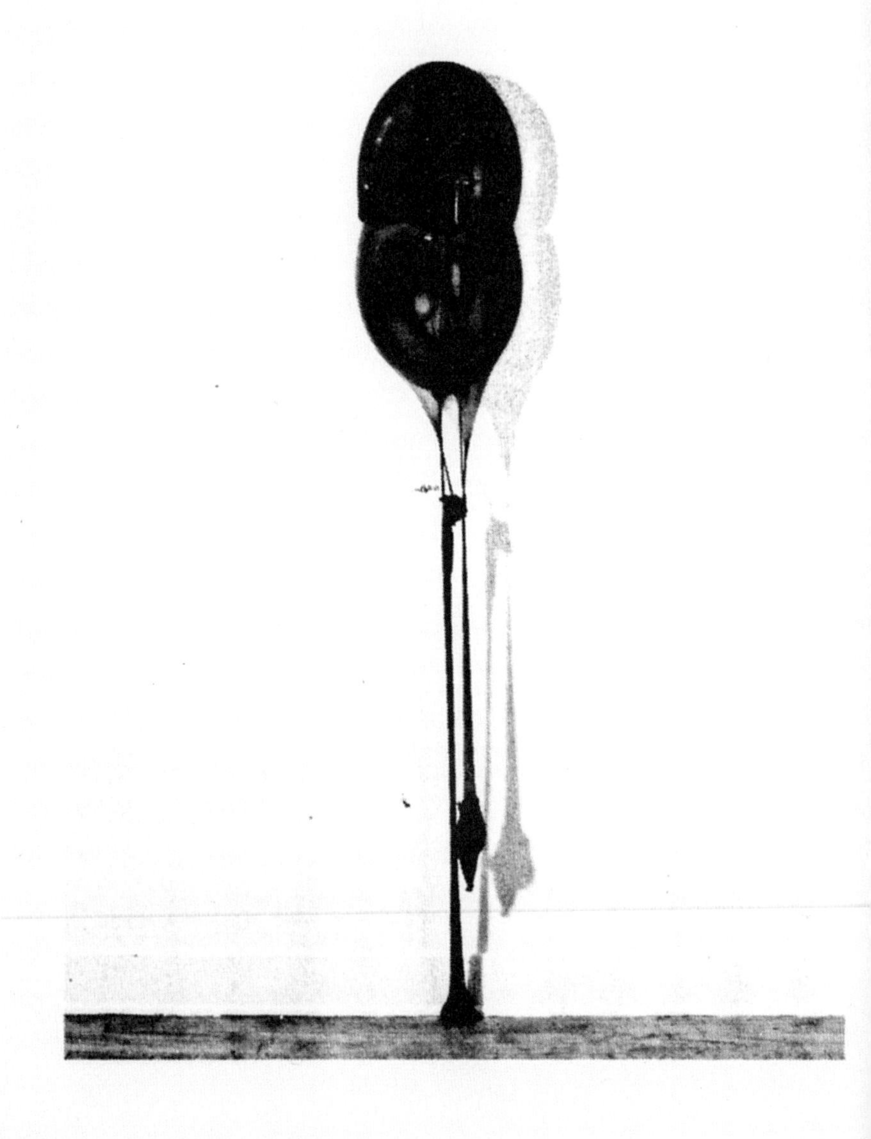

INVITATION CARD FOR *SENGA NENGUDI: NYLON MESH SERIES*, PEARL C. WOODS GALLERY, LOS ANGELES, MAY 13-29, 1977

NYLON MESH SERIES

RECENT WORK

SENGA NENGUDI

RECEPTION: MAY 13, 8-10 P.M.

PEARL C. WOOD GALLERY
TRIANGULAR CHURCH OF RELIGIOUS SCIENCE, UPSTAIRS
1938 S. WESTERN AVE., LOS ANGELES, CA.
CONTINUES THROUGH MAY 29, THURS.-SUN. 3-7 P.M.
(213) 731-1194

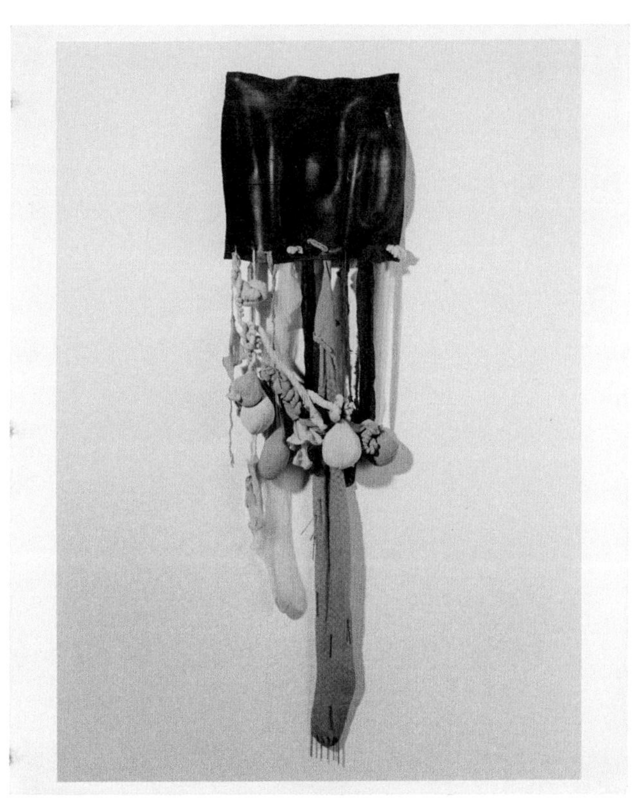

INSTALLATION VIEWS, *NYLON MESH SERIES*

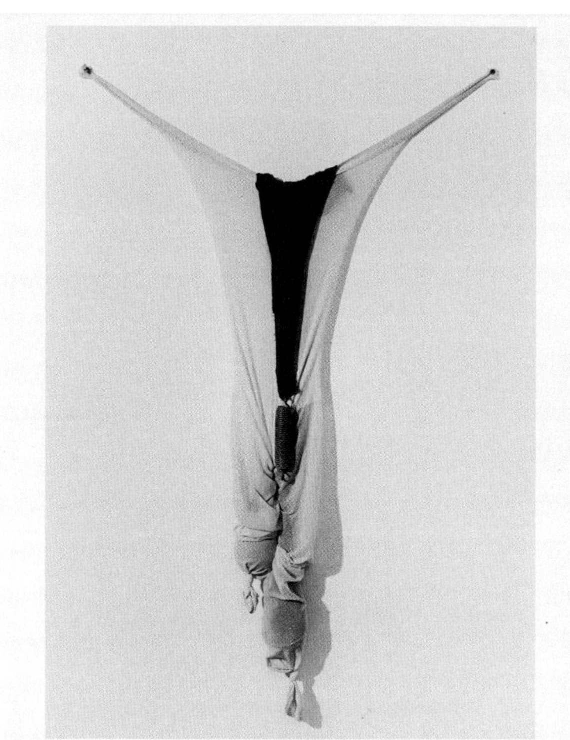

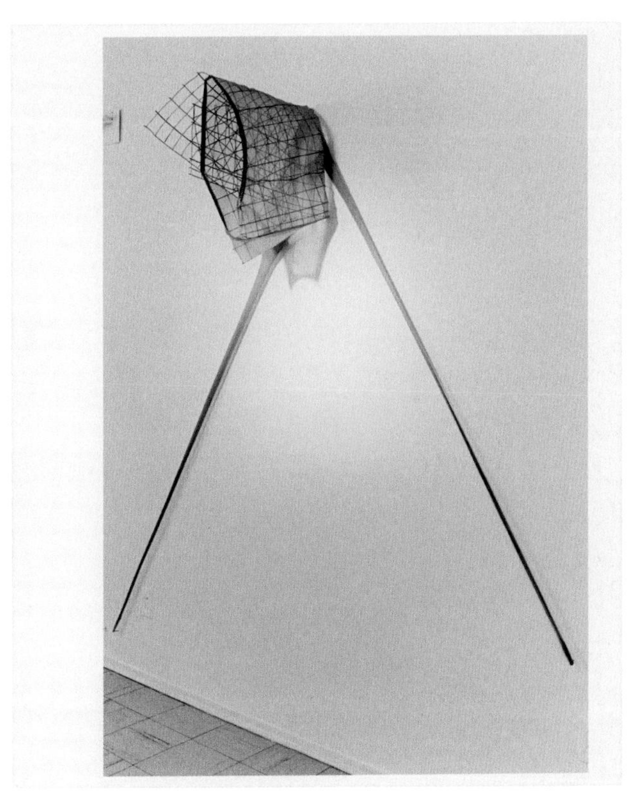

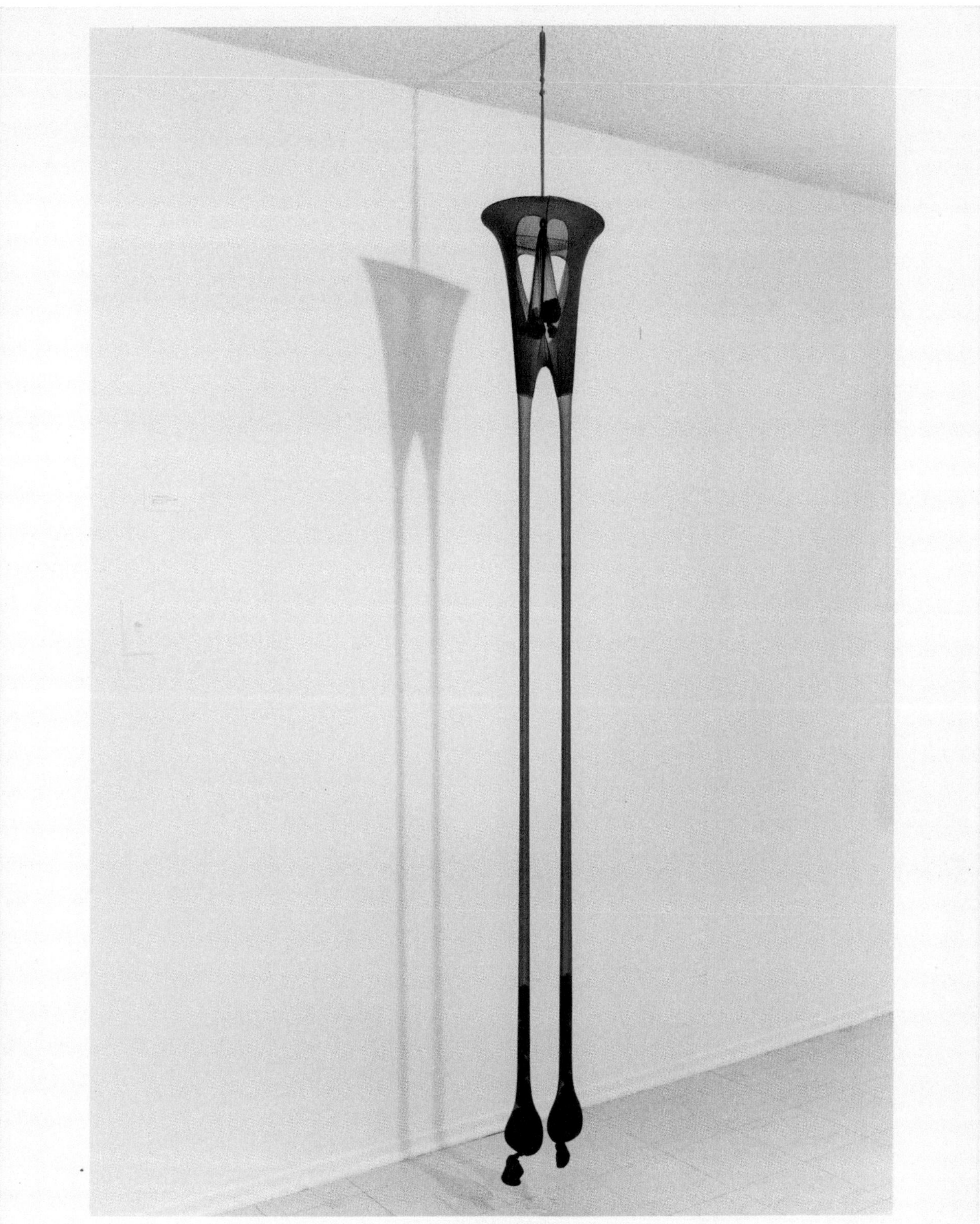

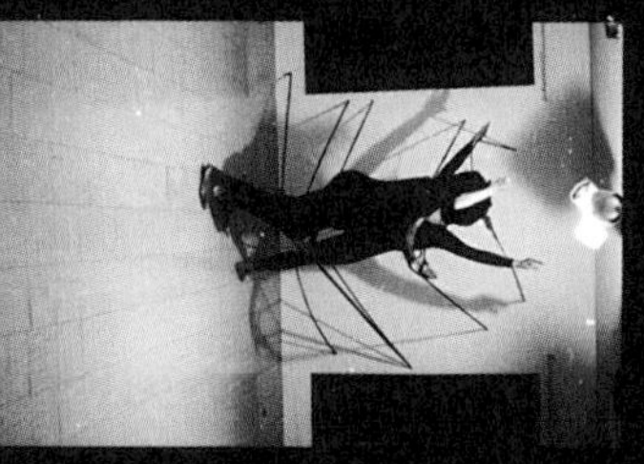
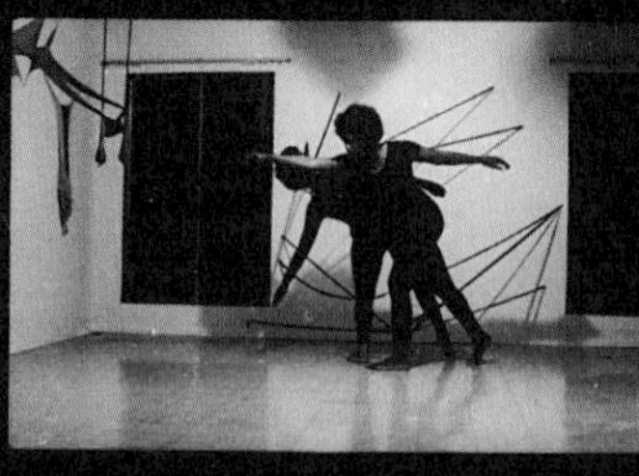
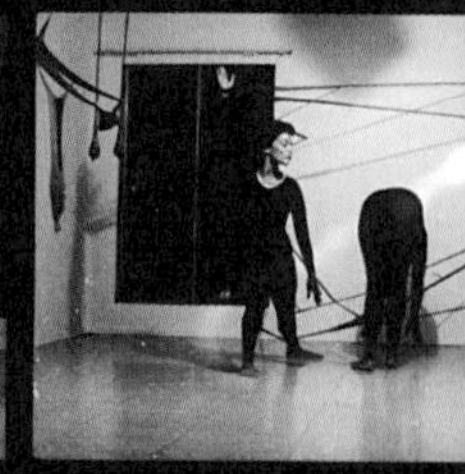
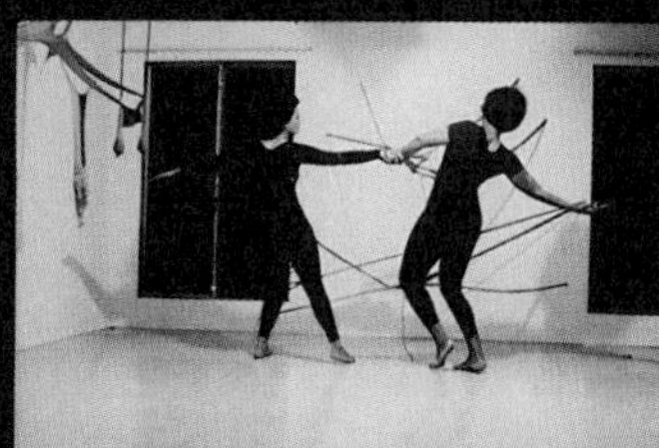
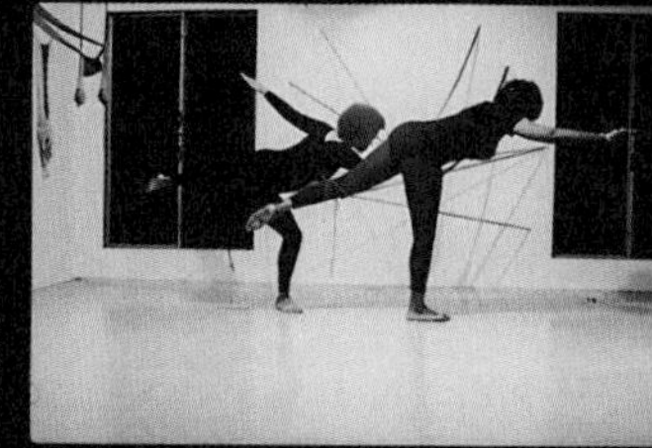
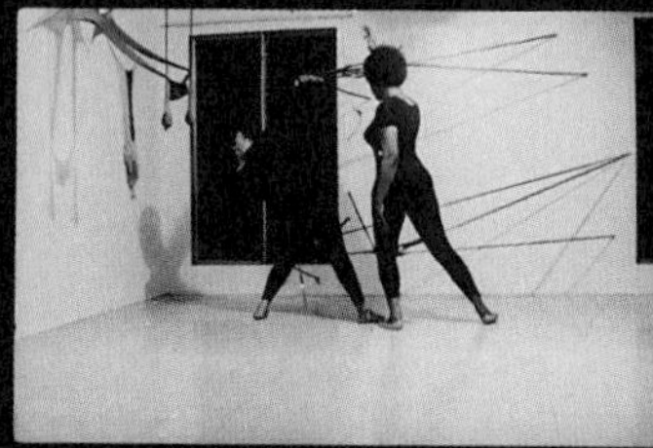
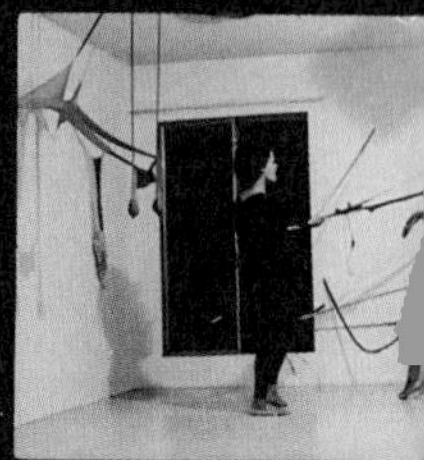
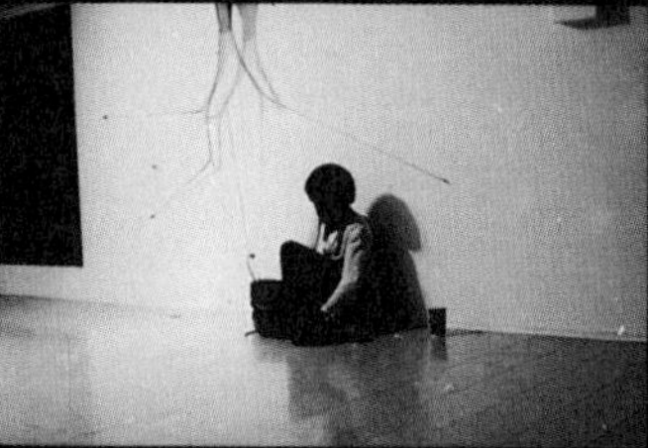
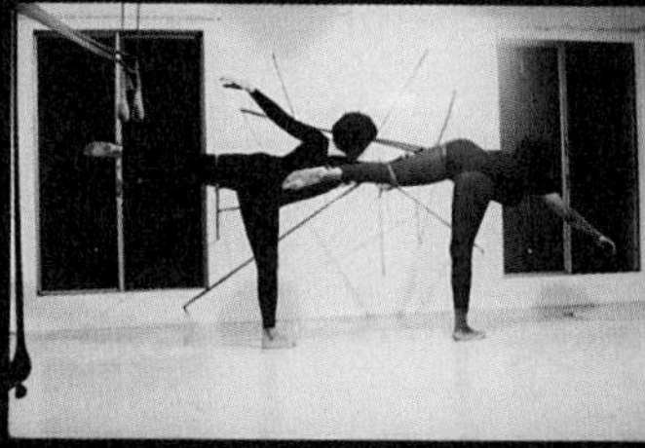
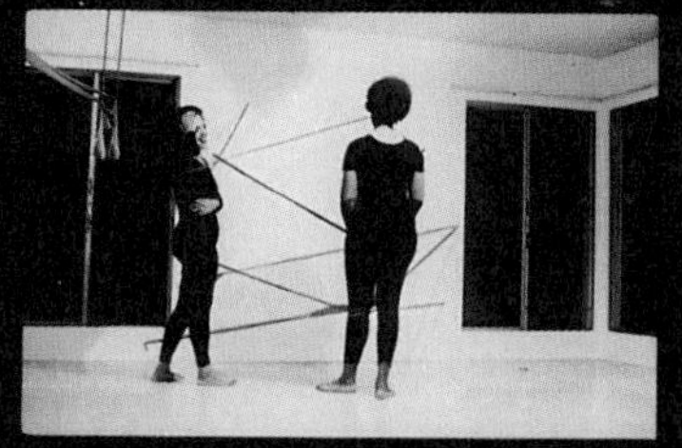
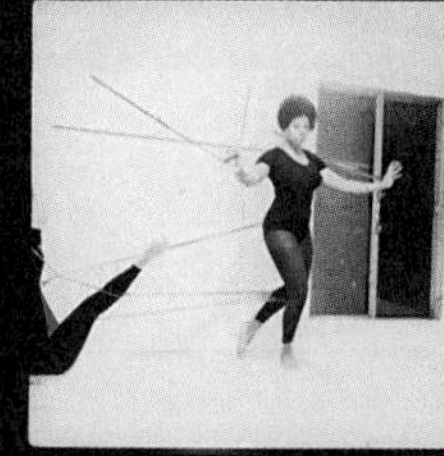
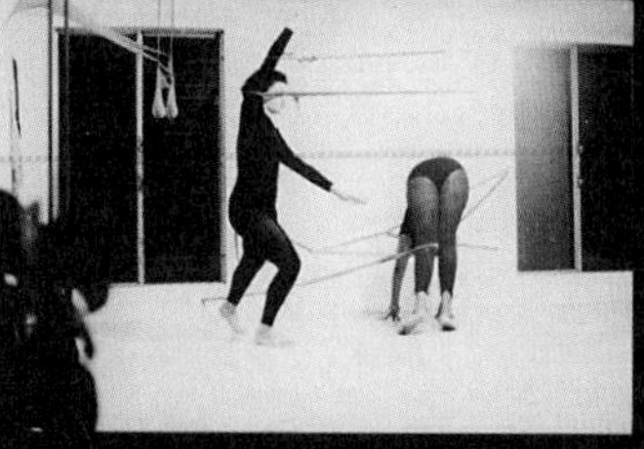
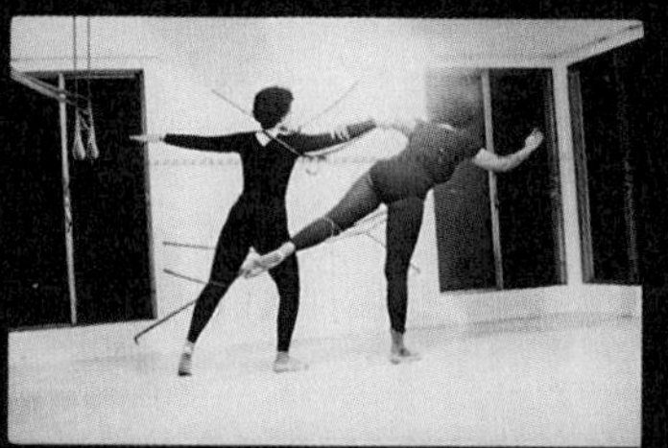
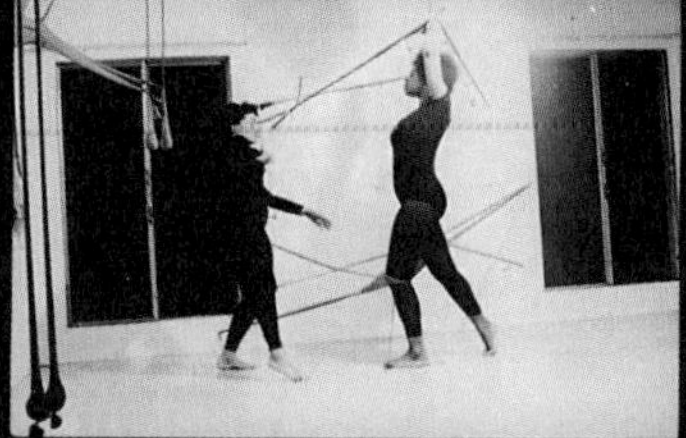
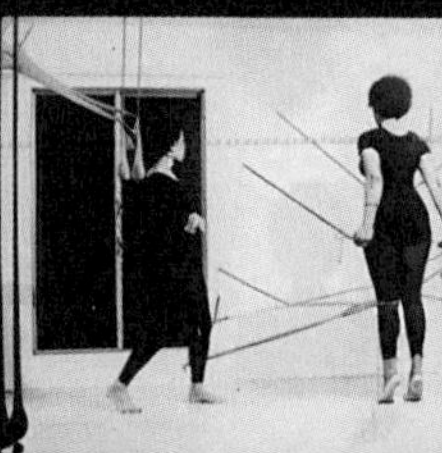
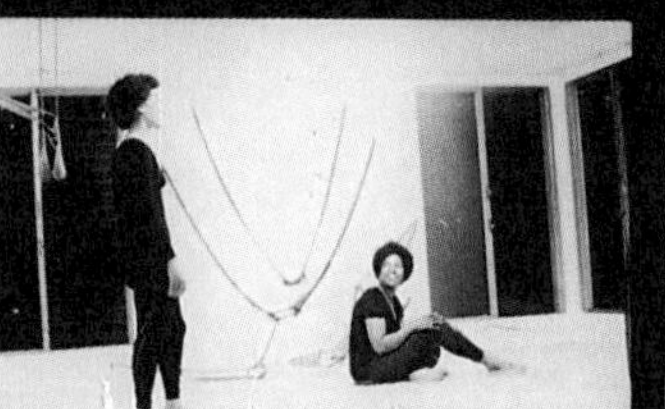
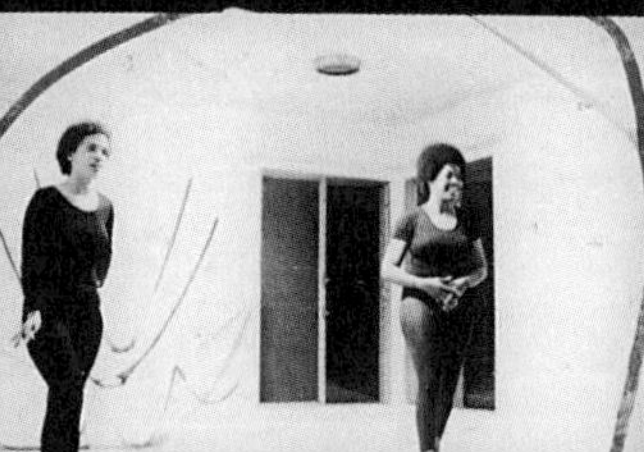
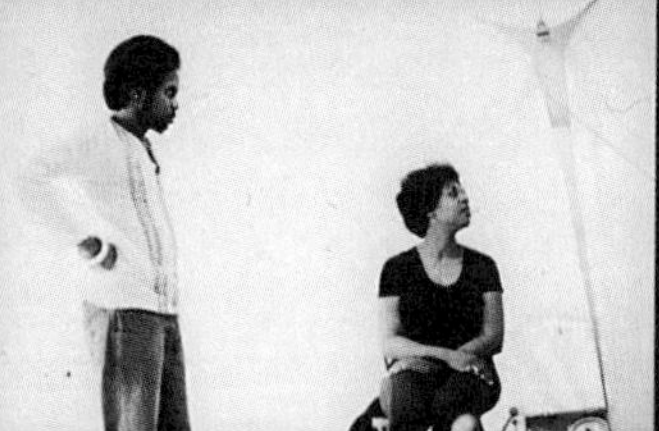
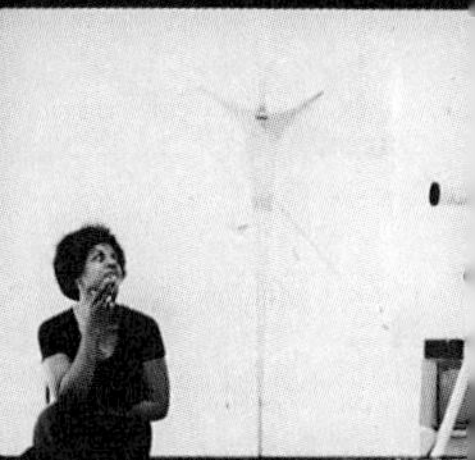

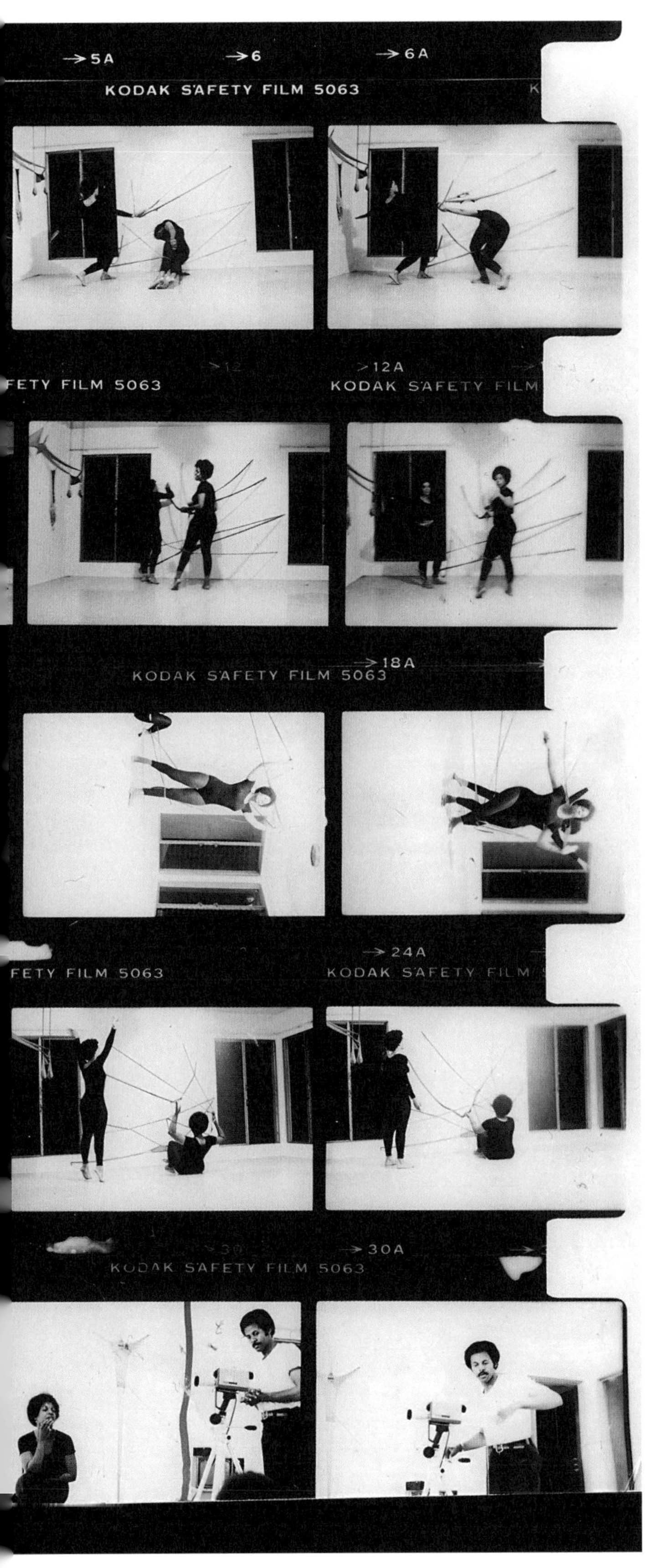

CONTACT SHEET OF NENGUDI AND MAREN HASSINGER
REHEARSING, PEARL C. WOODS GALLERY,
LOS ANGELES, 1977

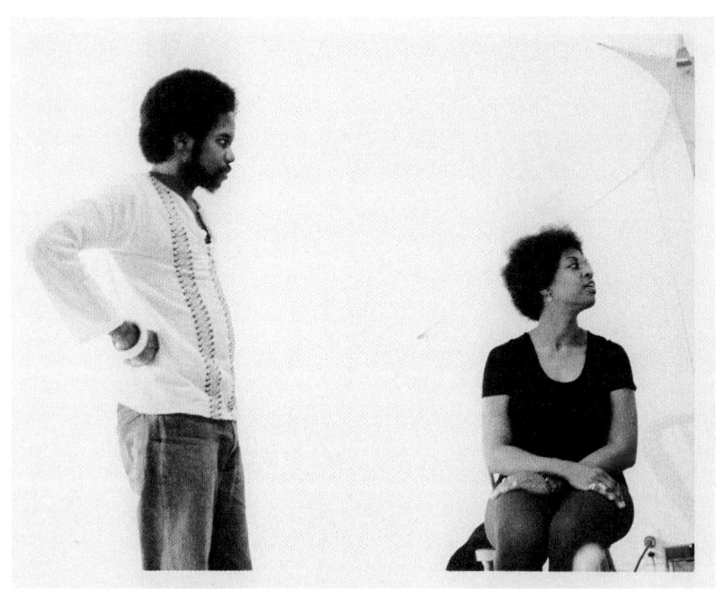

GREG PITTS AND NENGUDI DURING A REHEARSAL SESSION,
PEARL C. WOODS GALLERY, LOS ANGELES, 1977

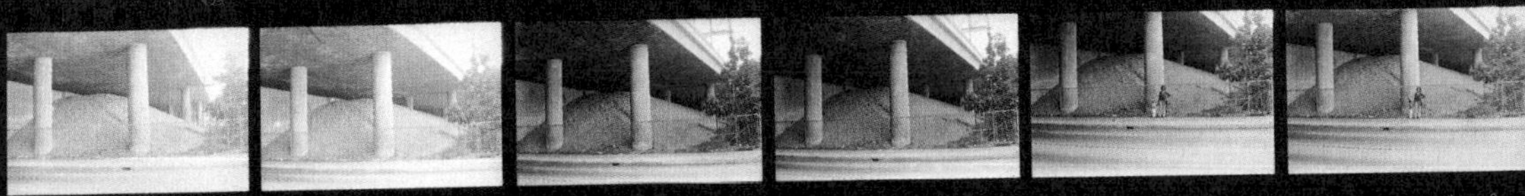

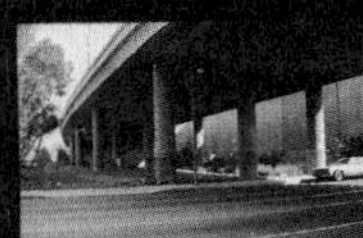
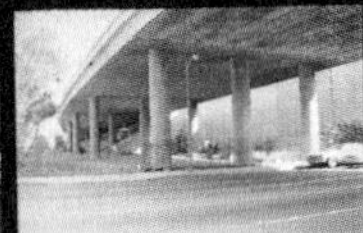
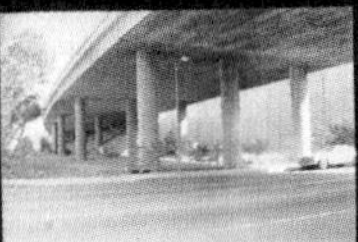
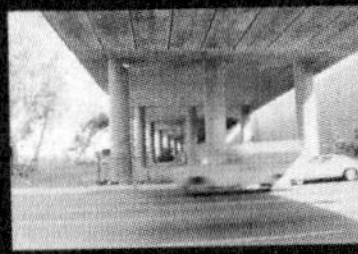
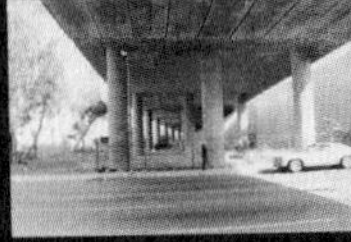
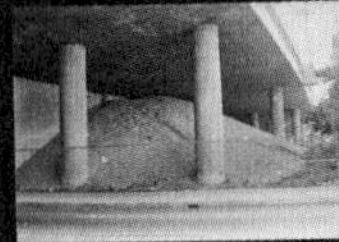

THE CAL-TRANS HIGHWAY ART PROGRAM IN CONJUNCTION WITH THE BGP/CETA TITLE VI
PROGRAM INVITES YOU TO ATTEND A CEREMONY FOR THE UNVEILING OF AN ENVIRONMENTAL

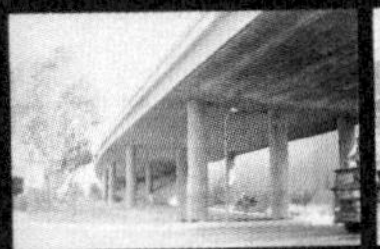
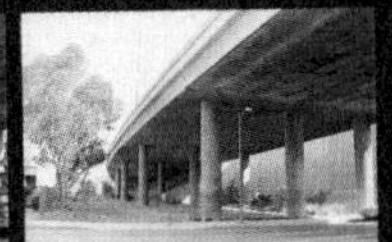
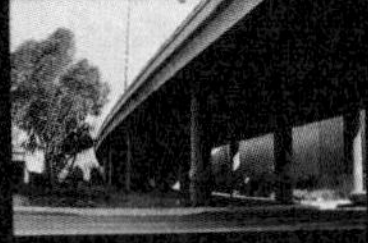
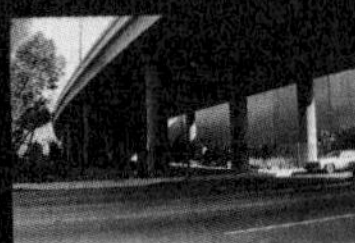

SCULPTURE BY ARTIST, SENGA NENGUDI, THURSDAY, 9:30AM/APRIL 13th-1327 W.PICO BL.

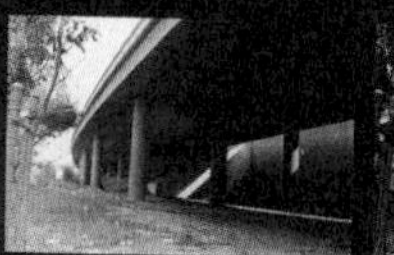
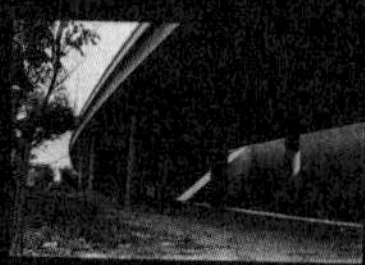
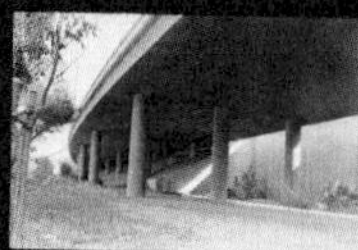
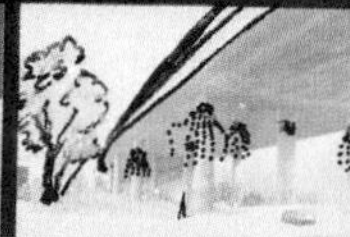

INVITATION CARD FOR *CEREMONY FOR FREEWAY FETS*,
1327 WEST PICO BOULEVARD, LOS ANGELES, APRIL 13, 1978
CHOREOGRAPHY AND COSTUMES BY NENGUDI
PERFORMED BY DAVID HAMMONS, MAREN HASSINGER
MUSIC BY FREEDOM N' EXPRESSION, FRANKLIN PARKER,
JOE RAY, ROHO, AND KENNETH SEVERIN

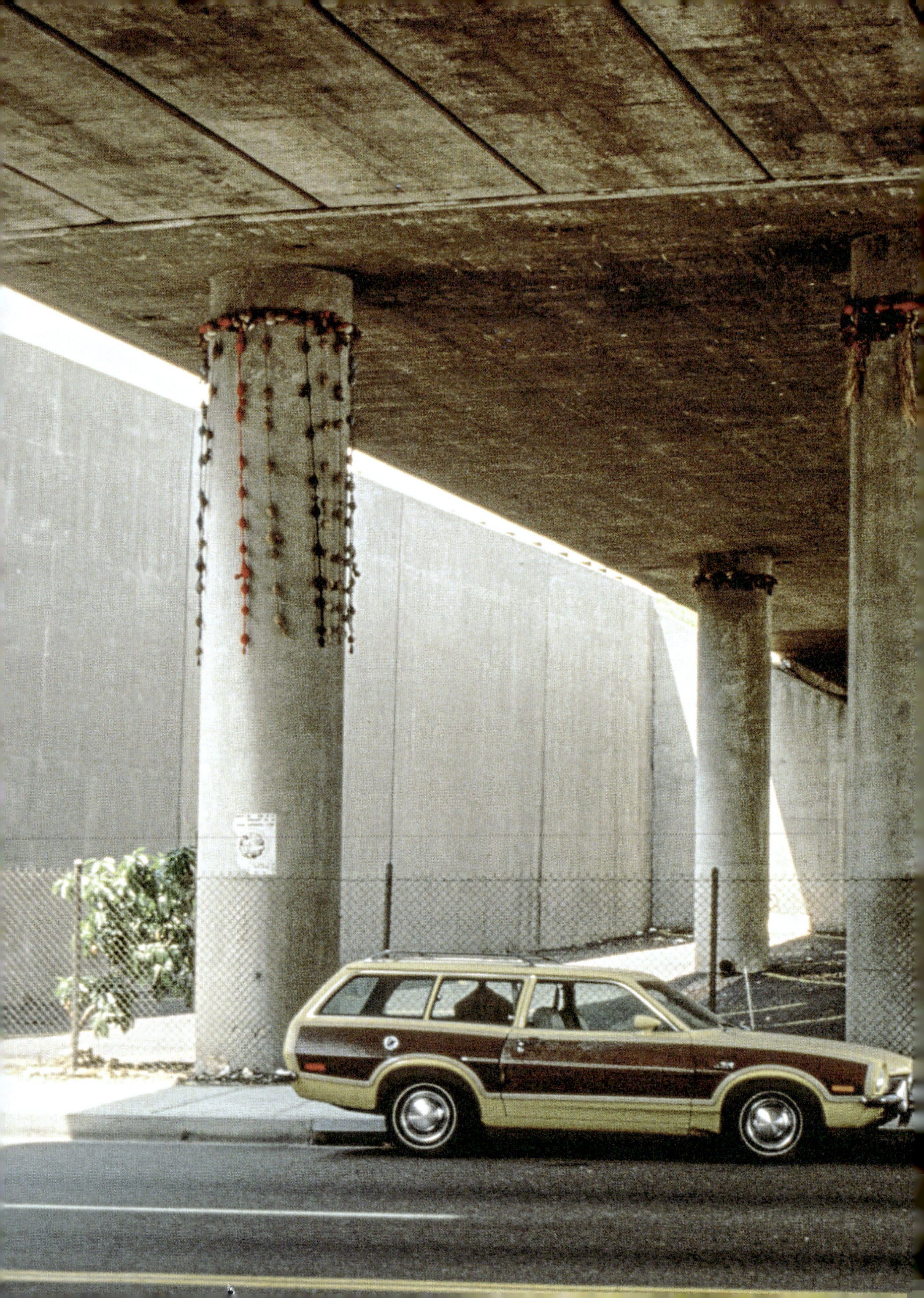

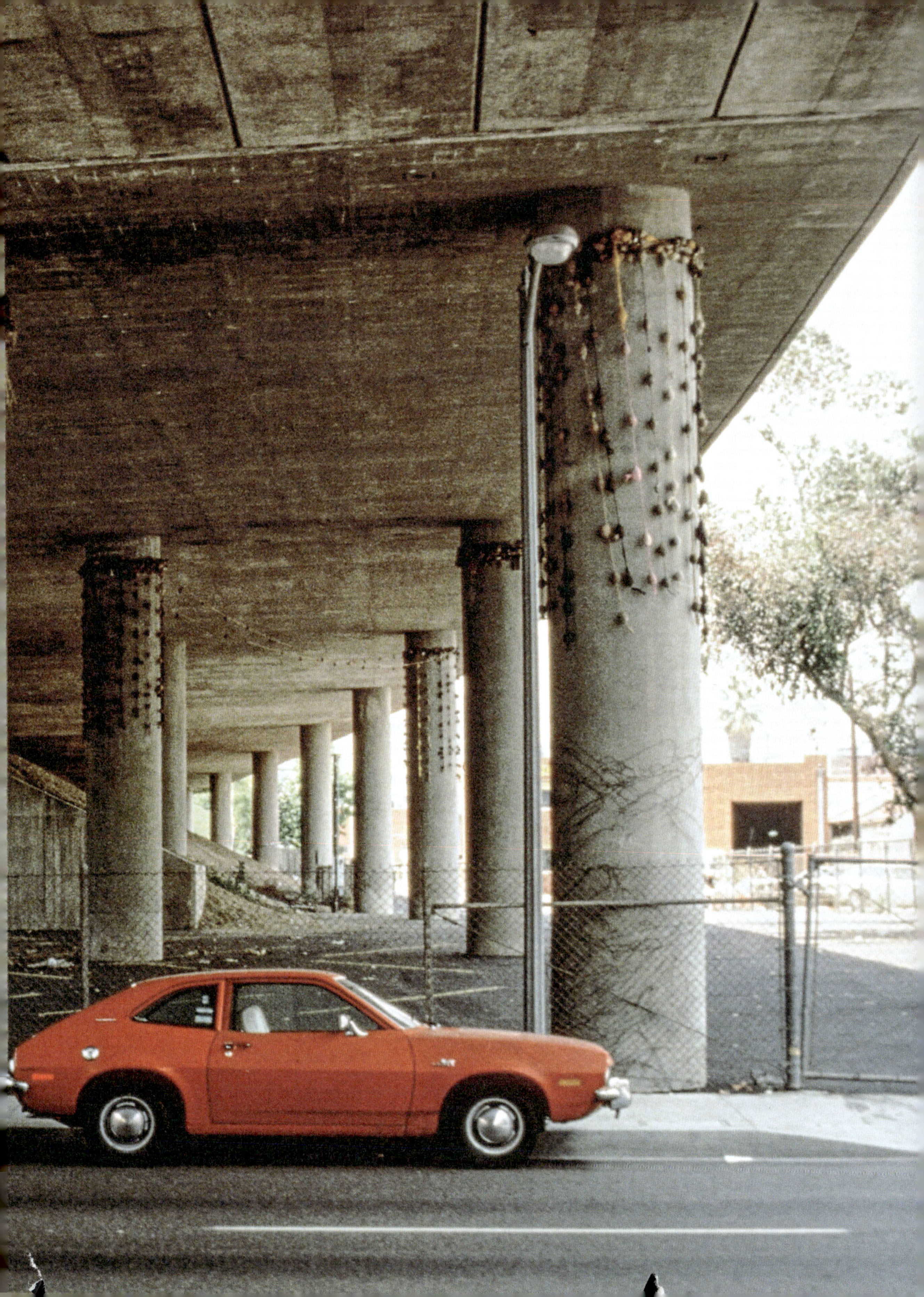

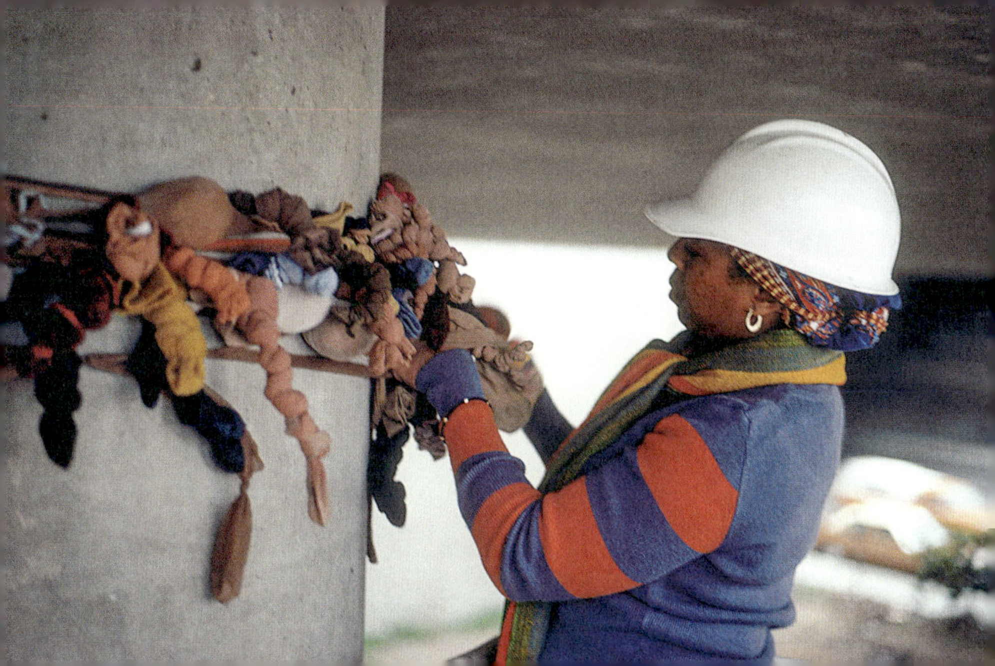

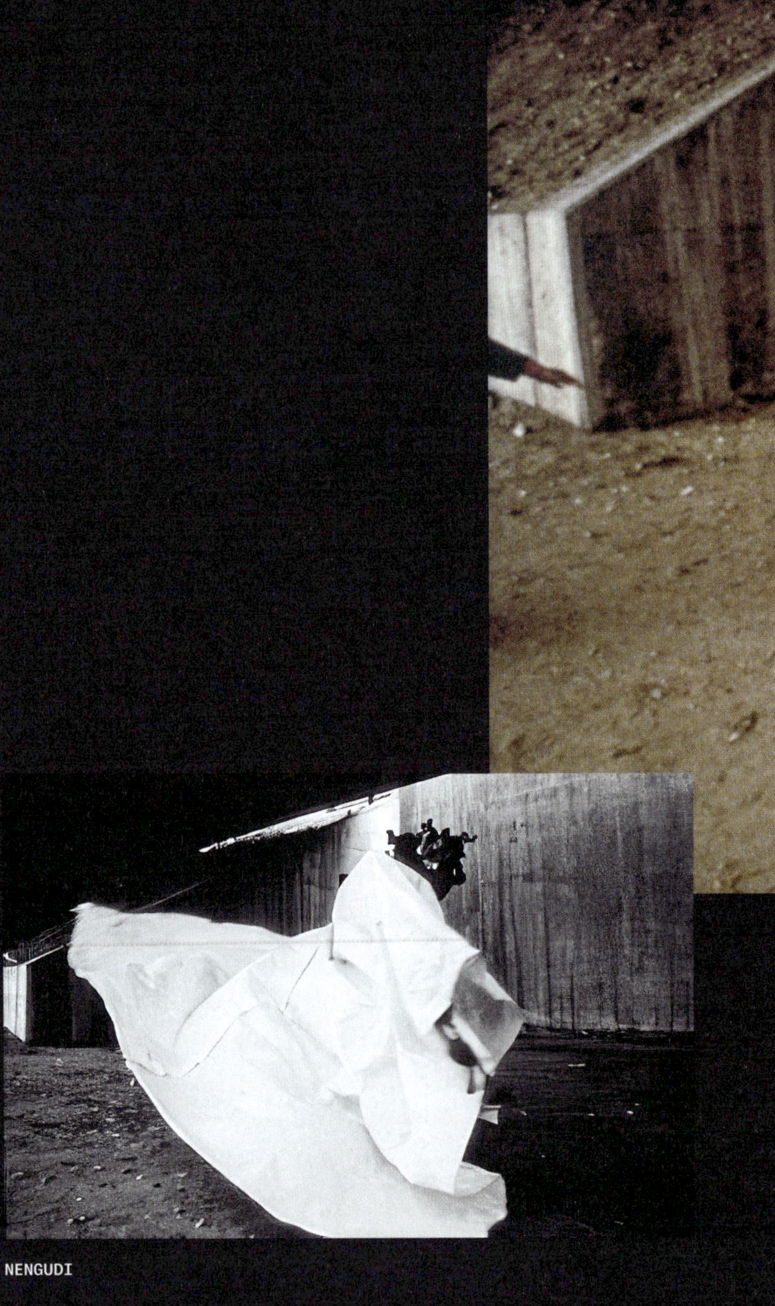

NENGUDI

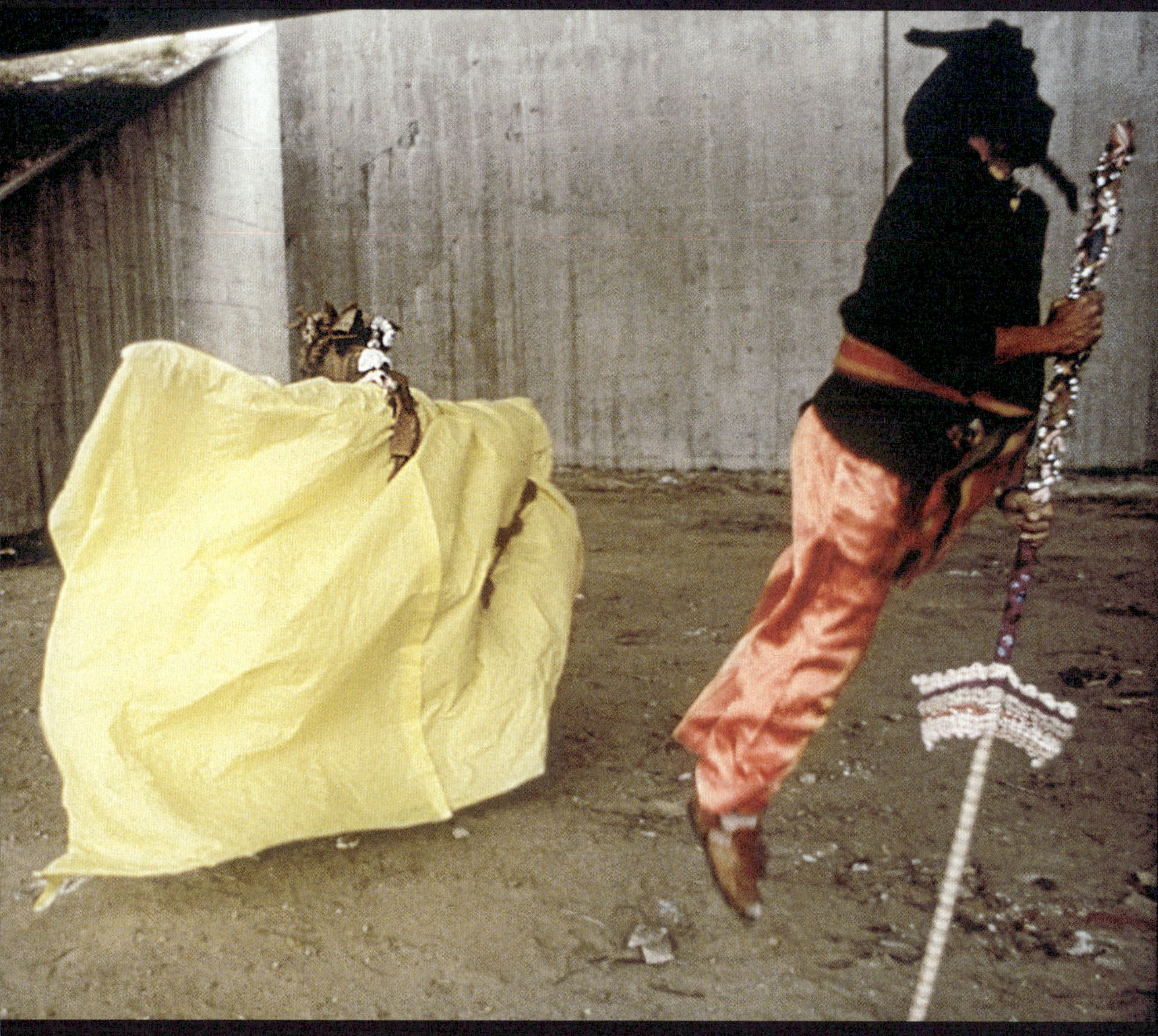

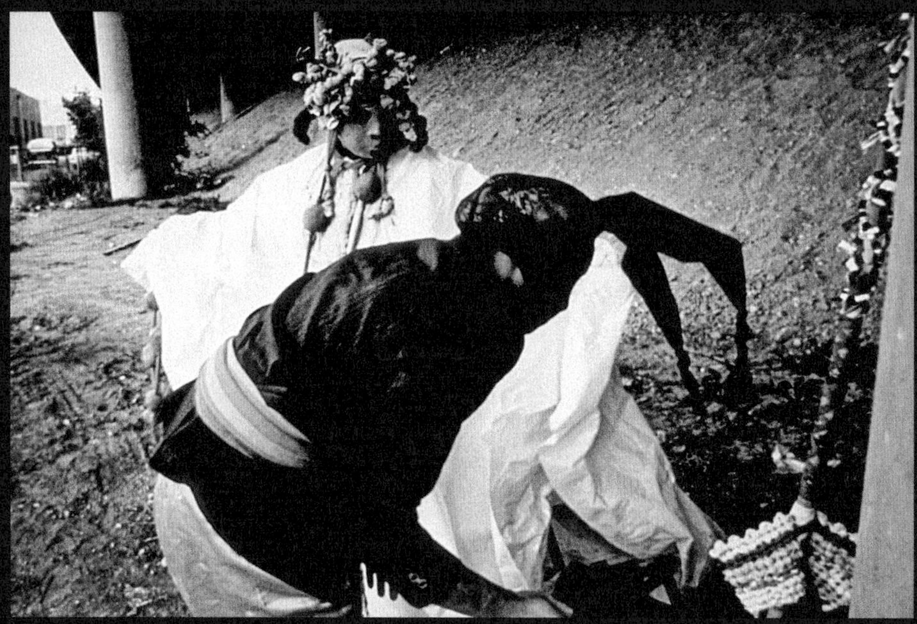

NENGUDI AND HAMMONS

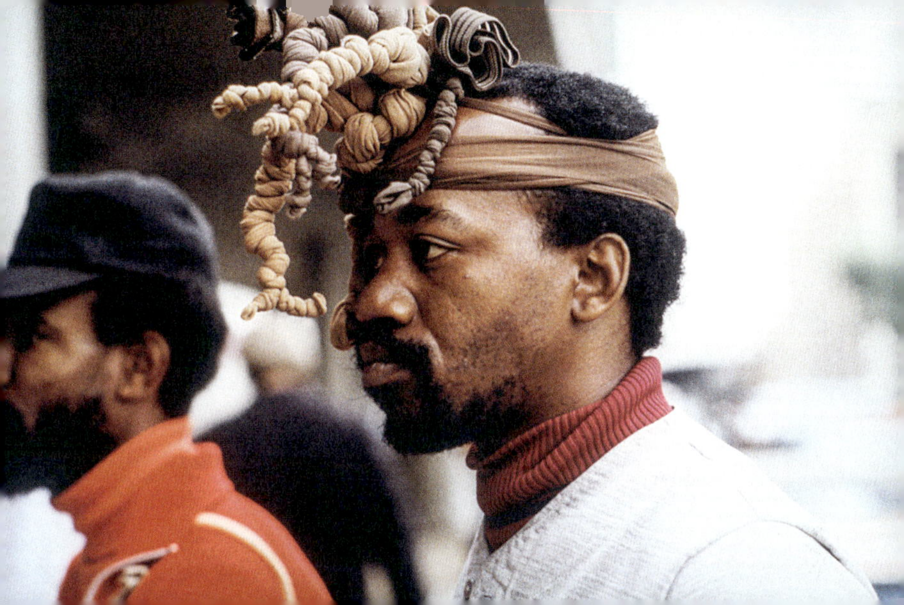

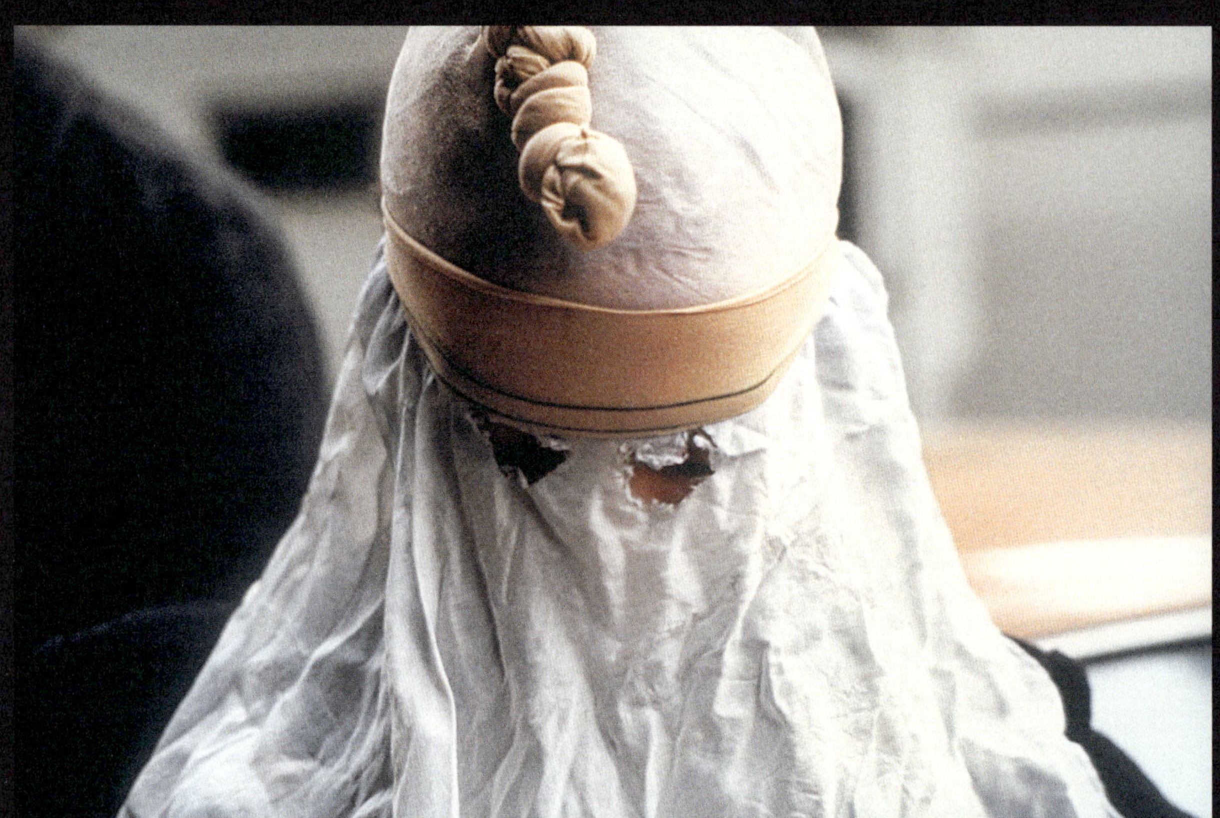

HASSINGER

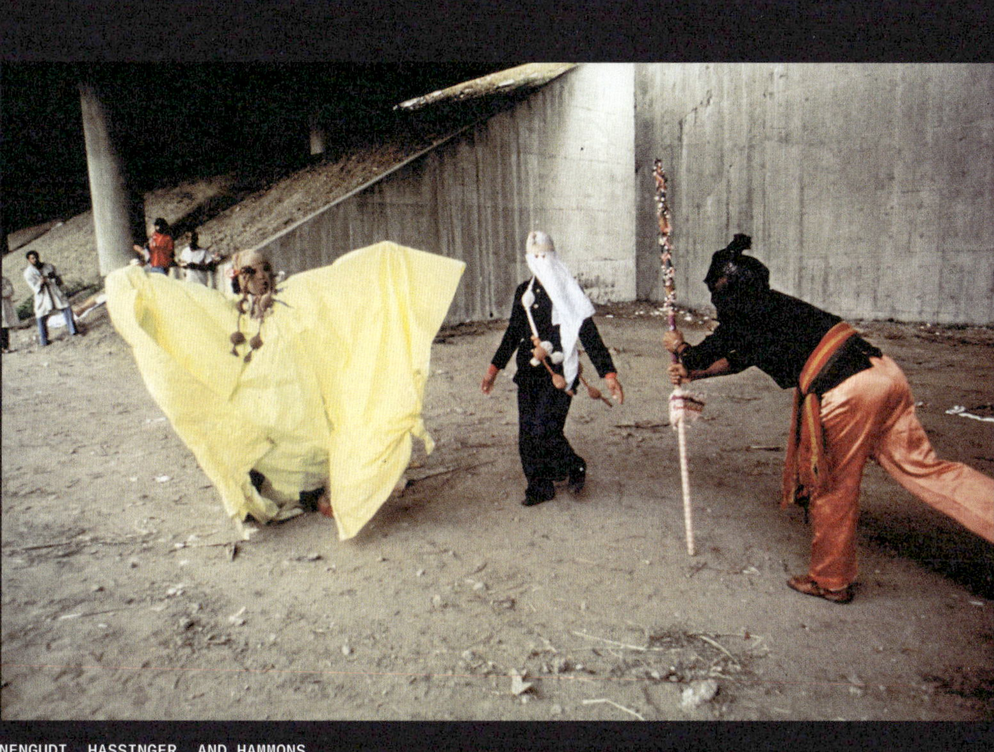

NENGUDI, HASSINGER, AND HAMMONS

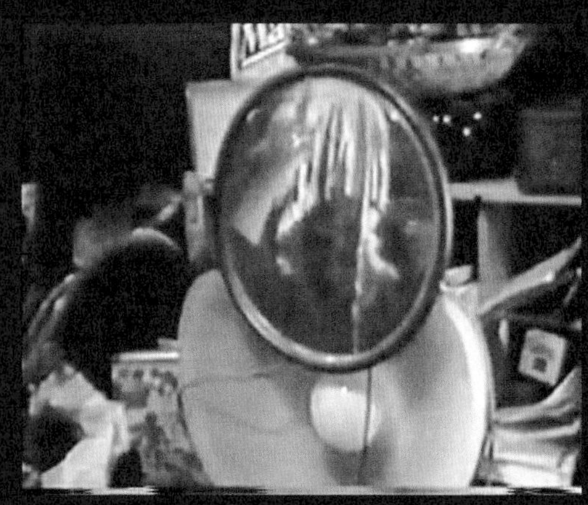

STILLS OF NENGUDI PERFORMING IN BARBARA MCCULLOUGH'S *SHOPPING BAG SPIRITS AND FREEWAY FETISHES: REFLECTIONS ON RITUAL SPACE*, 1981
VIDEO, 60 MIN.

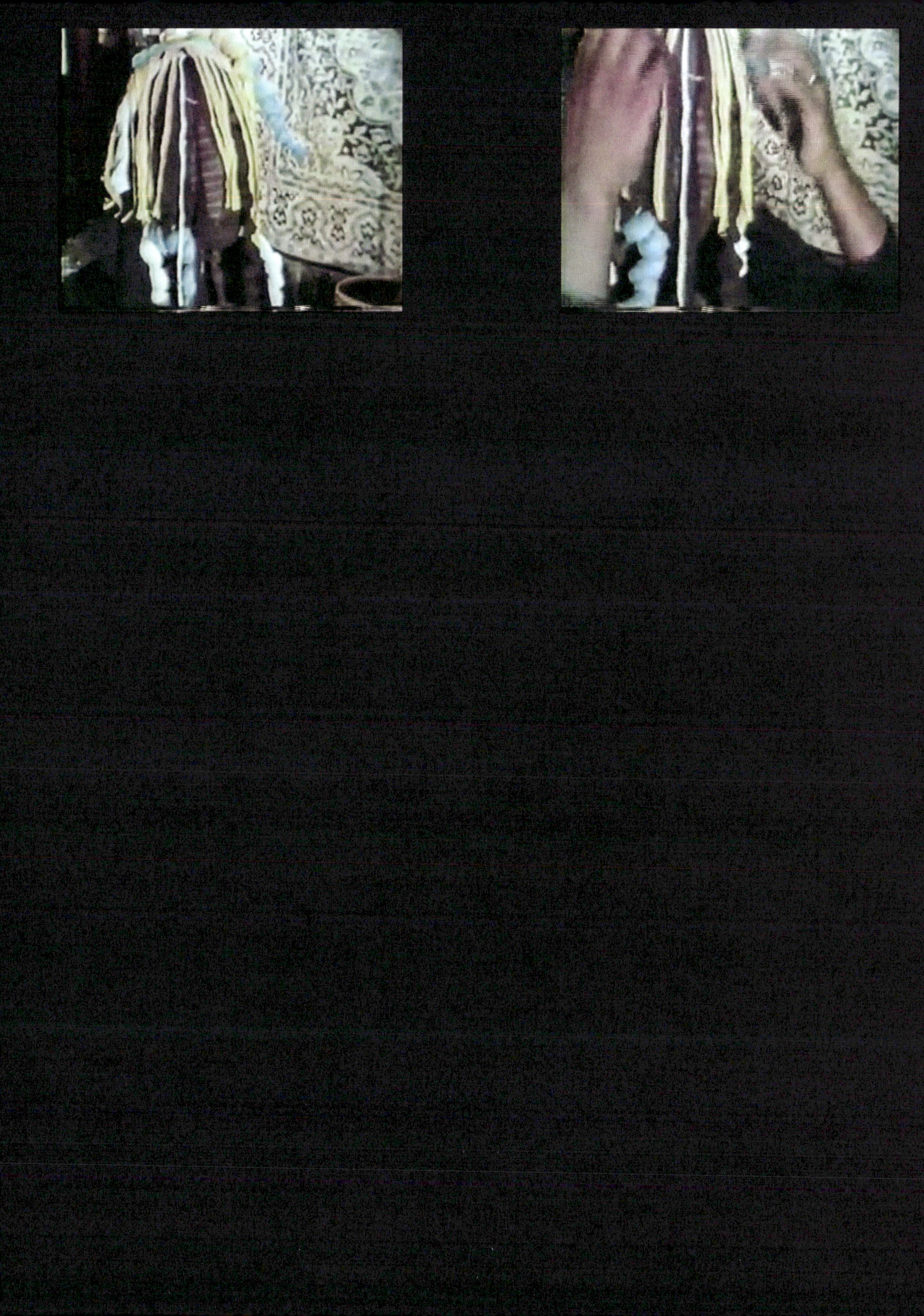

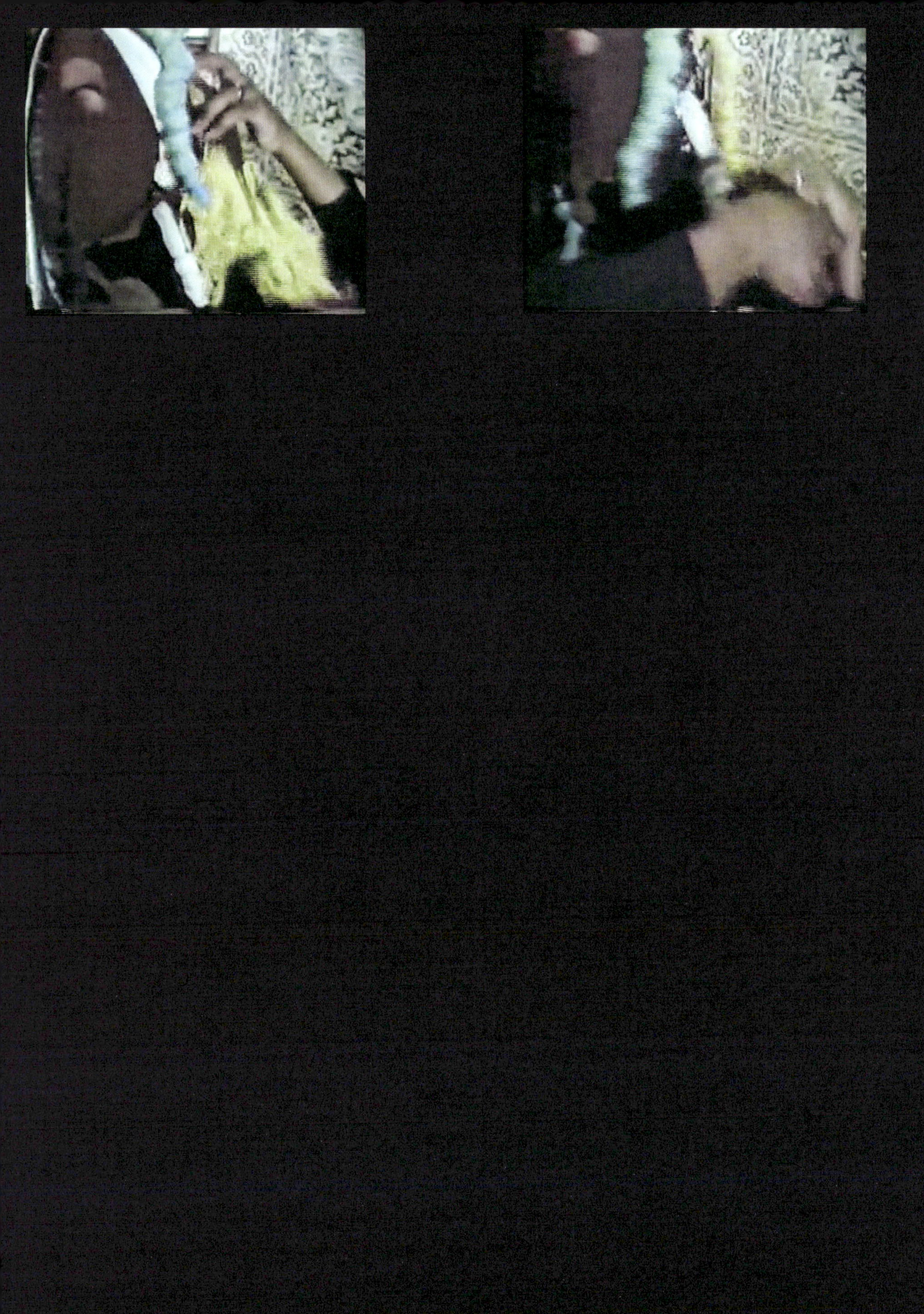

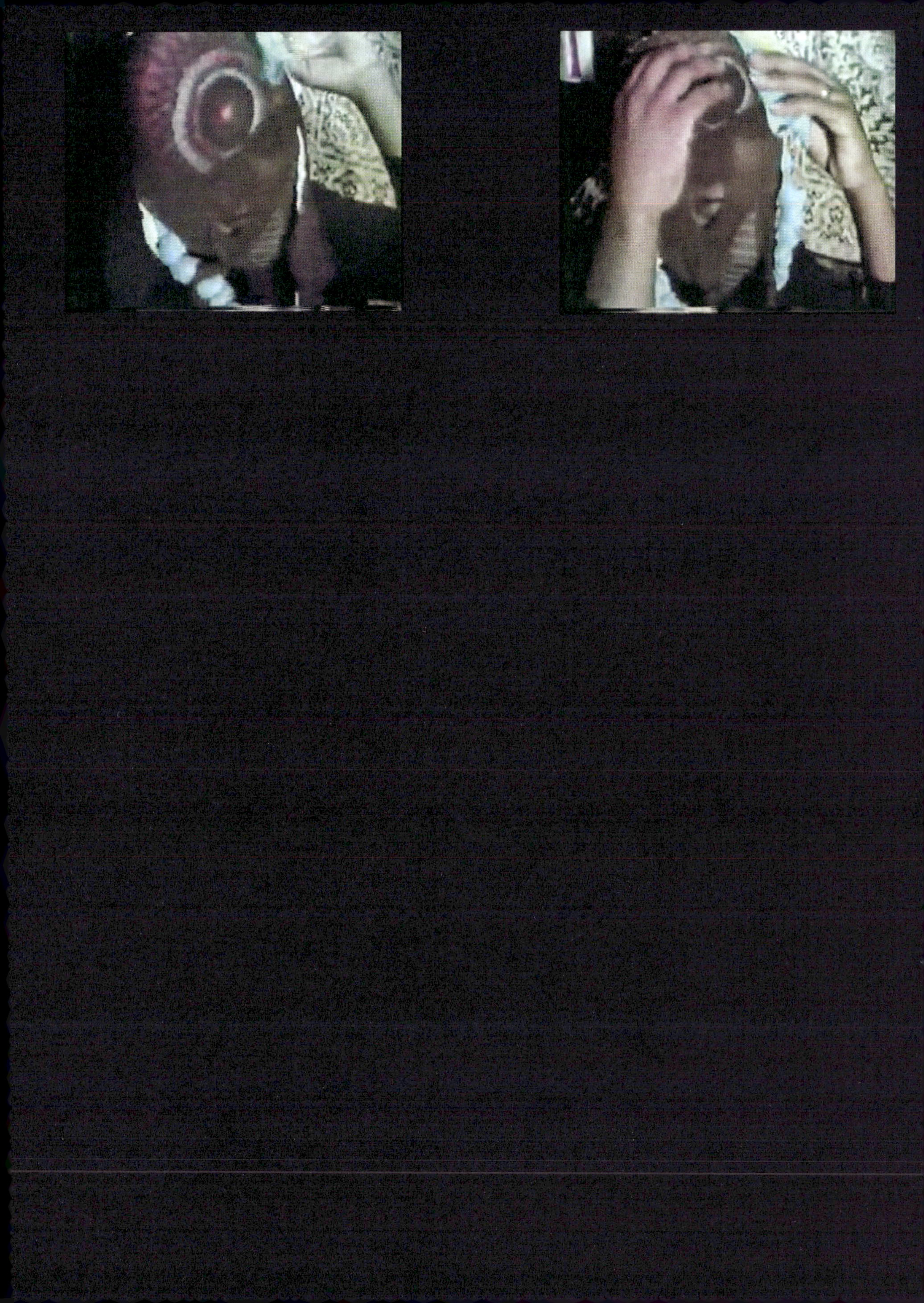

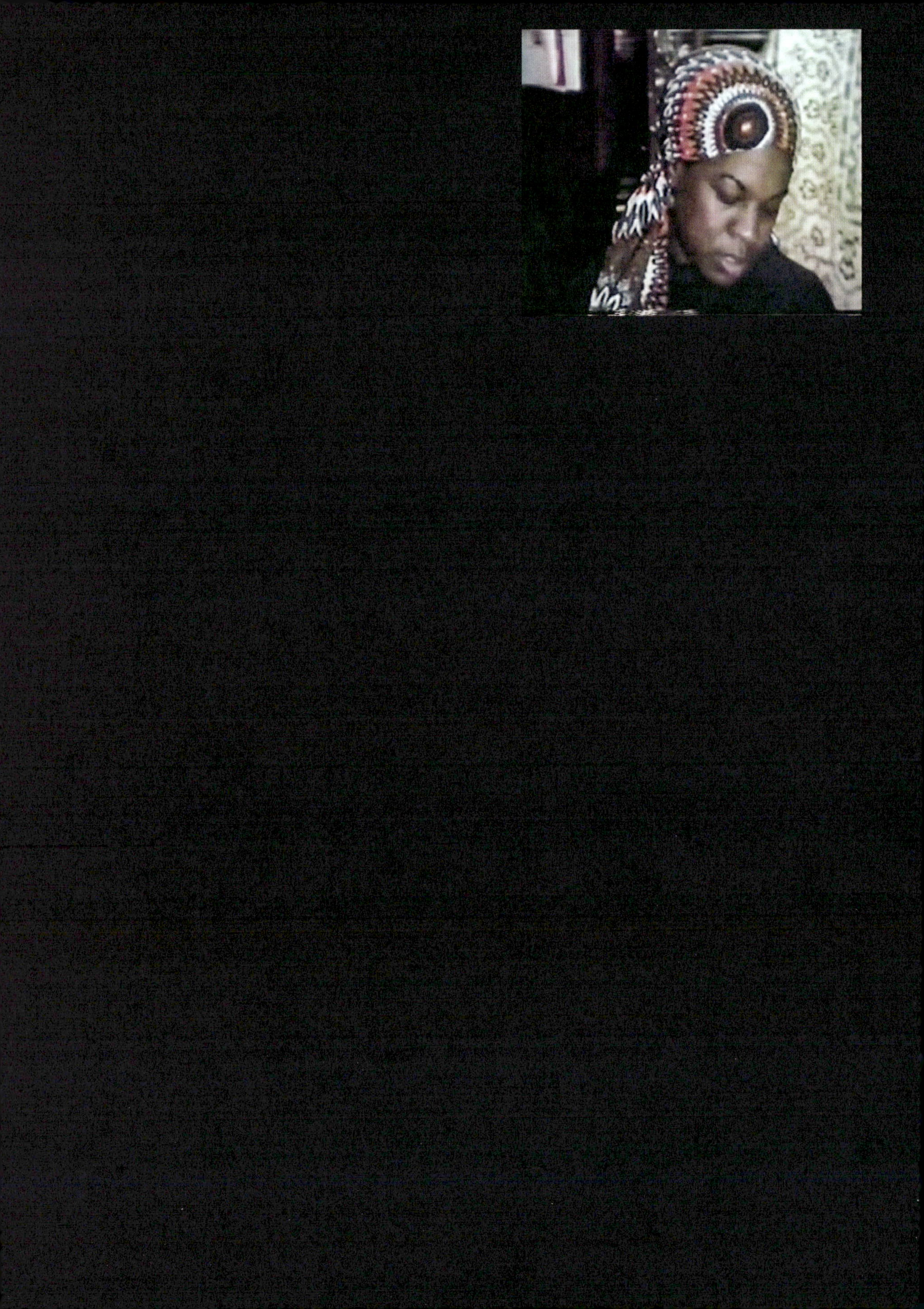

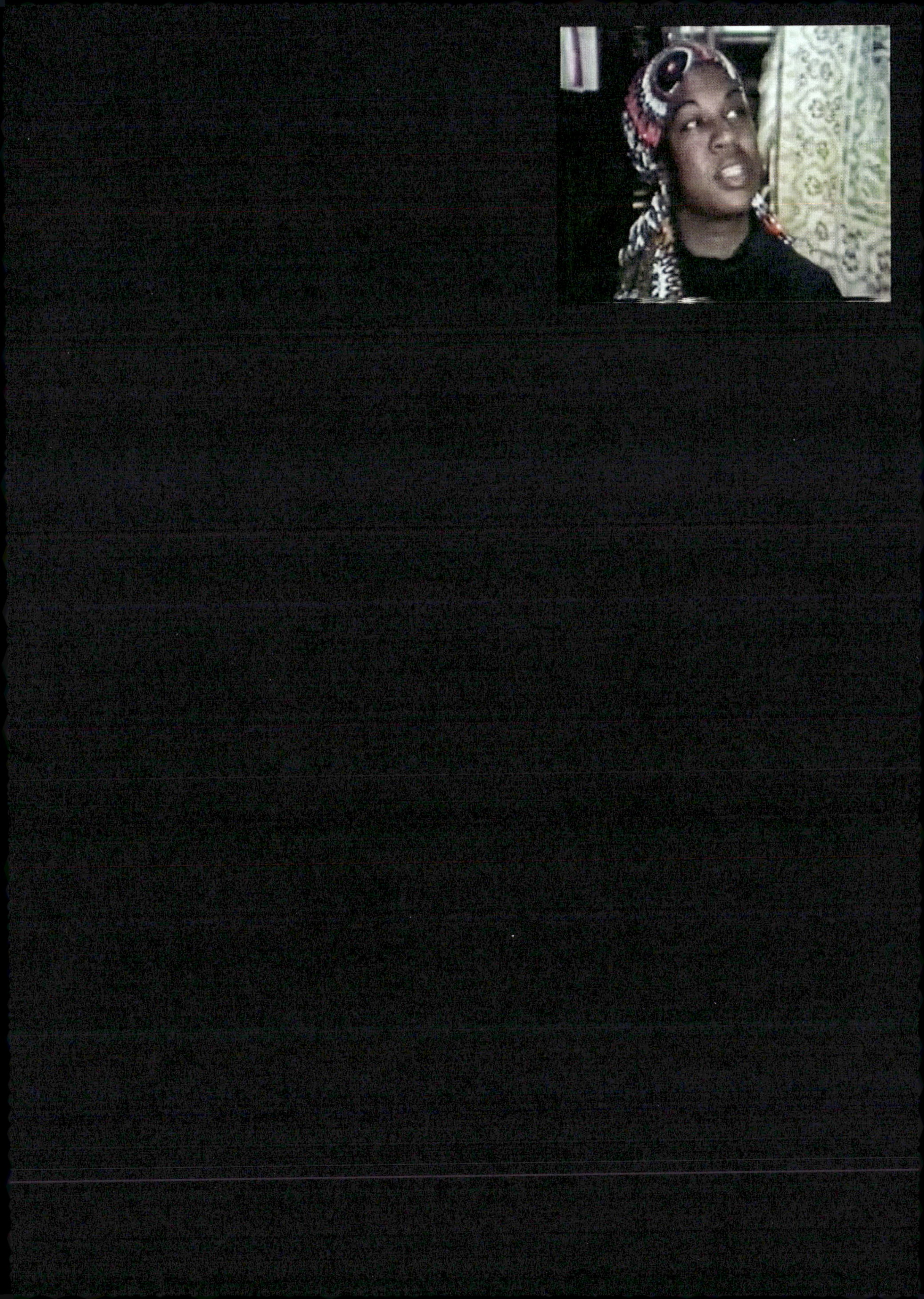

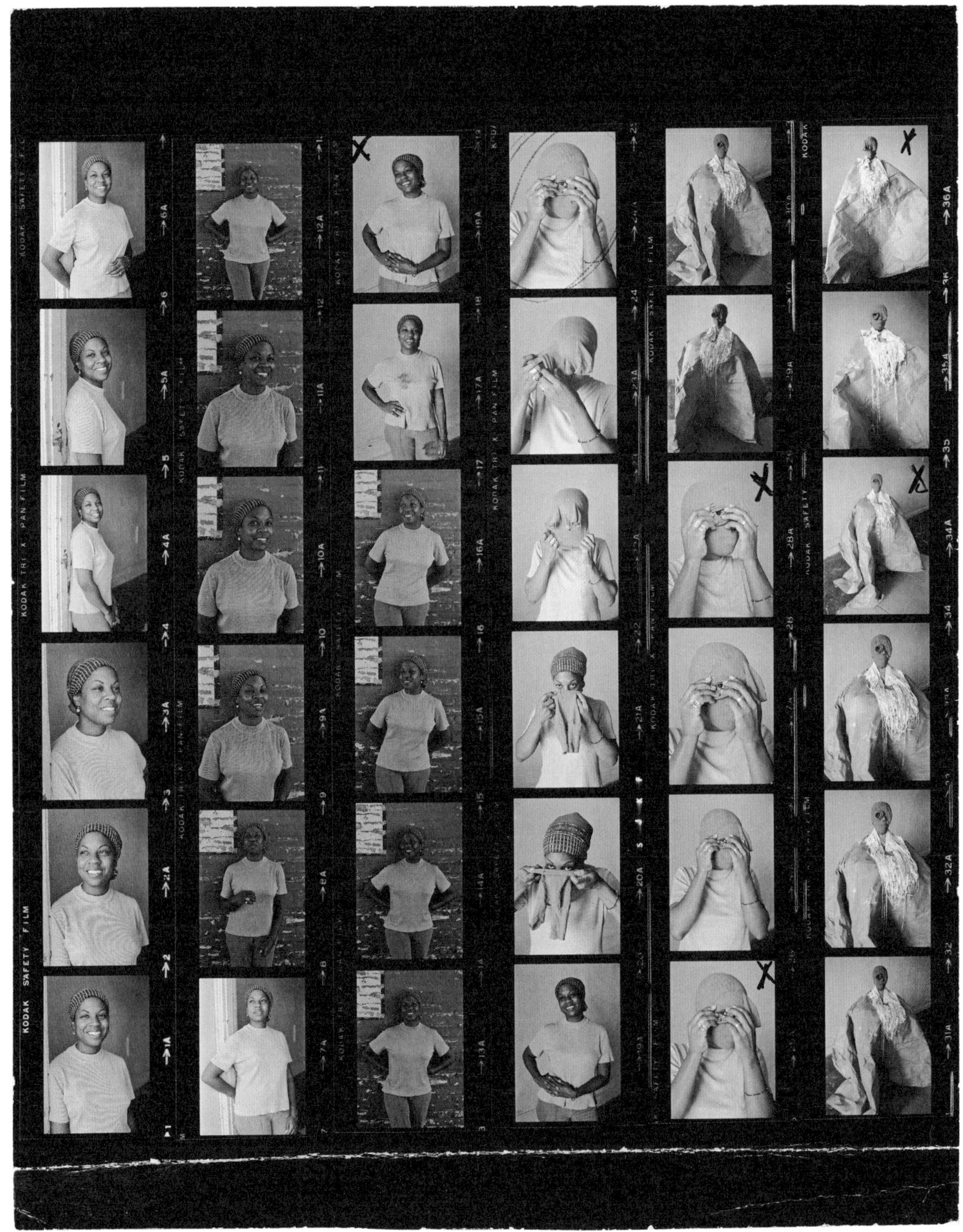

CONTACT SHEET FOR *MESH MIRAGE*,
STUDIO PERFORMANCE, WEST ADAMS,
LOS ANGELES, 1978

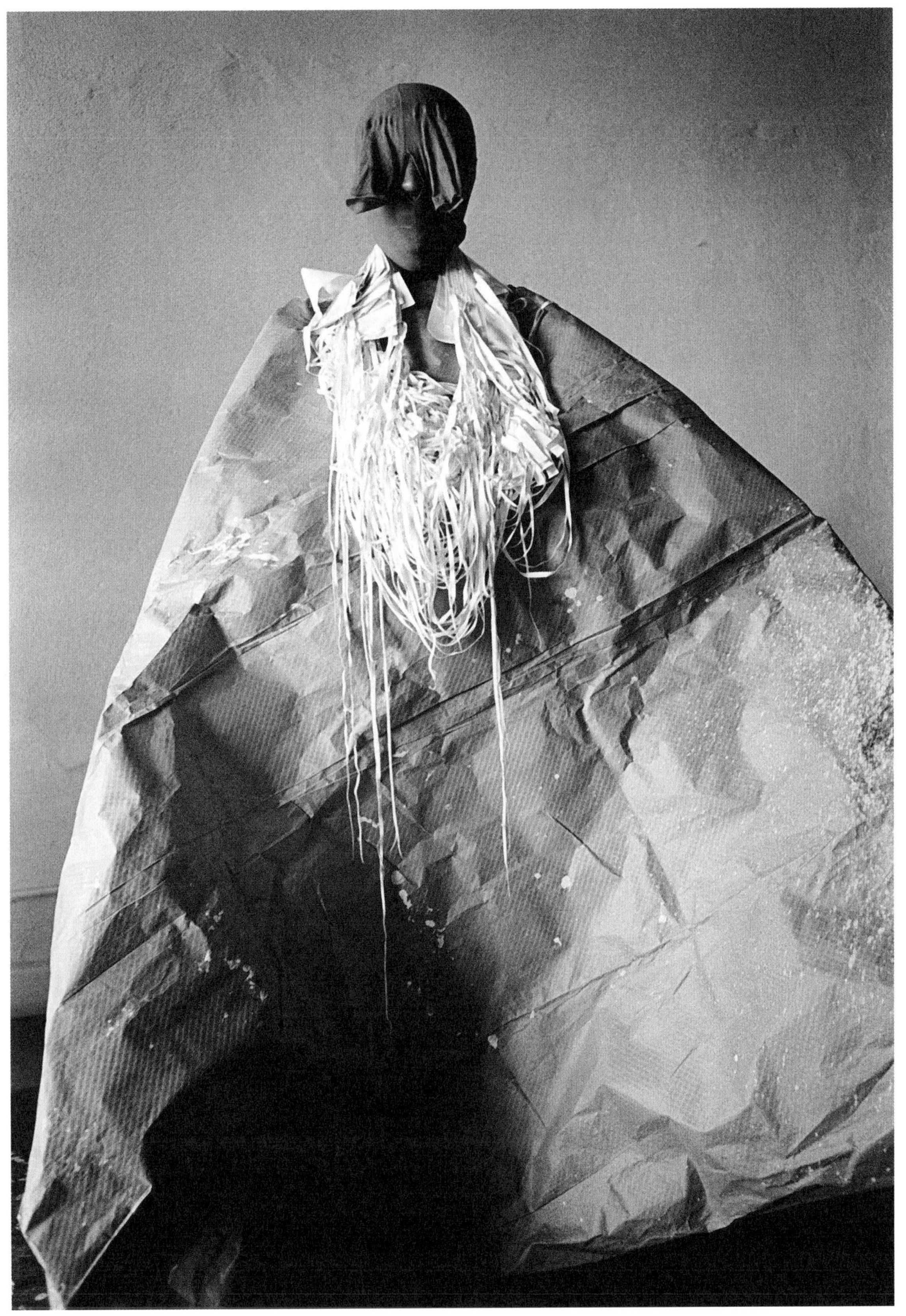

MESH MIRAGE, 1978
GELATIN SILVER PRINT,
40 × 30 INCHES (101.6 × 76.2 CM)
PHOTO: ADAM AVILA

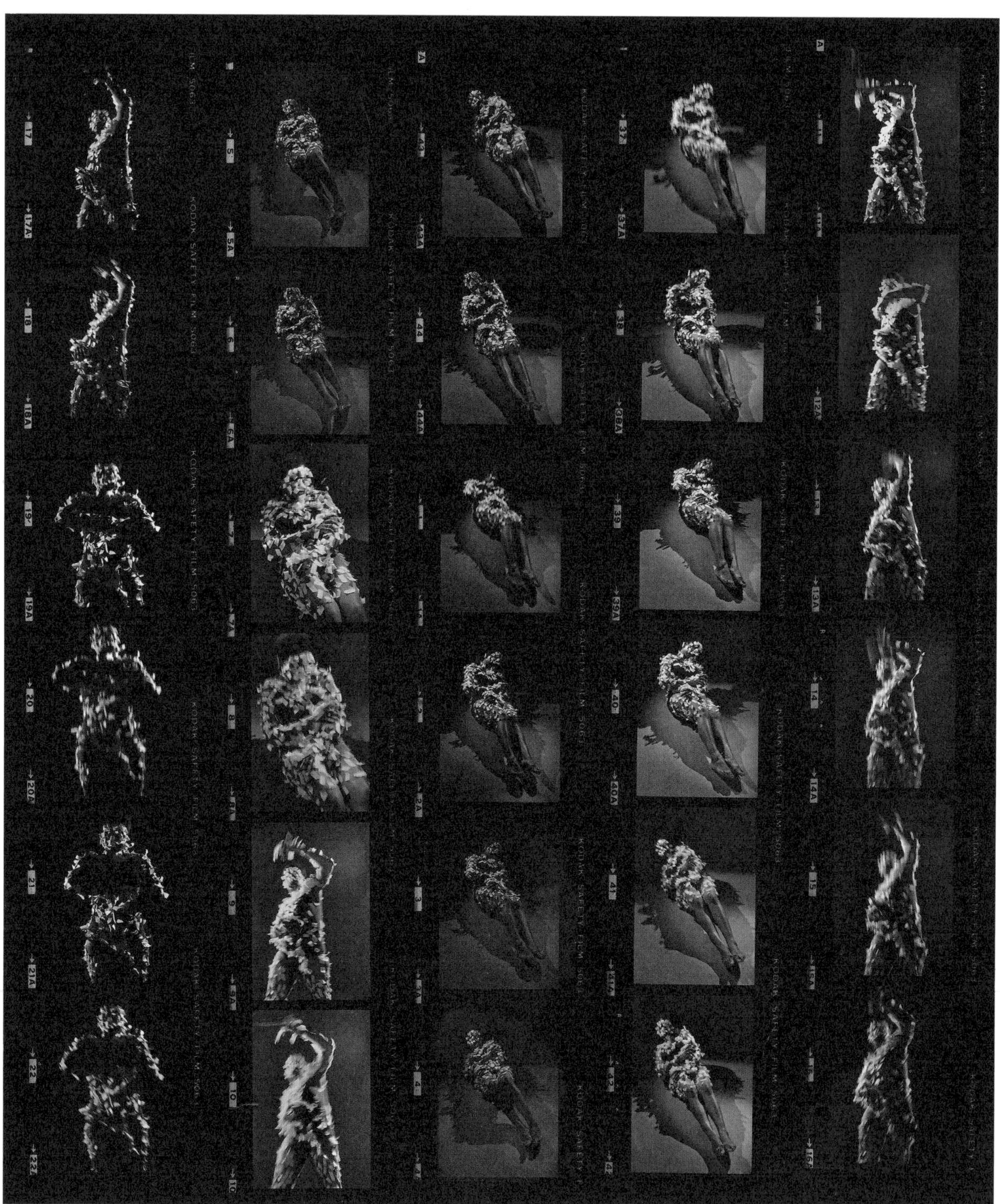

CONTACT SHEET FOR *MASKED TAPING*,
STUDIO PERFORMANCE,
WEST ADAMS, LOS ANGELES, 1978-79

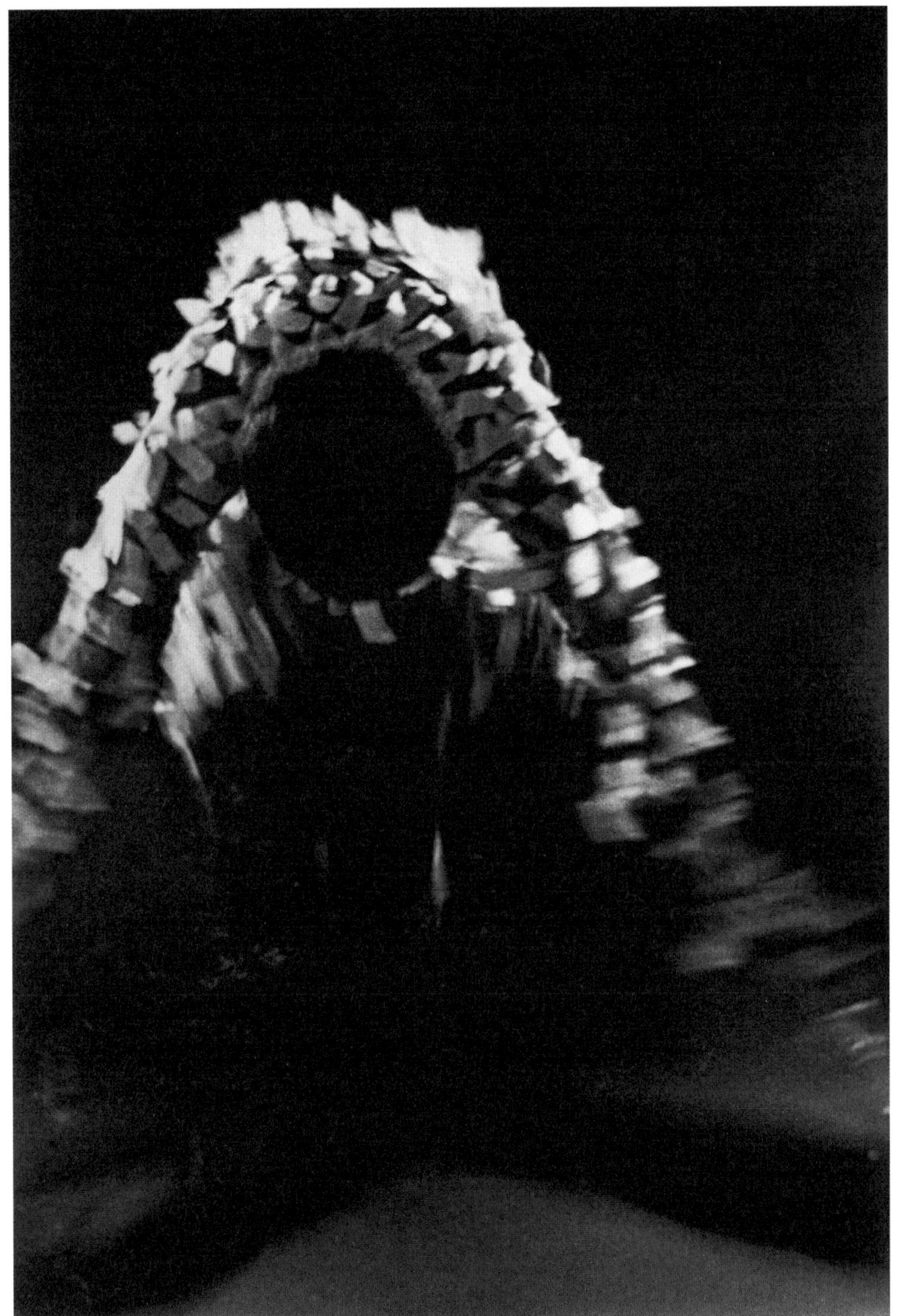

MASKED TAPING, 1978–79
GELATIN SILVER PRINT,
40 × 26¾ INCHES (101.6 × 67.9 CM)
PHOTO: ADAM AVILA

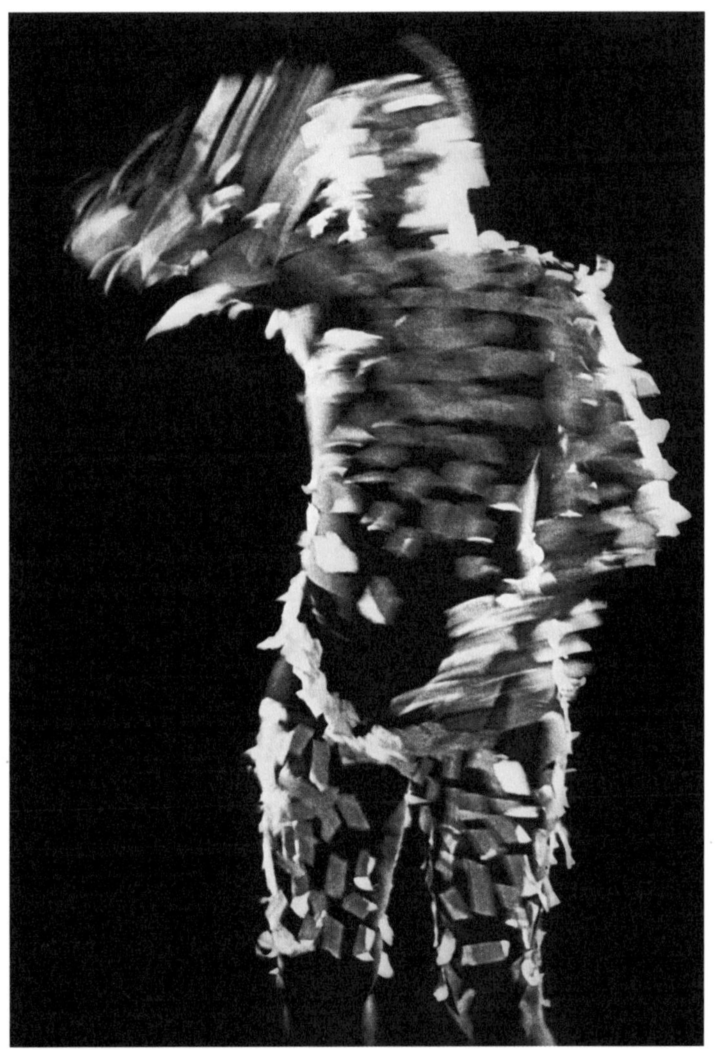

MASKED TAPING, 1978–79
GELATIN SILVER PRINT,
40 × 26¾ INCHES (101.6 × 67.9 CM)
PHOTO: ADAM AVILA

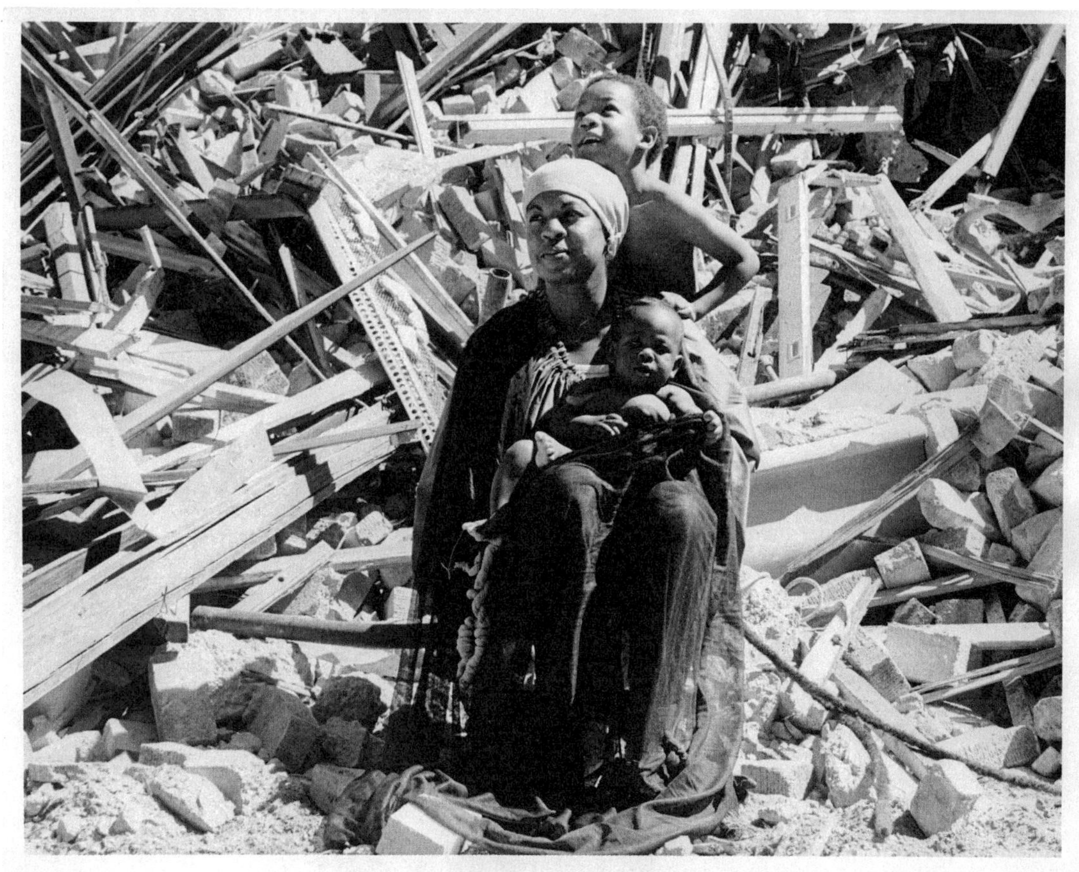

URBAN STUDY, 1980
GELATIN SILVER PRINT,
8 × 10 INCHES (20.3 × 25.4 CM)
PHOTO: BARBARA MCCULLOUGH

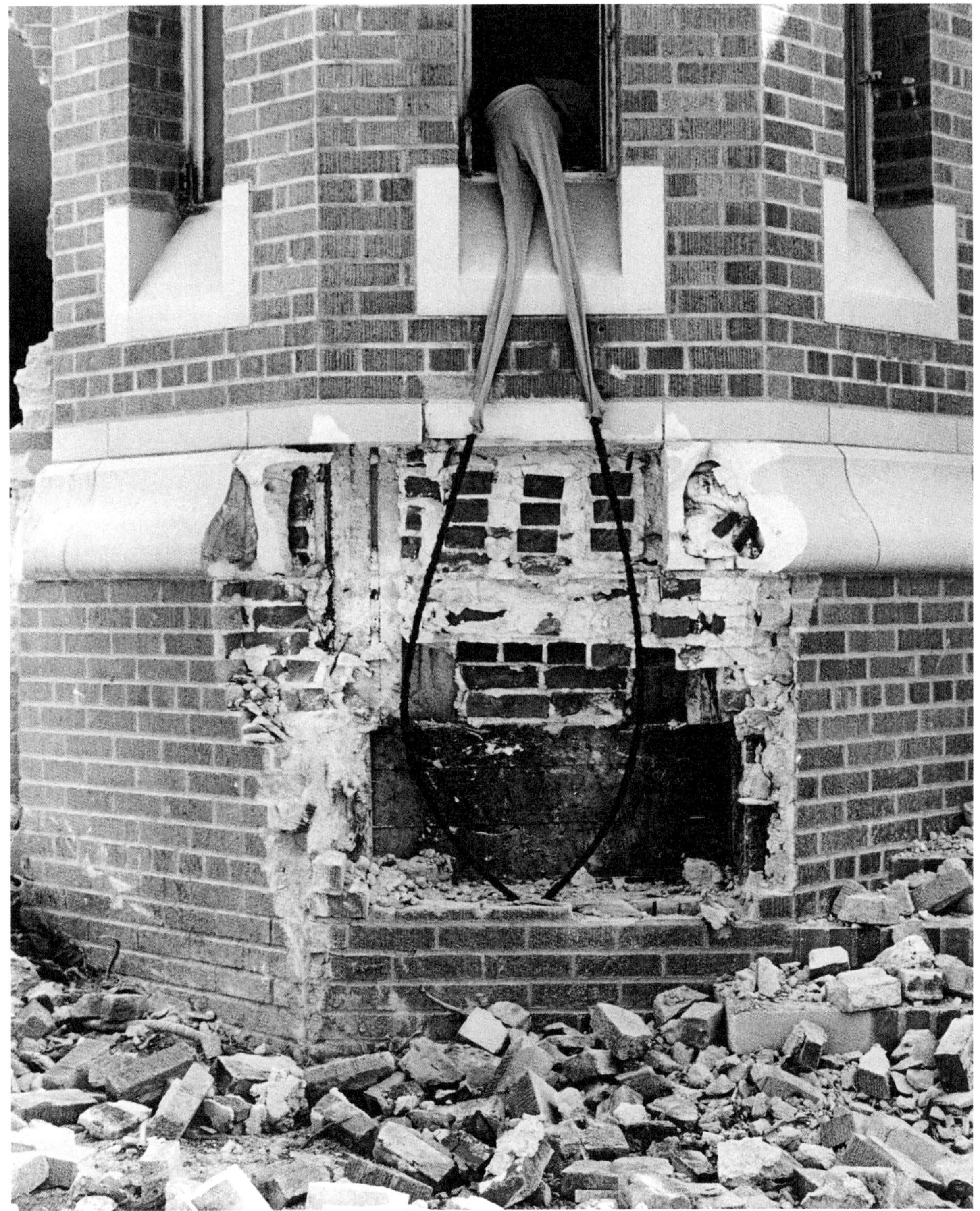

RAPUNZEL, 1980
FEATURING HAIR-AND-WIRE SCULPTURE BY DAVID HAMMONS
GELATIN SILVER PRINT,
40 × 32 INCHES (101.6 × 81.3 CM)
PHOTO: BARBARA MCCULLOUGH

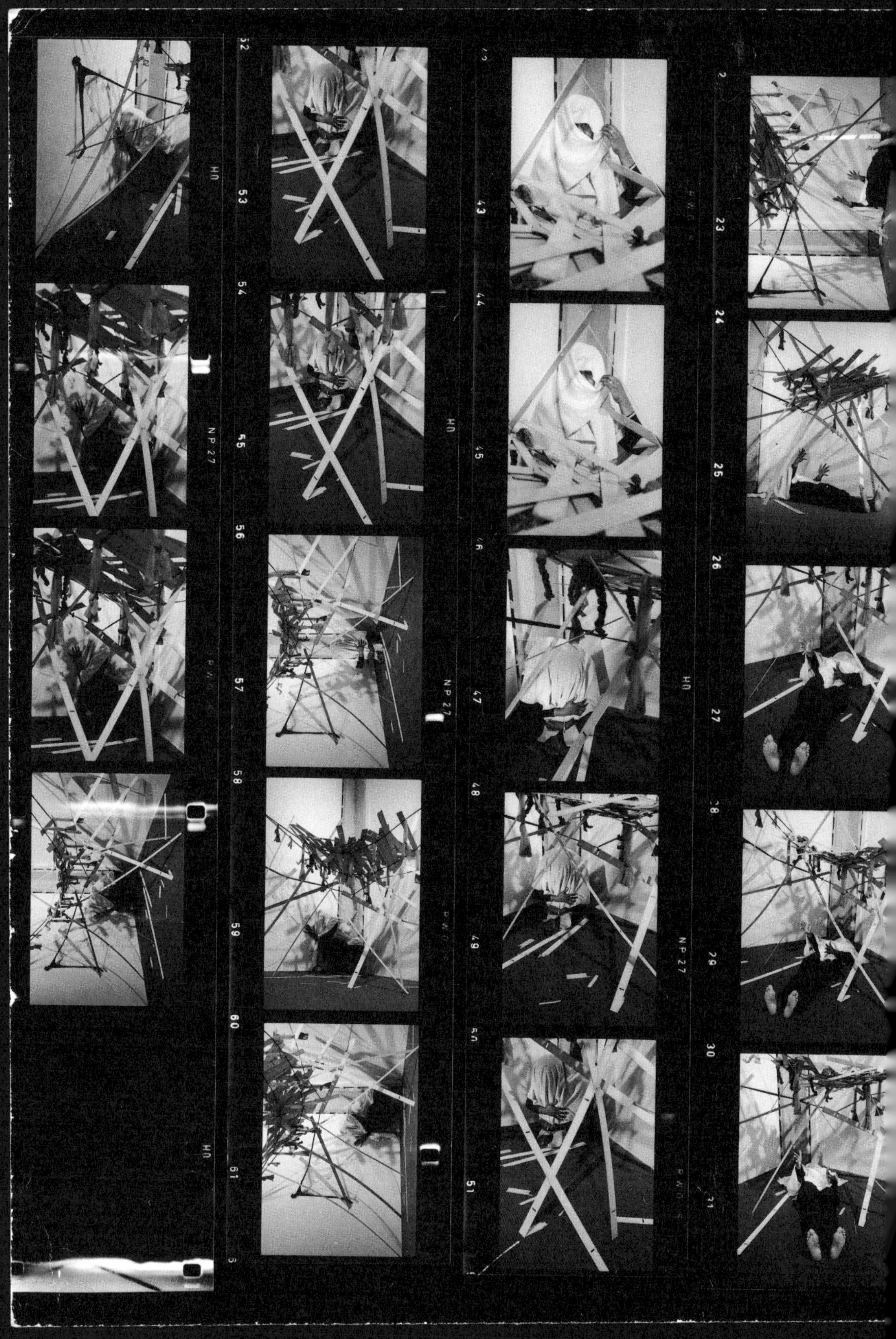

CONTACT SHEET FOR *NUKI-NUKI: ACROSS 118TH ST*, STUDIO PERFORMANCE, WEST ADAMS, LOS ANGELES, 1982

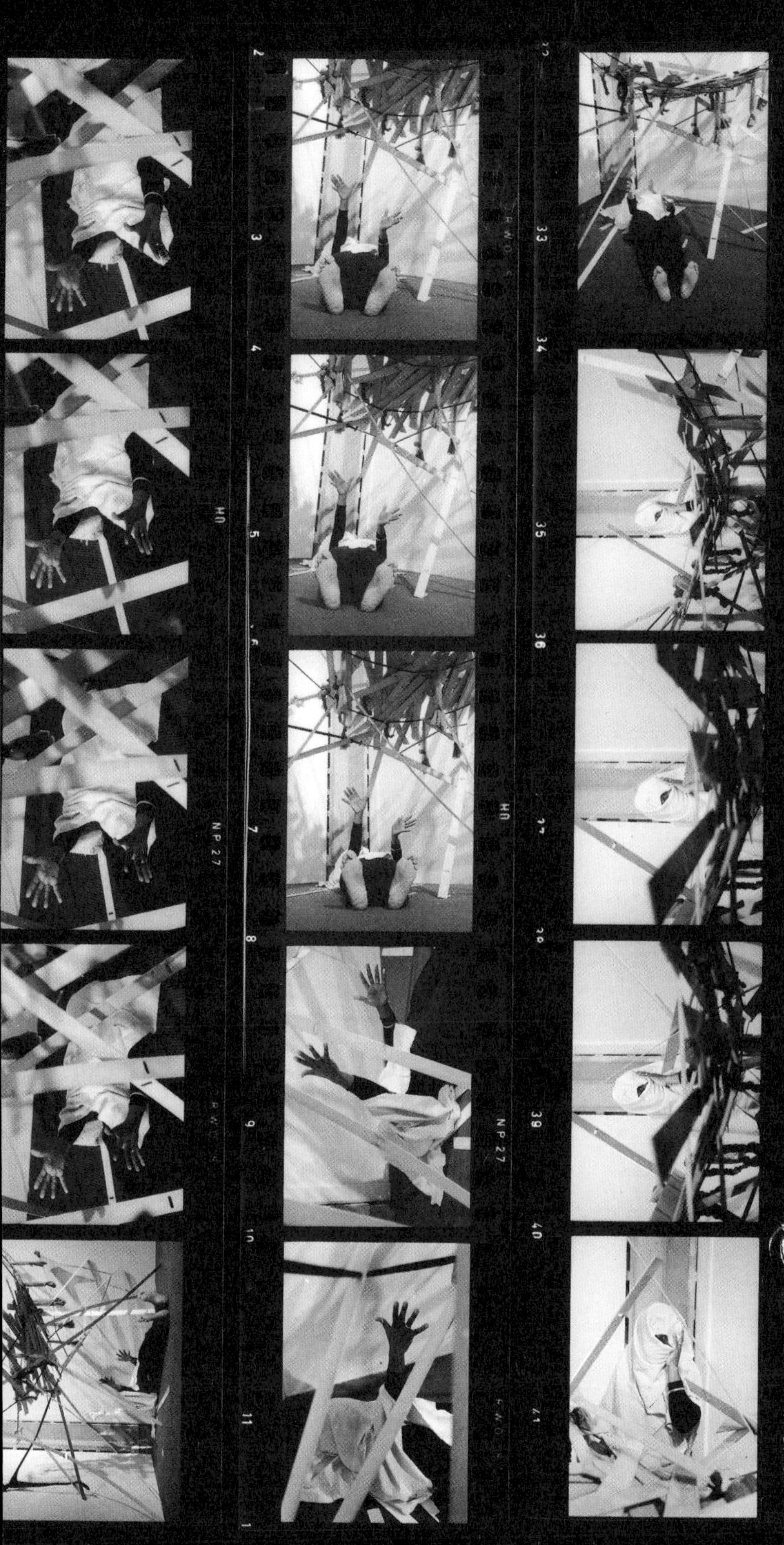

NUKI-NUKI: ACROSS 118TH ST, 1982
GELATIN SILVER PRINT, 8 × 10 INCHES (20.3 × 25.4 CM)
PHOTO: ADAM AVILA

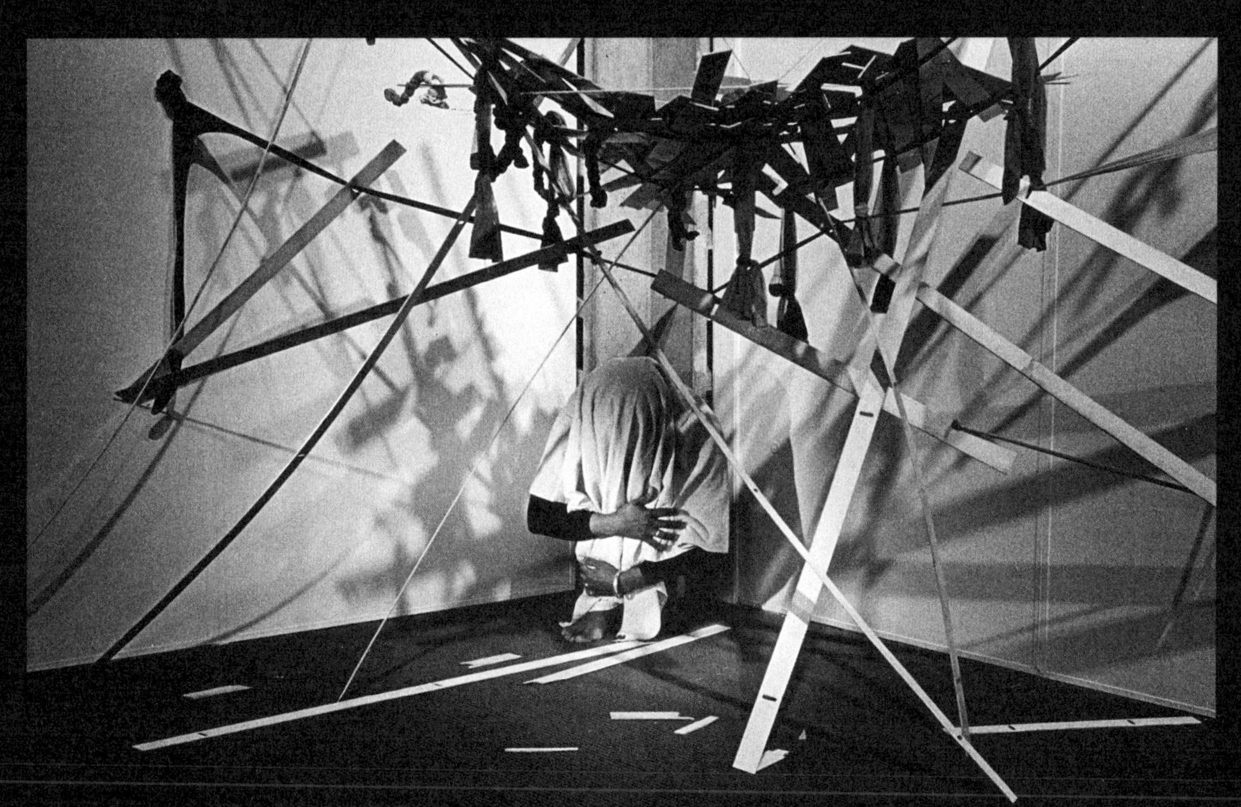

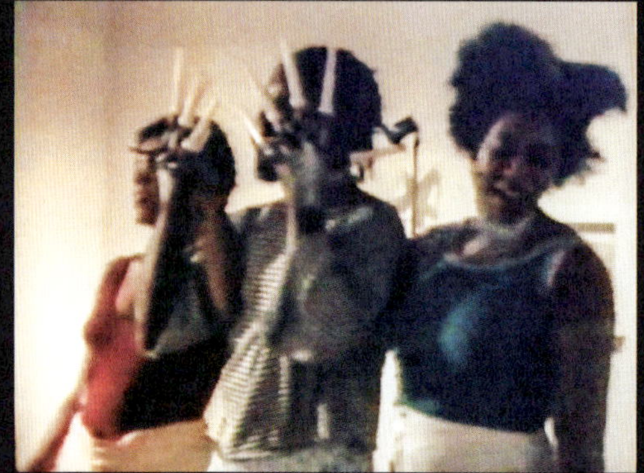

HASSINGER, PARKER, AND NENGUDI

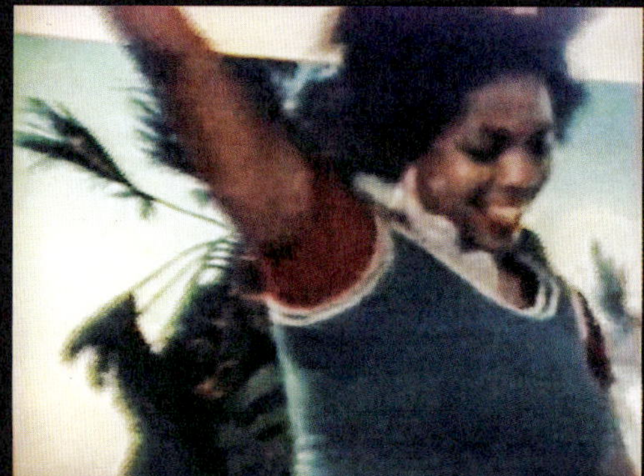

NENGUDI

FLIER FOR *ALIVE: KISS*, EXPLORATORIUM, UNIVERSITY-STUDENT UNION, CALIFORNIA STATE UNIVERSITY, LOS ANGELES, JULY 16, 1980
IMPROVISED PERFORMANCE BY MAREN HASSINGER, NENGUDI, AND FRANKLIN PARKER

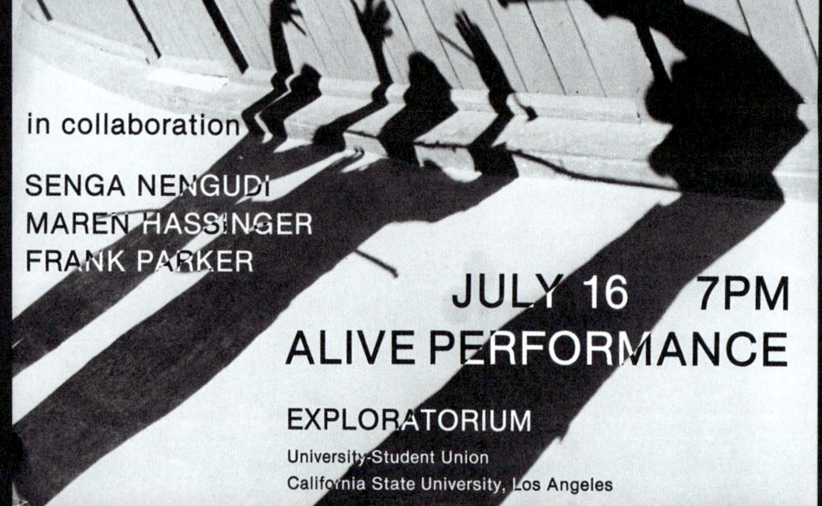

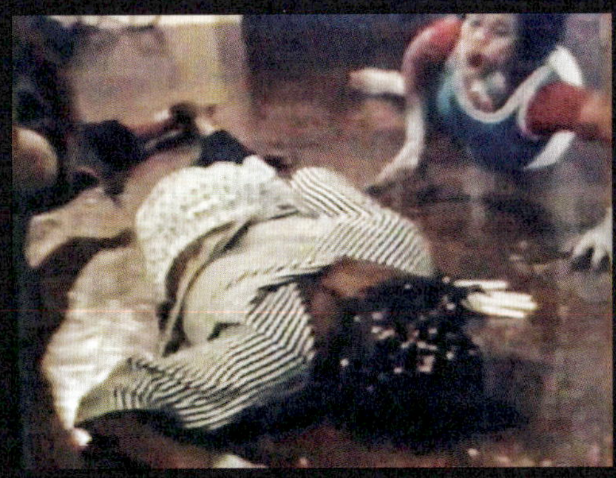

PARKER AND NENGUDI

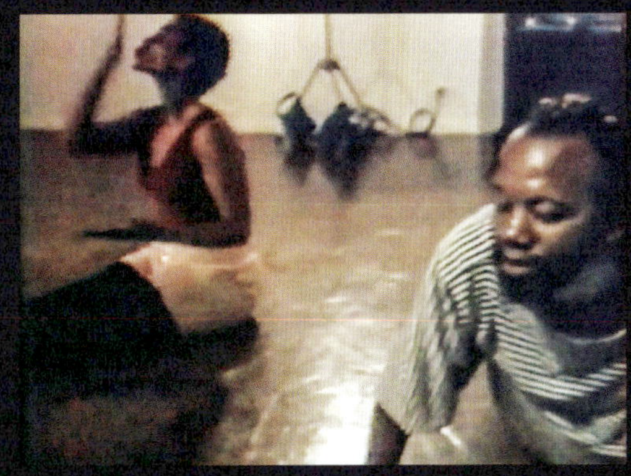

HASSINGER AND PARKER

STILLS OF *ALIVE: KISS*
VIDEO, 3 MIN.

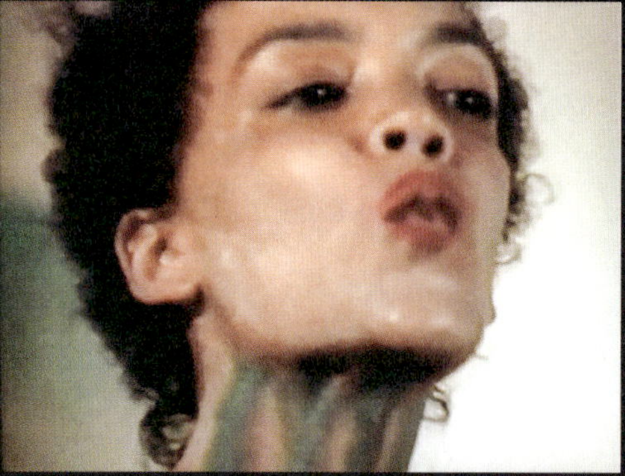

HASSINGER

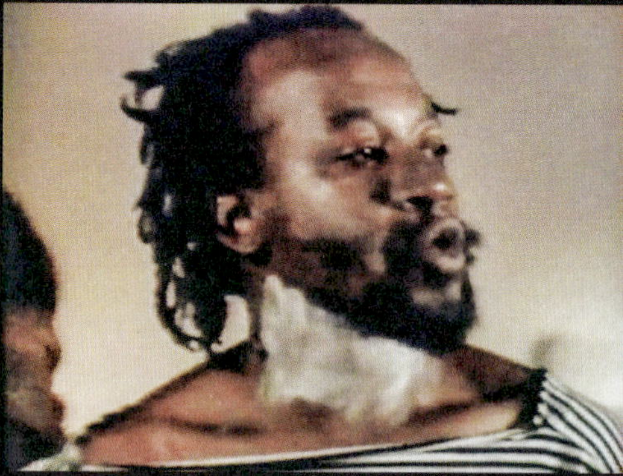

PARKER

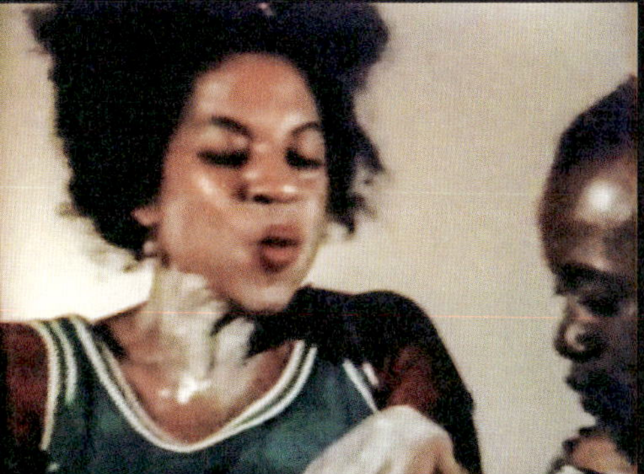

NENGUDI AND PARKER

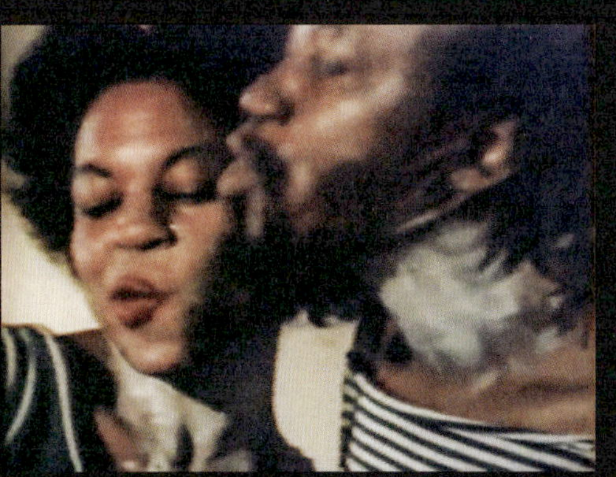

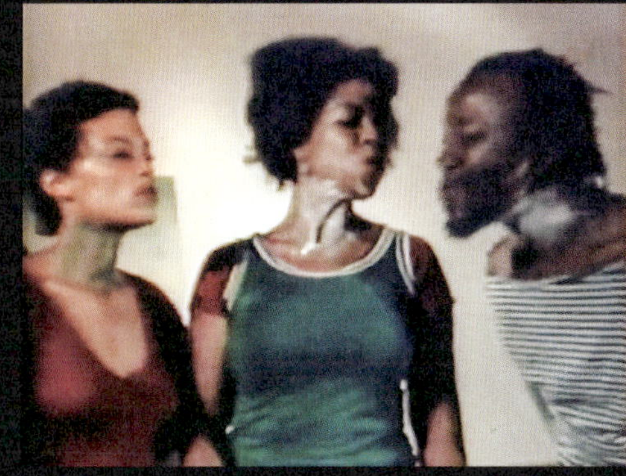

HASSINGER, NENGUDI, AND PARKER

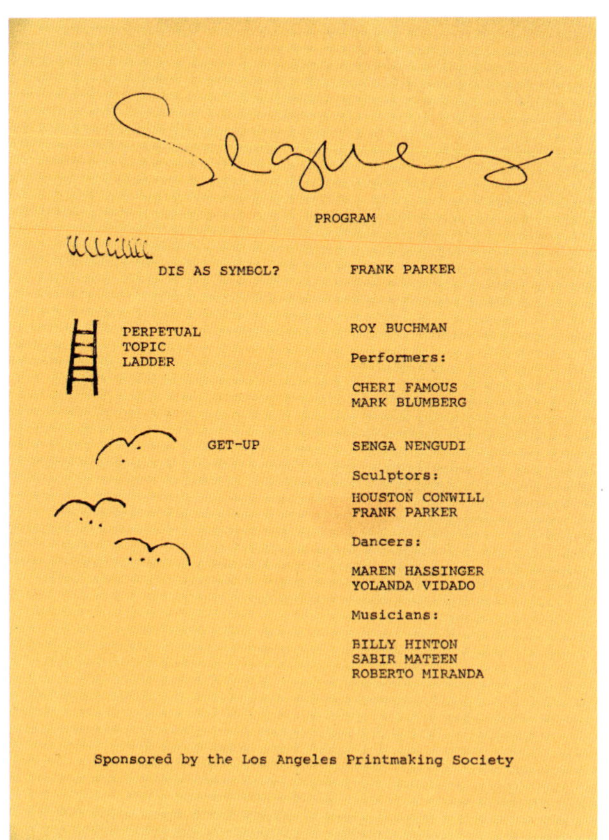

Segues

PROGRAM

DIS AS SYMBOL? — FRANK PARKER

PERPETUAL TOPIC LADDER — ROY BUCHMAN

Performers:

CHERI FAMOUS
MARK BLUMBERG

GET-UP — SENGA NENGUDI

Sculptors:

HOUSTON CONWILL
FRANK PARKER

Dancers:

MAREN HASSINGER
YOLANDA VIDADO

Musicians:

BILLY HINTON
SABIR MATEEN
ROBERTO MIRANDA

Sponsored by the Los Angeles Printmaking Society

PROGRAM FOR *SEGUES: A NIGHT OF PERFORMANCE* FEATURING *GET-UP*, THE PAPER MILL, LOS ANGELES PRINTMAKING SOCIETY, DECEMBER 1, 1980
CHOREOGRAPHY AND COSTUMES BY NENGUDI
PERFORMED BY HOUSTON CONWILL, MAREN HASSINGER, FRANKLIN PARKER, AND YOLANDA VIDADO

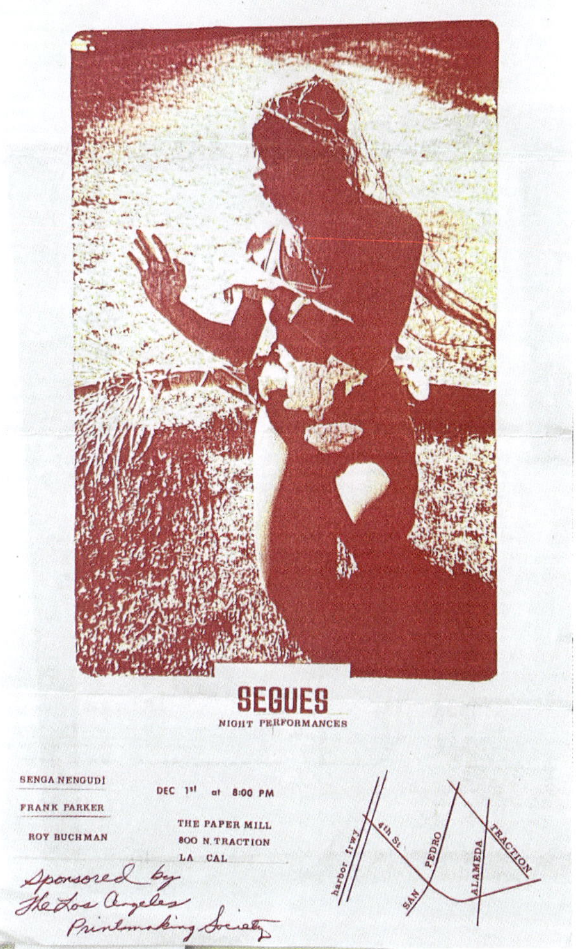

FLIER FOR *SEGUES*

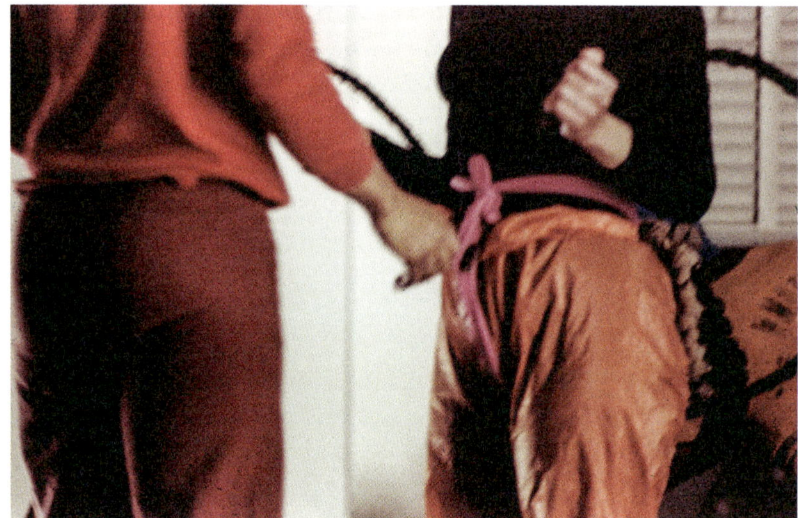

CONWILL AND HASSINGER

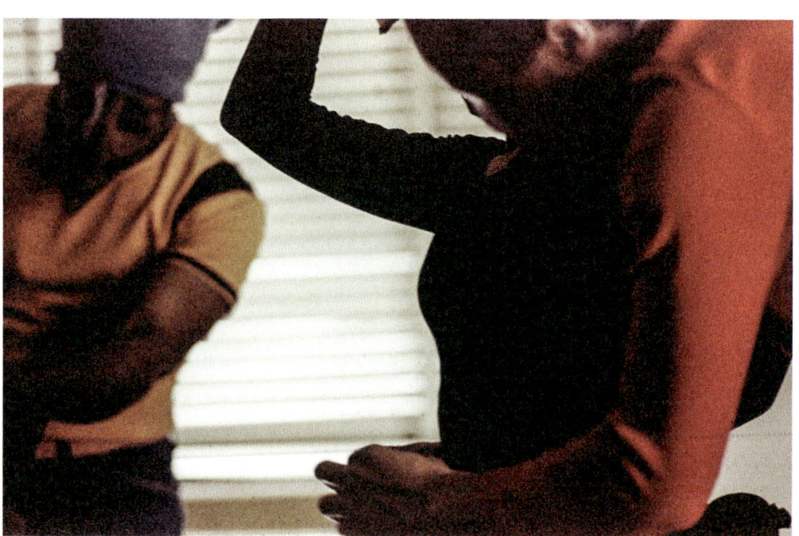

PARKER, HASSINGER, AND CONWILL

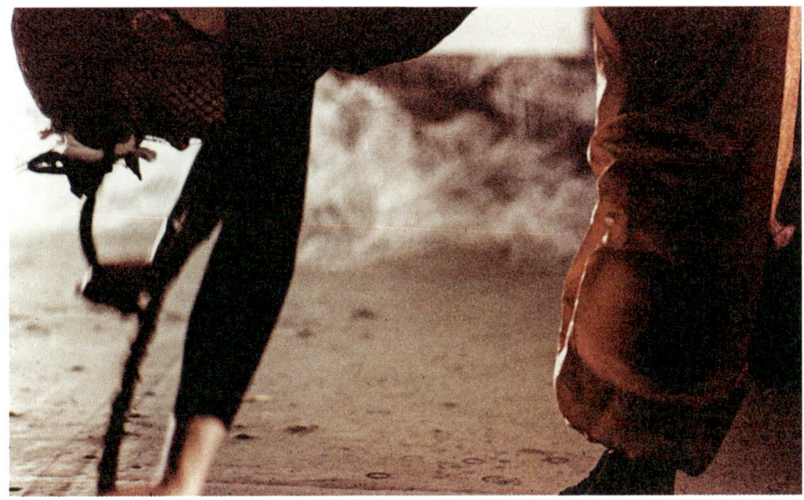

HASSINGER

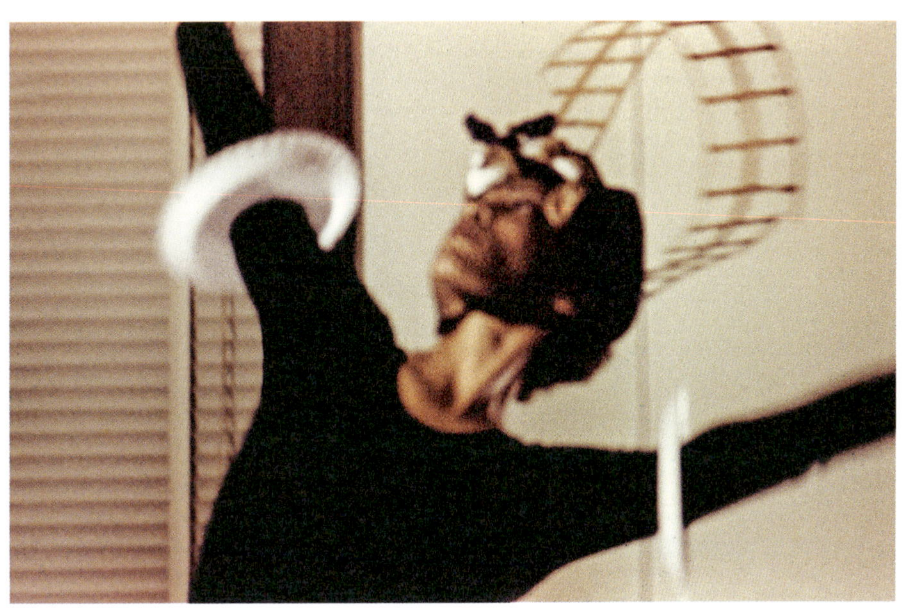

HASSINGER

VIDADO

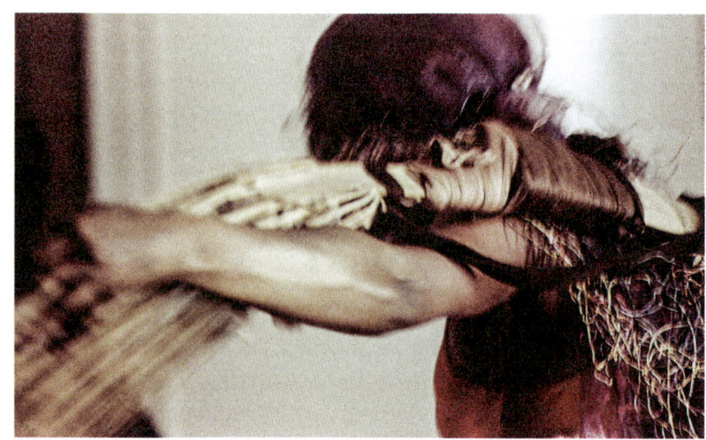

HASSINGER AND CONWILL

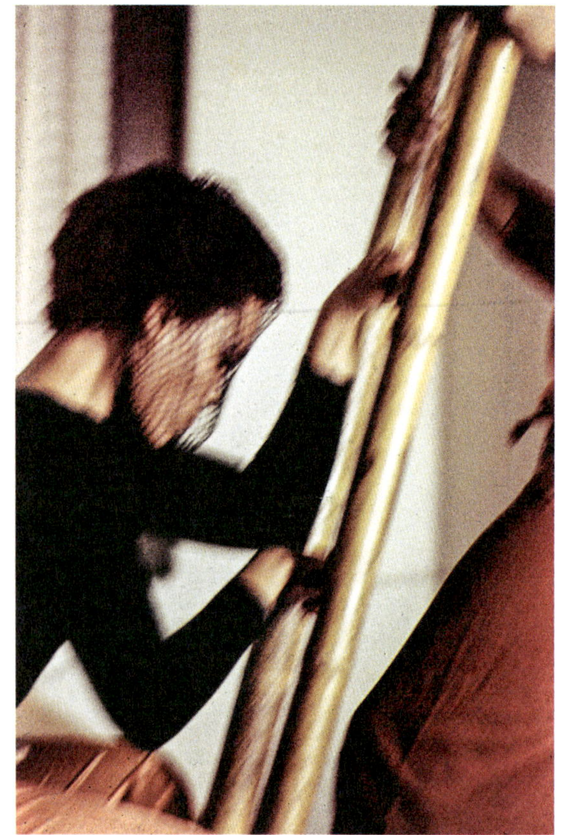

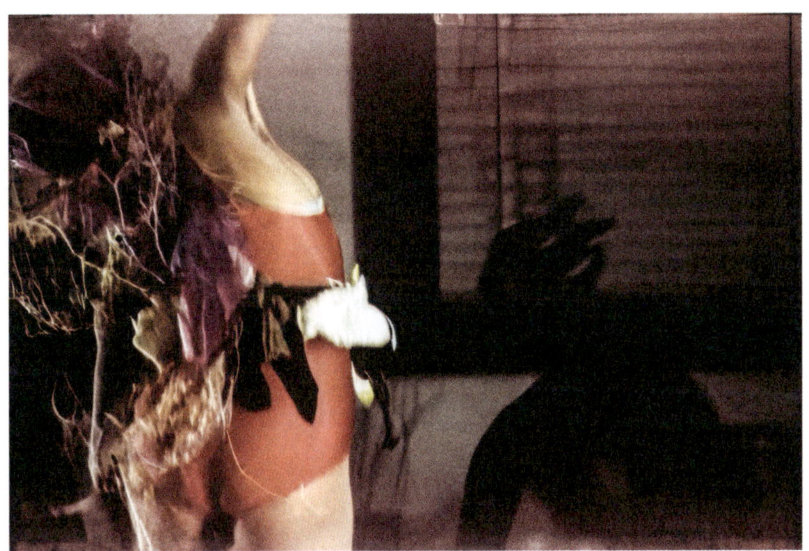

VIDADO

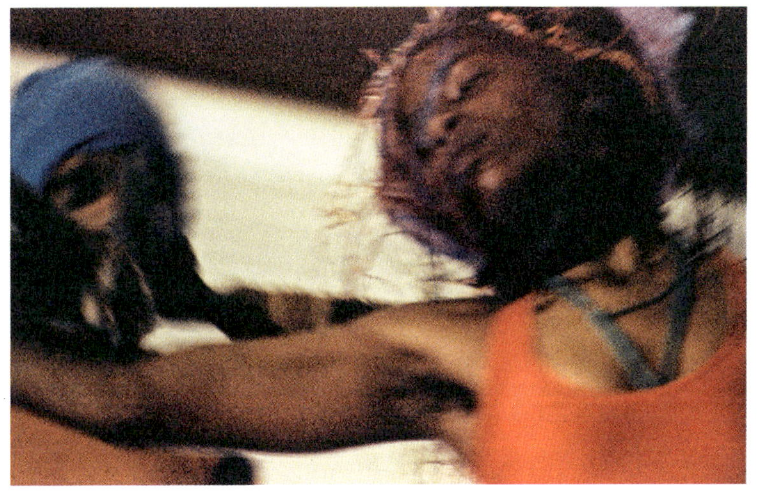

PARKER AND VIDADO

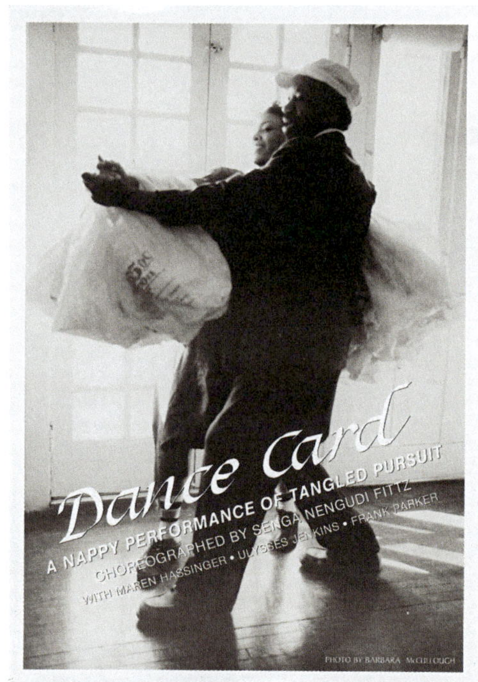

FLIER FOR *DANCE CARD*, BARBARA MCCULLOUGH'S HOMEBASE, LOS ANGELES, 1986
CHOREOGRAPHY BY NENGUDI
PERFORMED BY MAREN HASSINGER, ULYSSES JENKINS, AND FRANKLIN PARKER

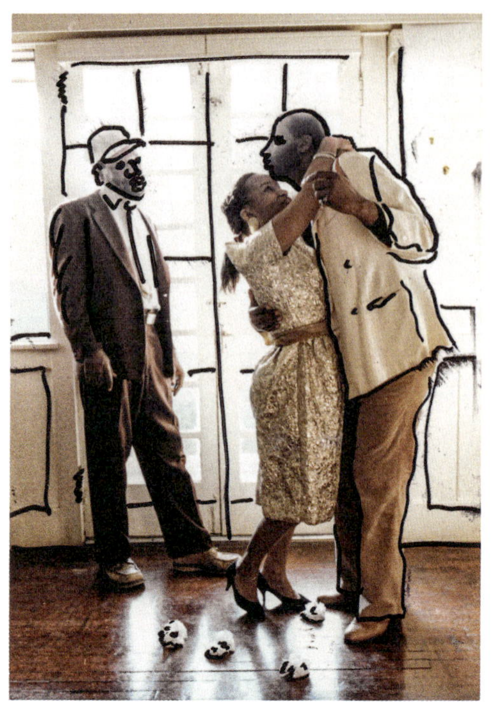

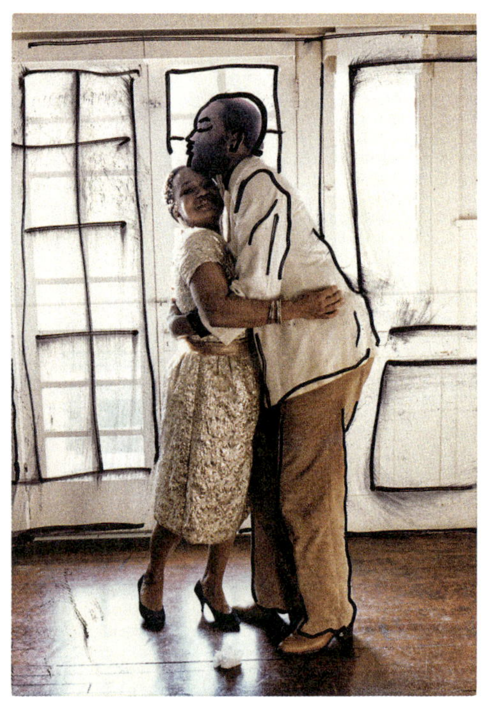

DANCE CARD REDUX, 1986
MARKER ON CHROMOGENIC PRINTS,
5 × 3½ INCHES (12.7 × 8.9 CM) EACH
PHOTO: BARBARA MCCULLOUGH

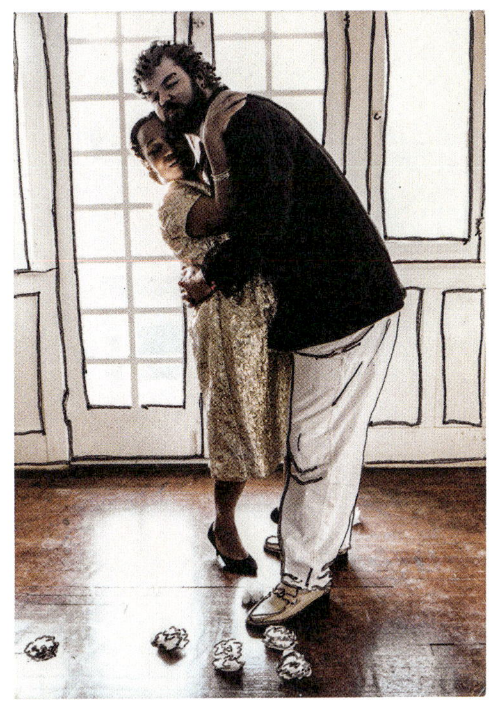

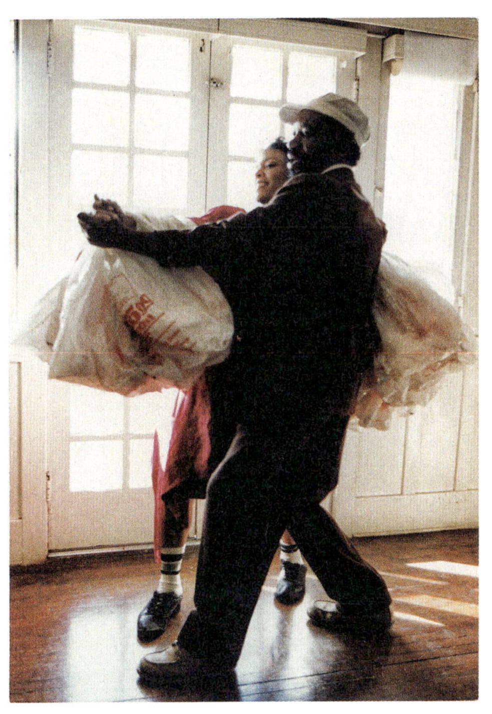

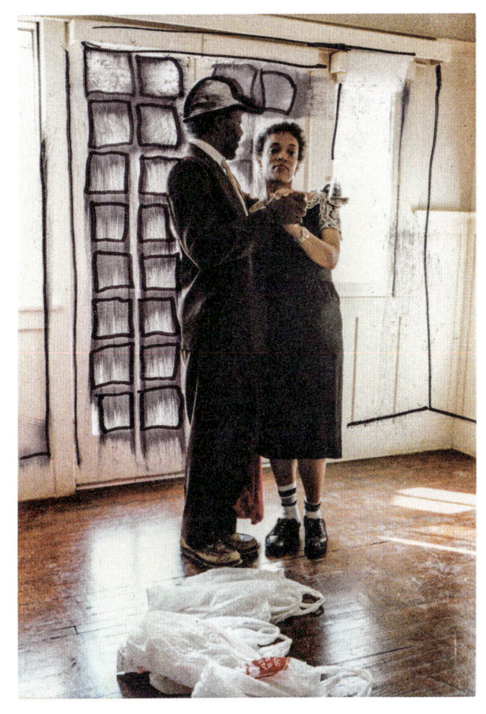

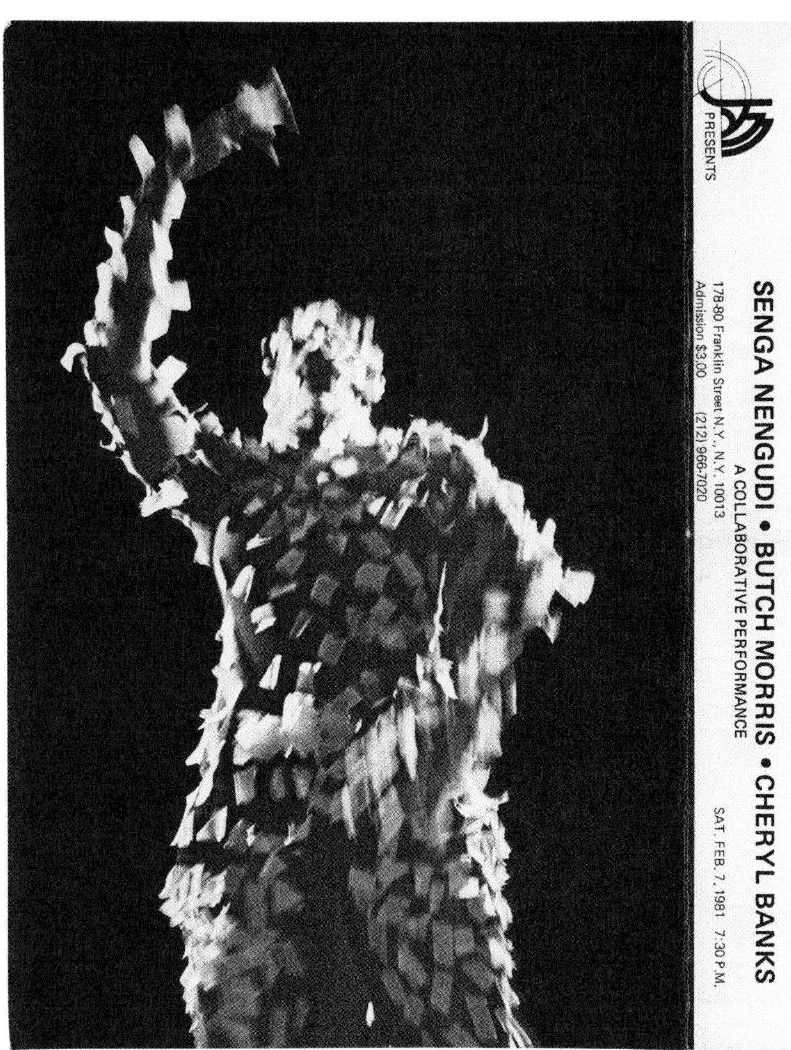

FLIER FOR *AIR PROPO*, JUST ABOVE MIDTOWN GALLERY,
NEW YORK, FEBRUARY 7, 1981
CHOREOGRAPHY AND COSTUMES BY NENGUDI
PERFORMED BY CHERYL BANKS, LAWRENCE "BUTCH" MORRIS,
AND NENGUDI

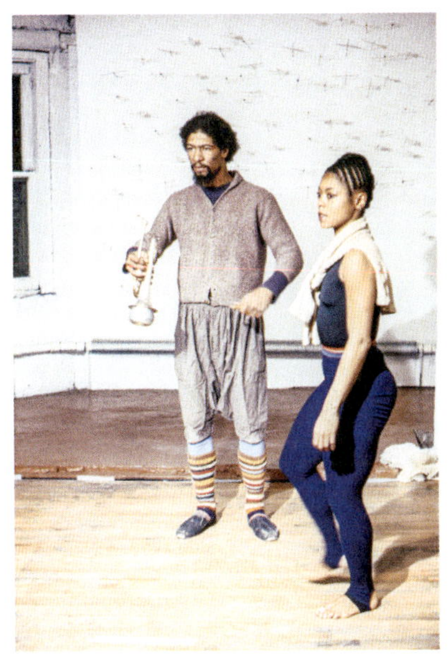
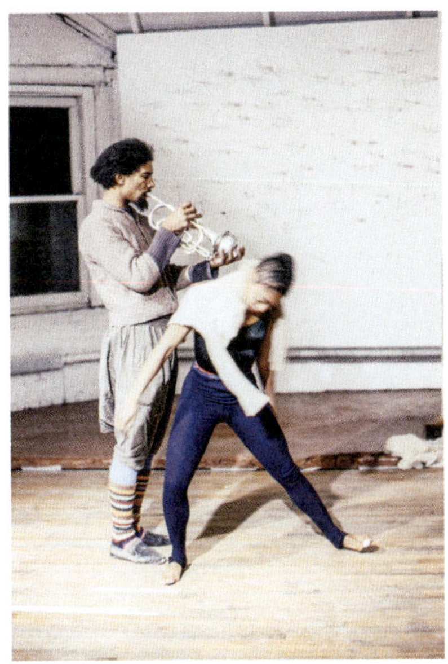
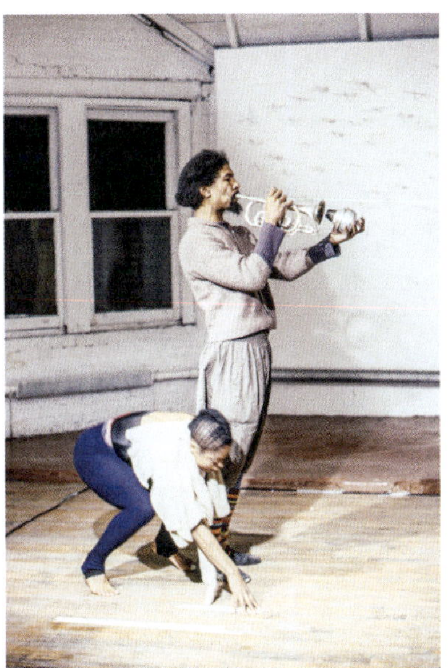

MORRIS AND BANKS

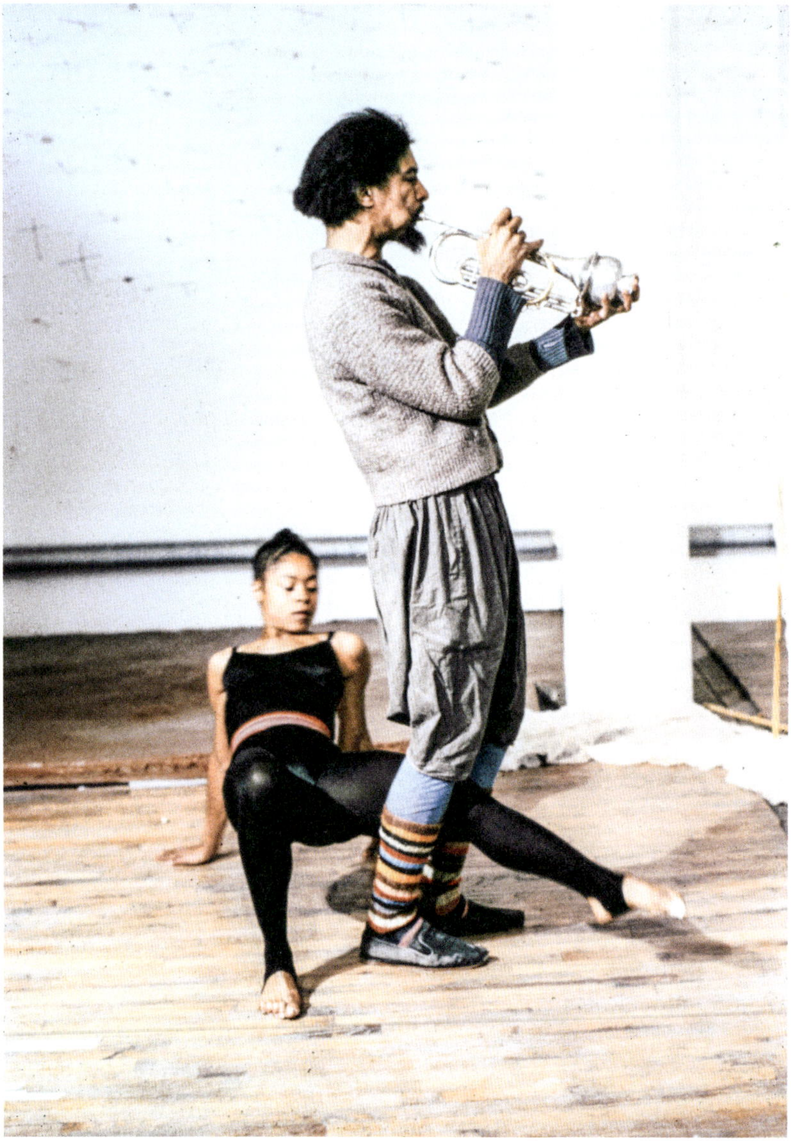

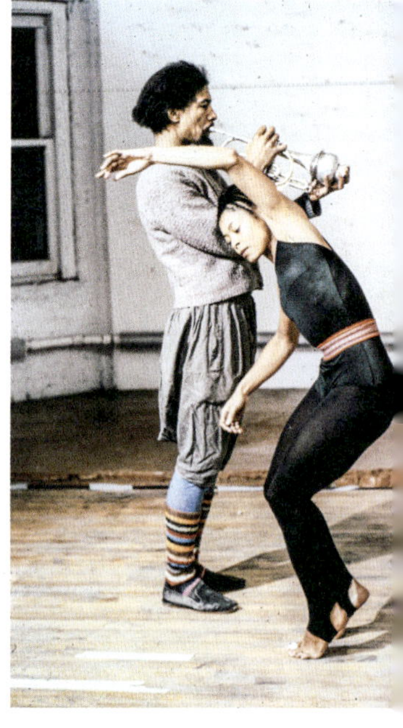

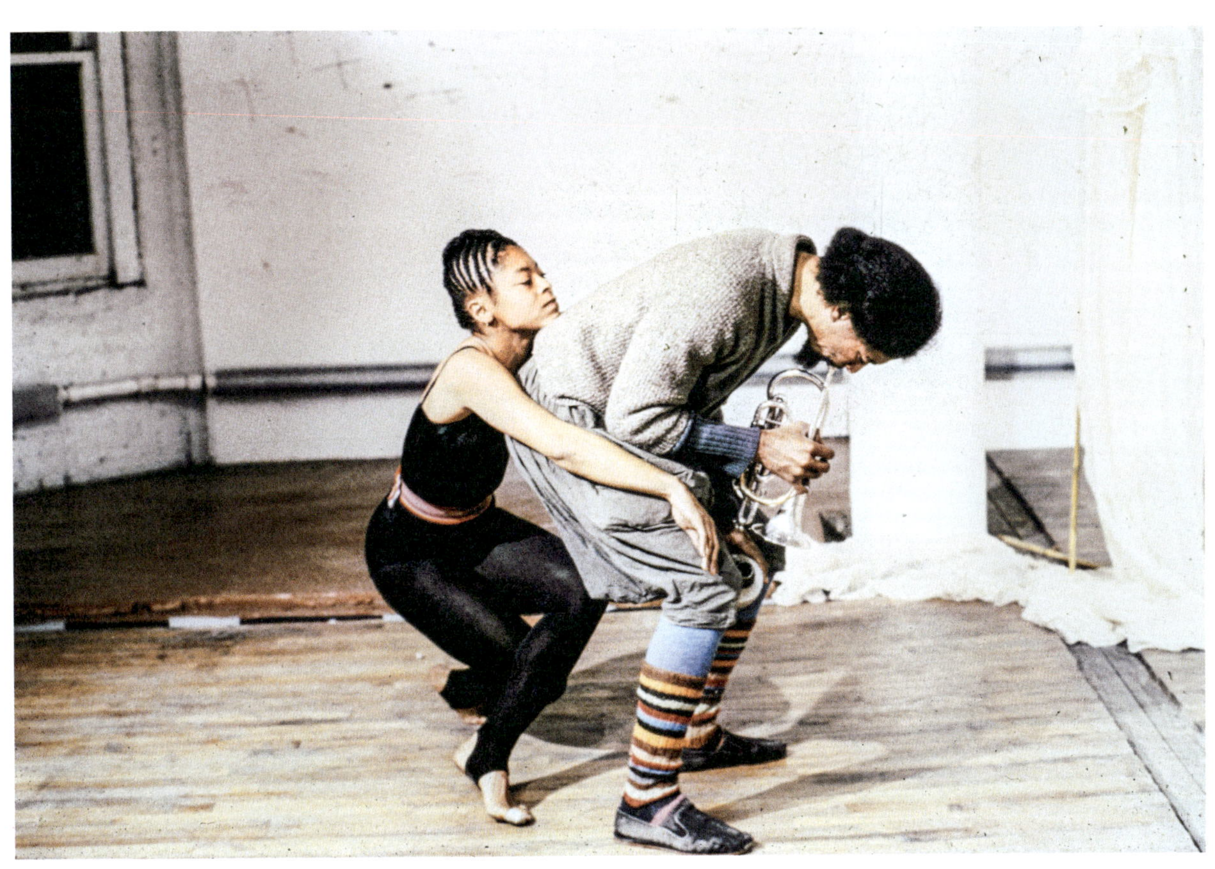

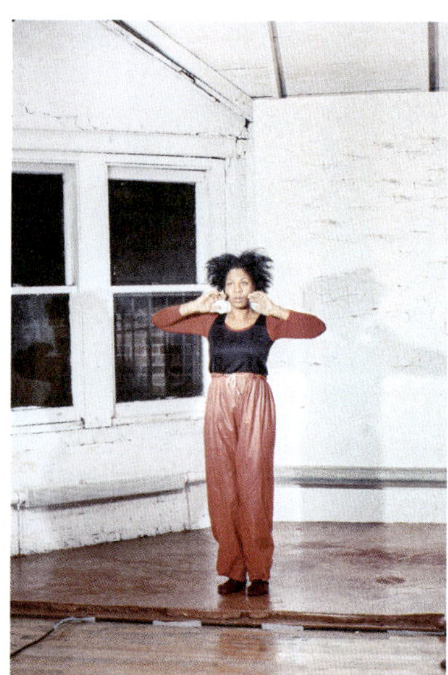

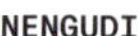
NENGUDI

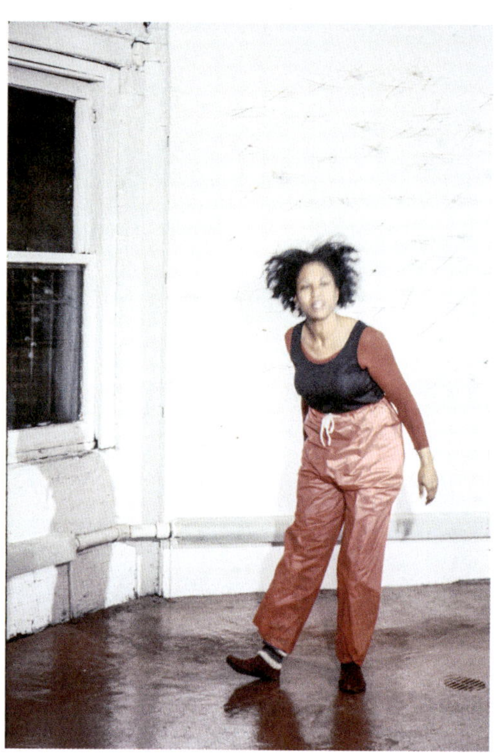

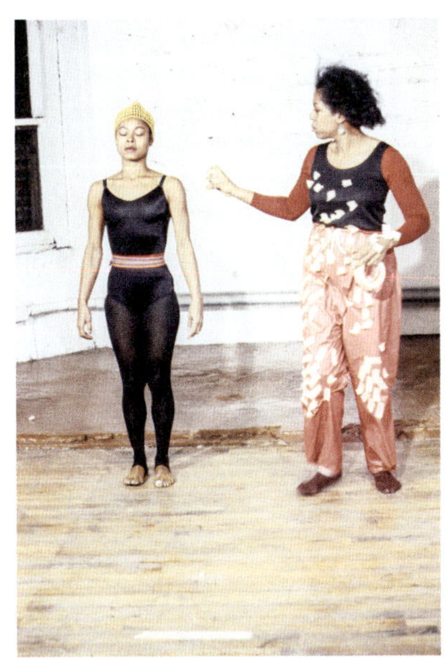
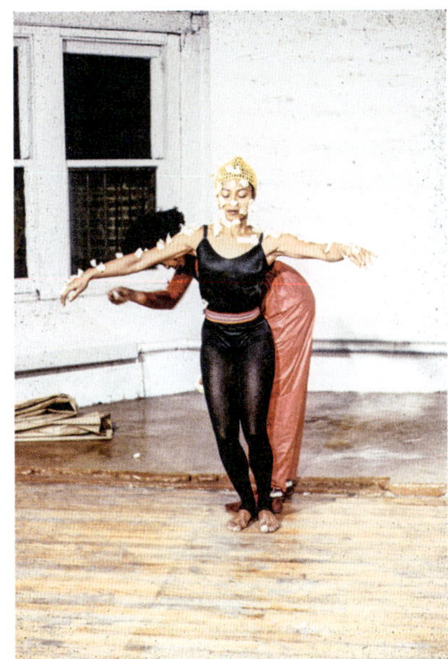
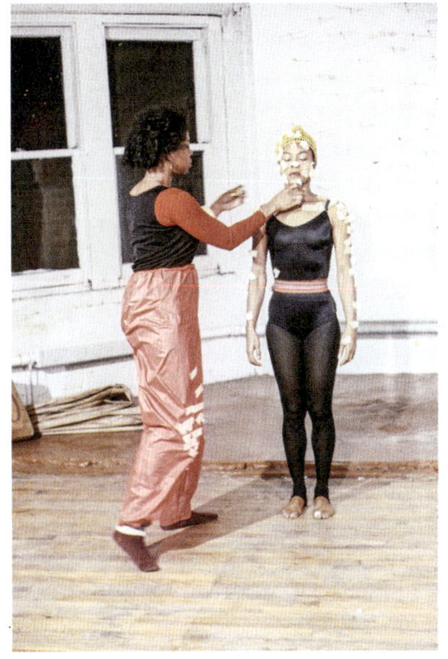

BANKS AND NENGUDI

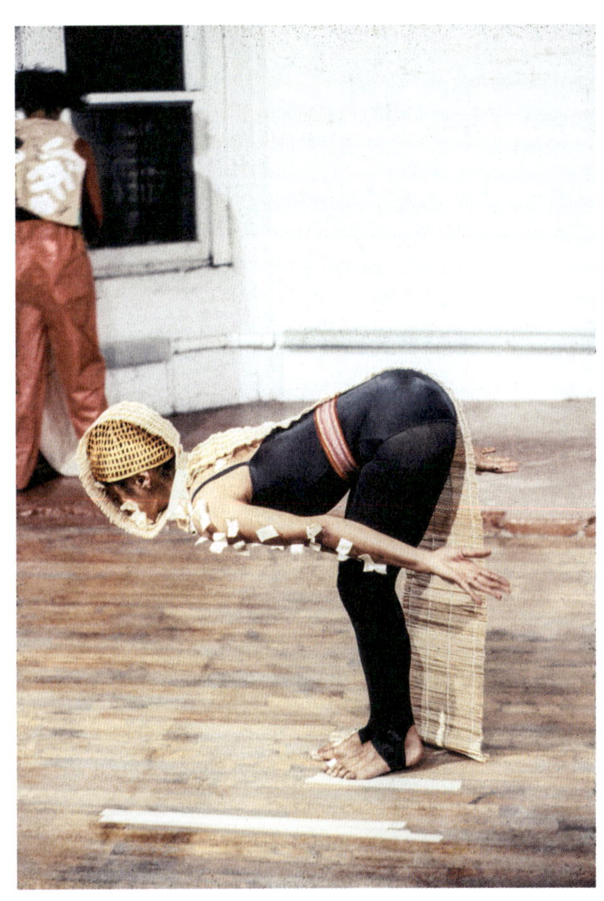

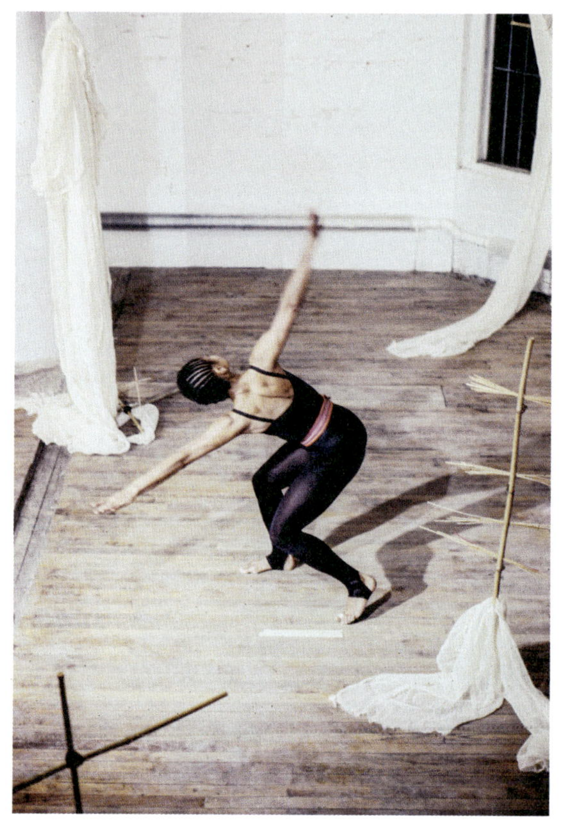

BANKS

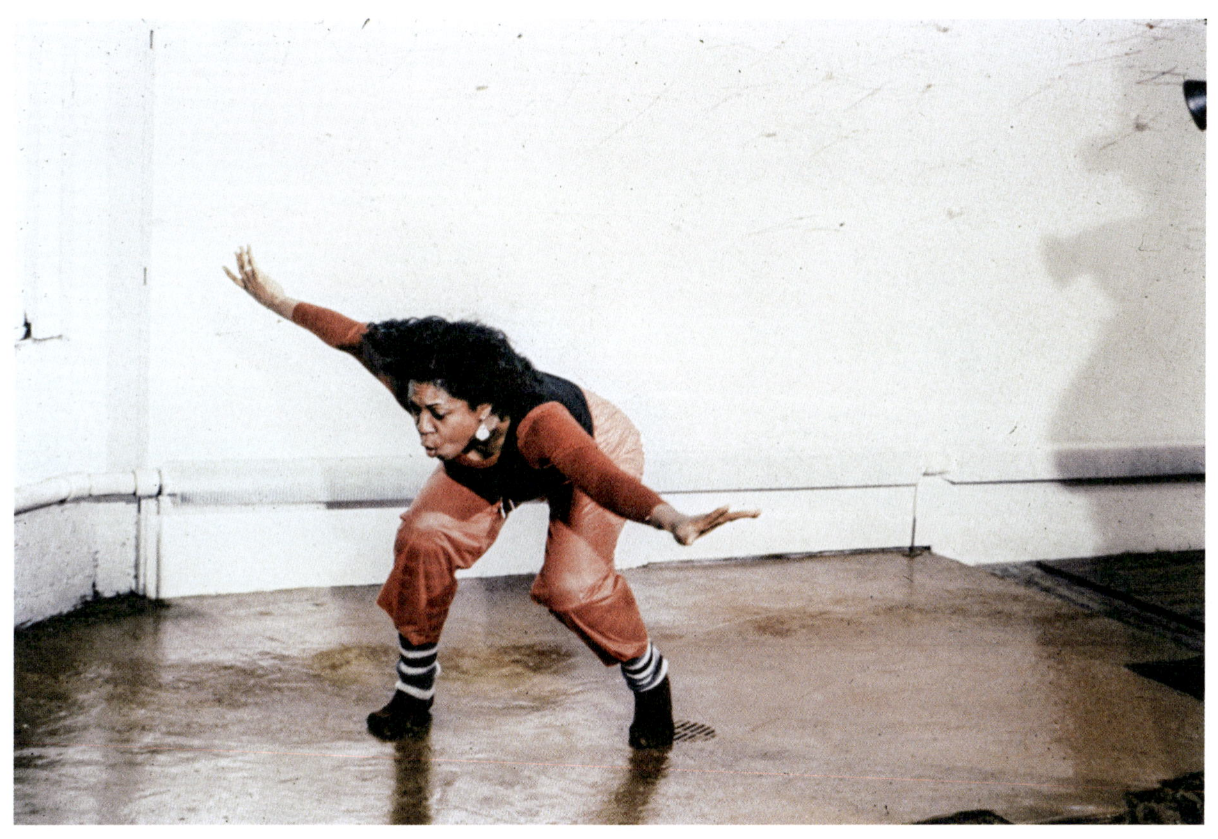

NENGUDI

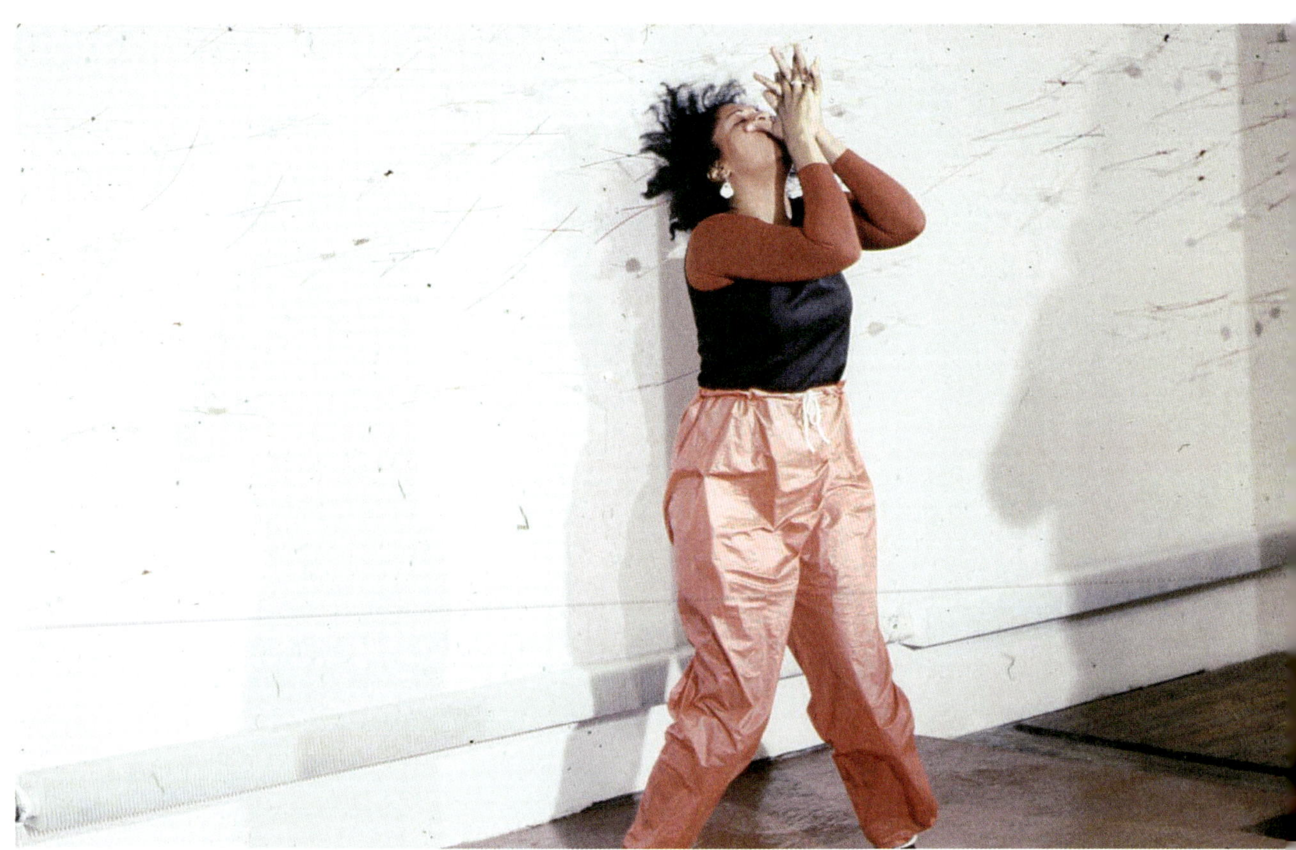

NENGUDI

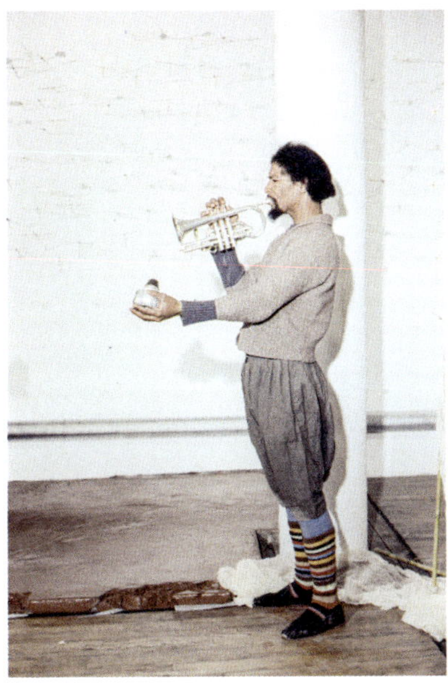

MORRIS

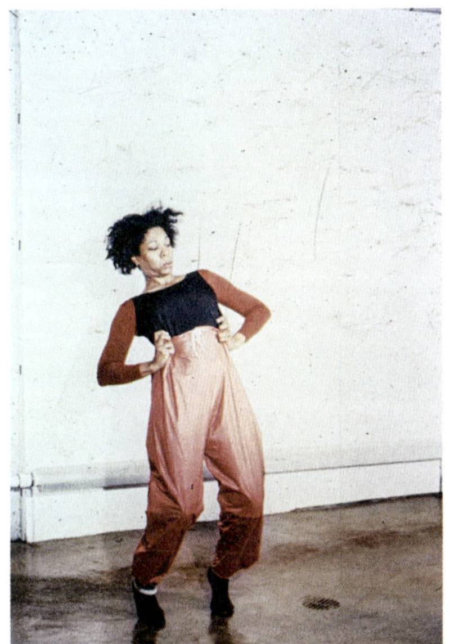

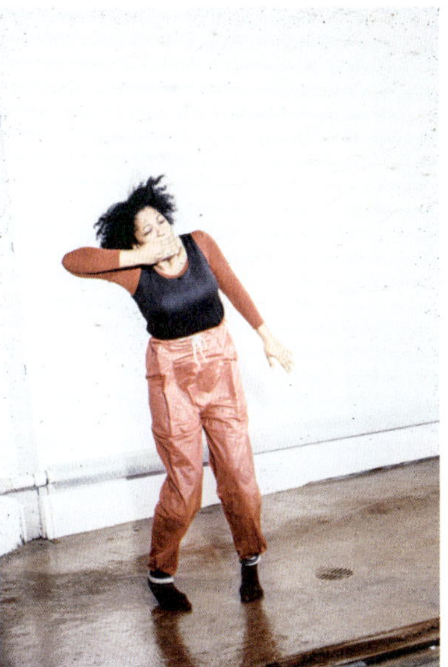

NENGUDI

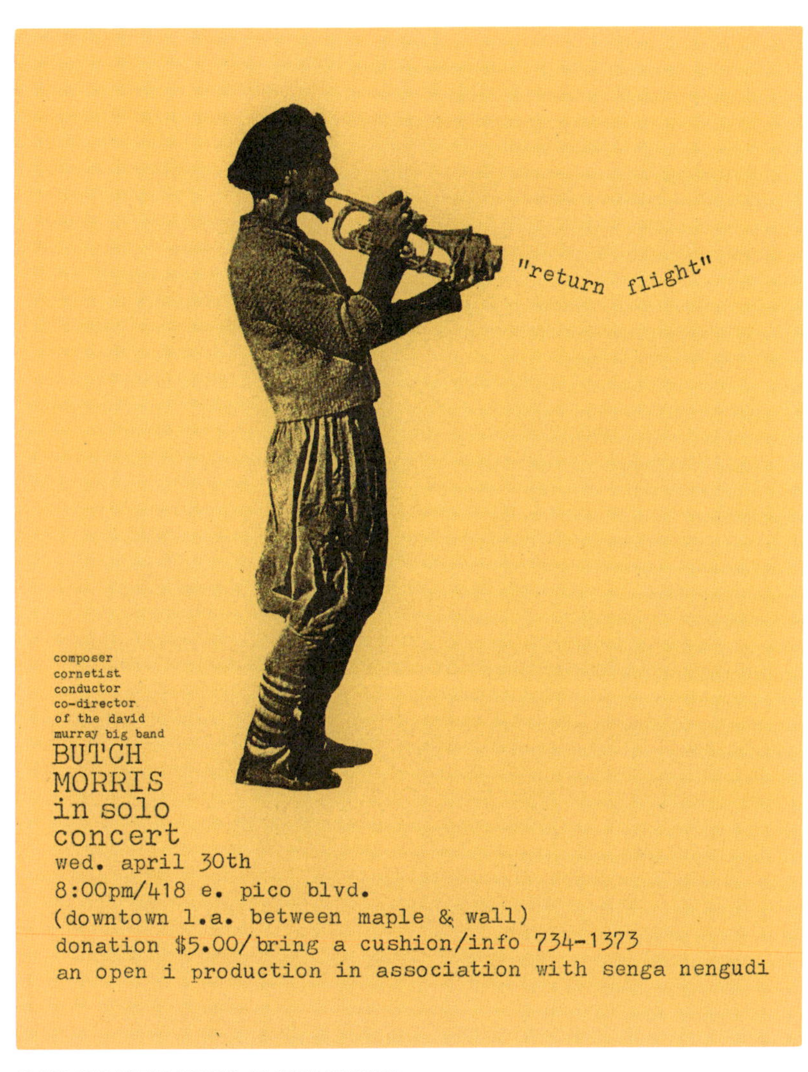

FLIER FOR *BUTCH MORRIS IN SOLO CONCERT*,
418 EAST PICO BOULEVARD, LOS ANGELES, APRIL 30, 1981
PRODUCED BY NENGUDI AND BARBARA MCCULLOUGH

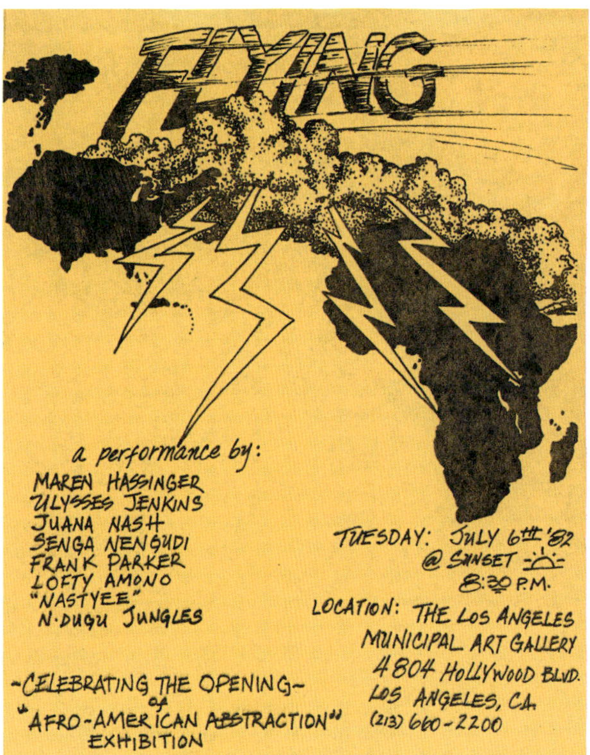

FLIER FOR *FLYING*, PRESENTED IN CONJUNCTION WITH THE *AFRO-AMERICAN ABSTRACTION* EXHIBITION OPENING, LOS ANGELES MUNICIPAL ART GALLERY, JULY 6, 1982
FLIER DESIGN BY ULYSSES JENKINS
PERFORMED BY MAREN HASSINGER, JENKINS, NENGUDI, AND FRANKLIN PARKER, WITH JUANA NASH, "NASTYEE" AND N'DUGU JUNGLES

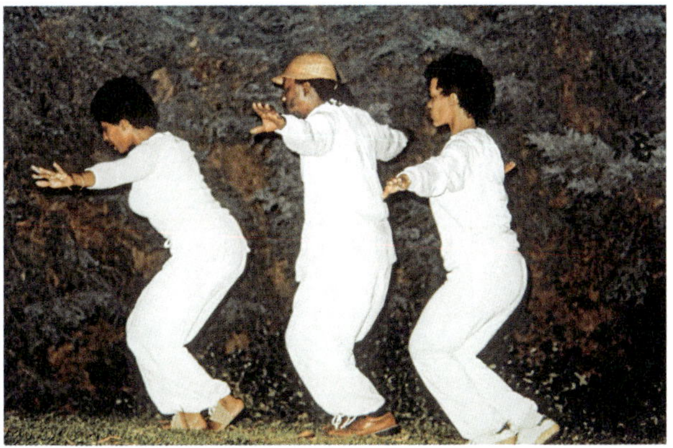

NENGUDI, PARKER, AND HASSINGER

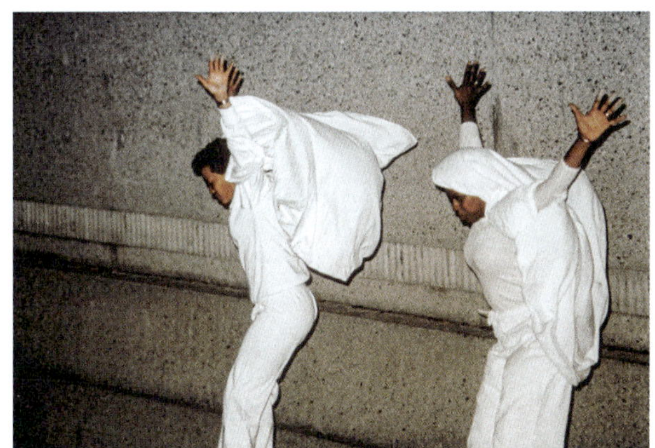

HASSINGER AND NENGUDI

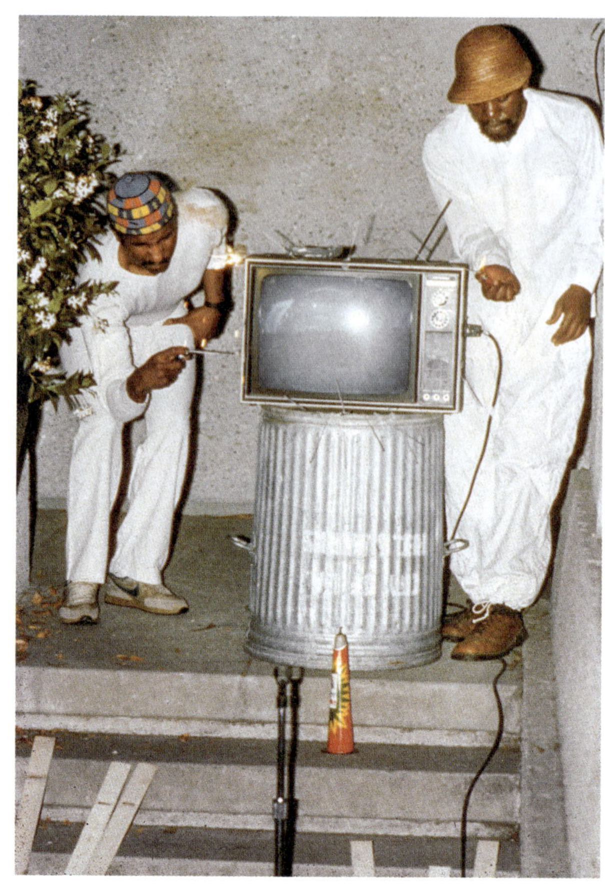

JENKINS AND PARKER

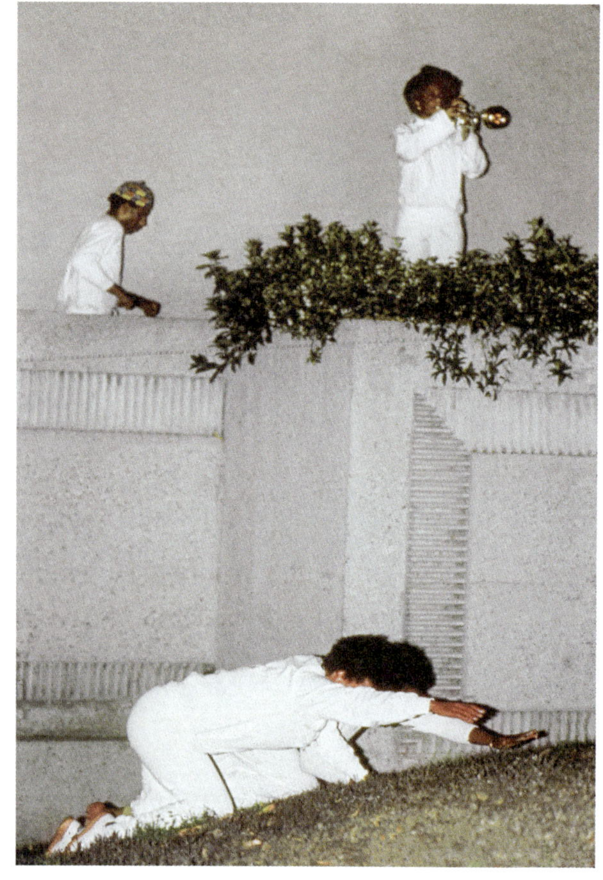

JENKINS, NASH, HASSINGER, AND NENGUDI

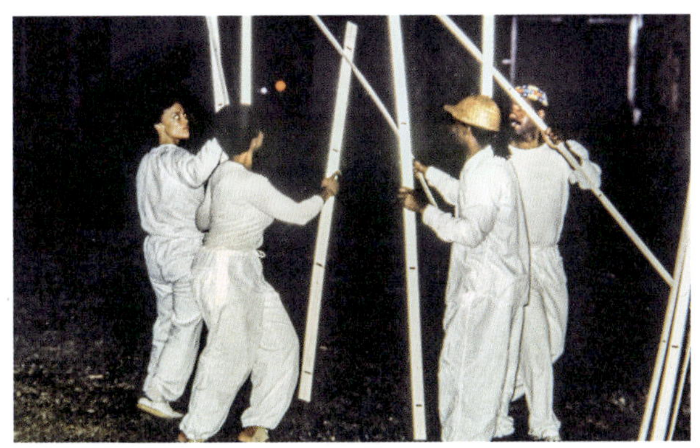

HASSINGER, NENGUDI, PARKER, AND JENKINS

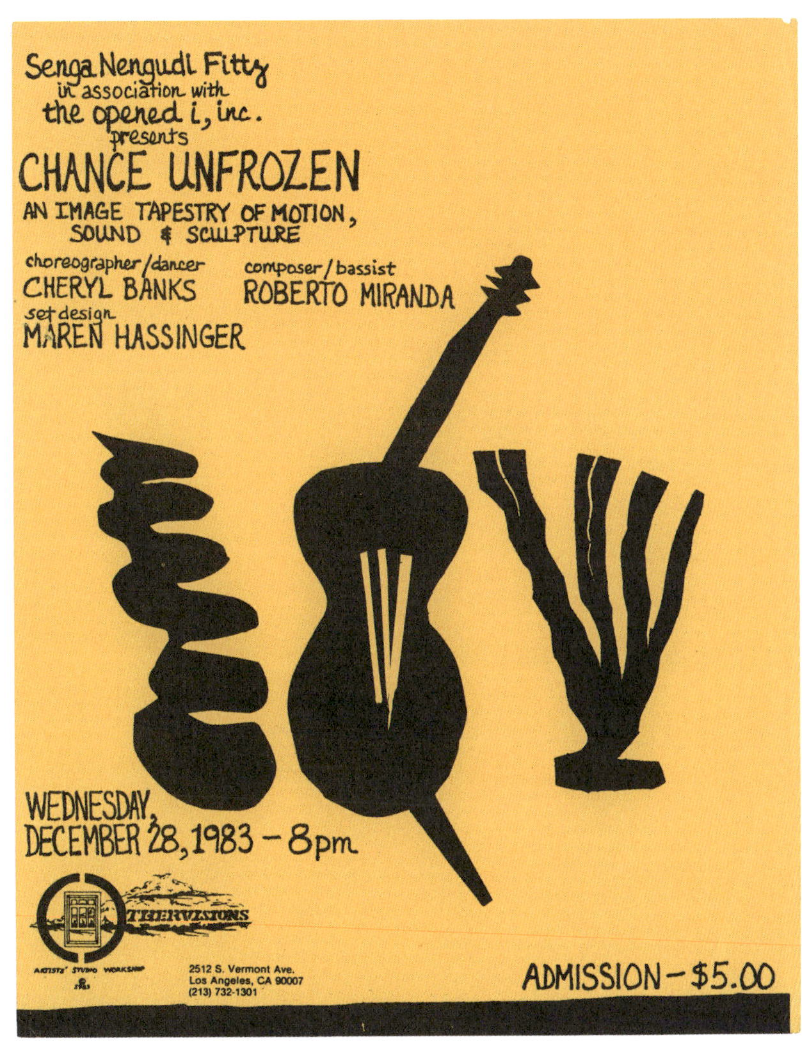

FLIER FOR *CHANCE UNFROZEN*, OTHERVISIONS STUDIO,
LOS ANGELES, DECEMBER 28, 1983
PRODUCED BY NENGUDI AND BARBARA MCCULLOUGH

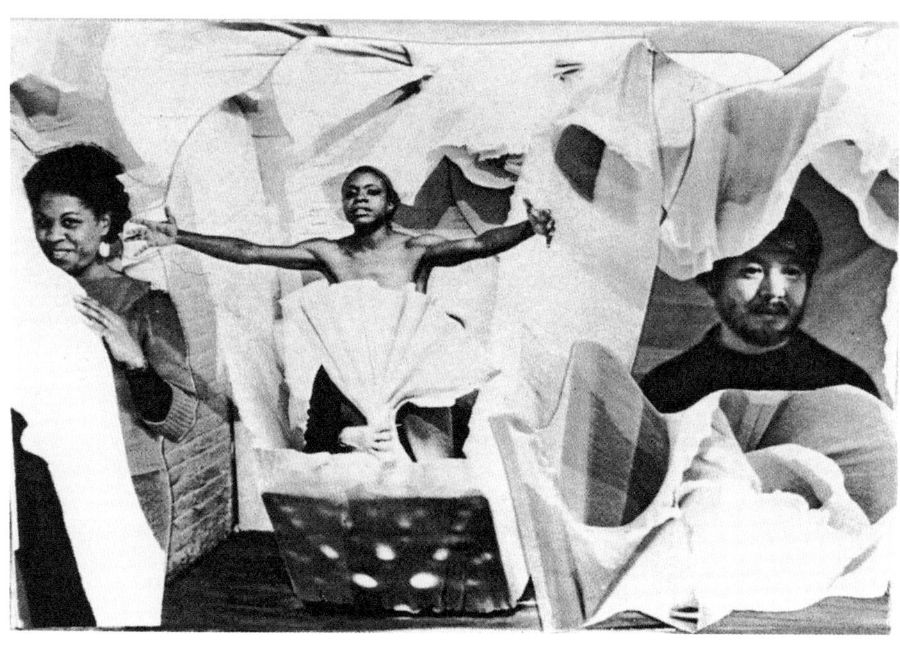

POSTCARD FOR *BLIND DATES*, JUST ABOVE MIDTOWN GALLERY AT WHITE DOG PERFORMANCE STUDIO, NEW YORK, NOVEMBER 20, 1982
SCRIPTED AND PERFORMED BY BLONDELL CUMMINGS, NENGUDI, AND YASUNAO TONE

I am from California. I want a photo of you to take home as a momento of my visit. If you don't want your picture taken, cover your face with this card or any way you choose. Thank You.

- Senga Nengudi

" Smile "

PERFORMANCE SCORE FOR *SMILE*, PART OF *BLIND DATES*, SIGNED BY CUMMINGS, NENGUDI, AND TONE

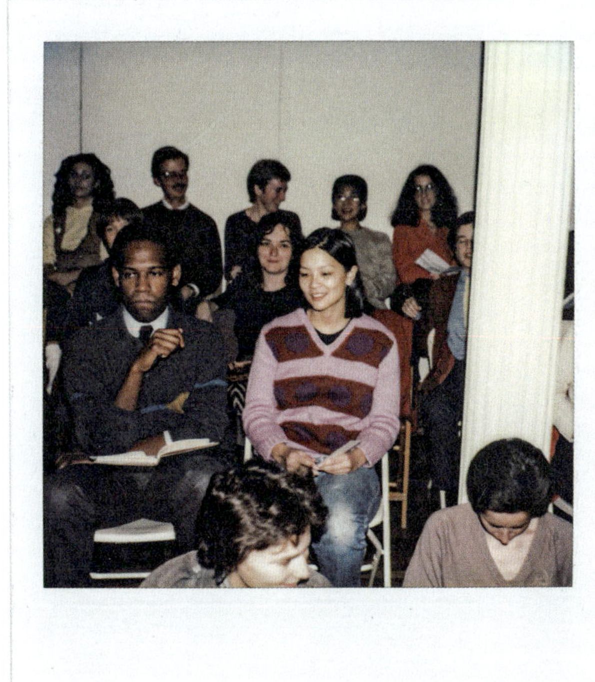

POLAROIDS OF *SMILE*

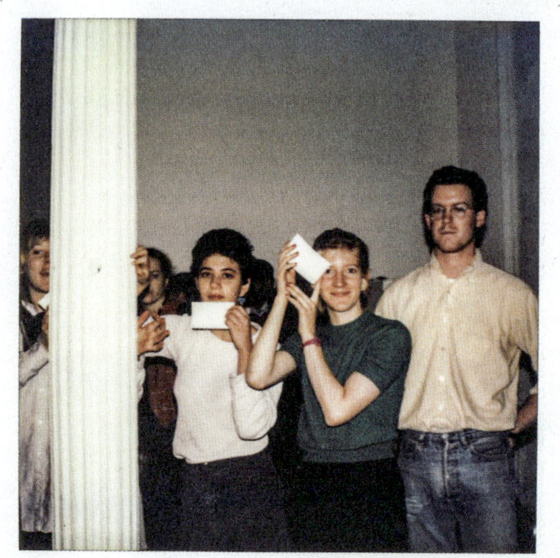

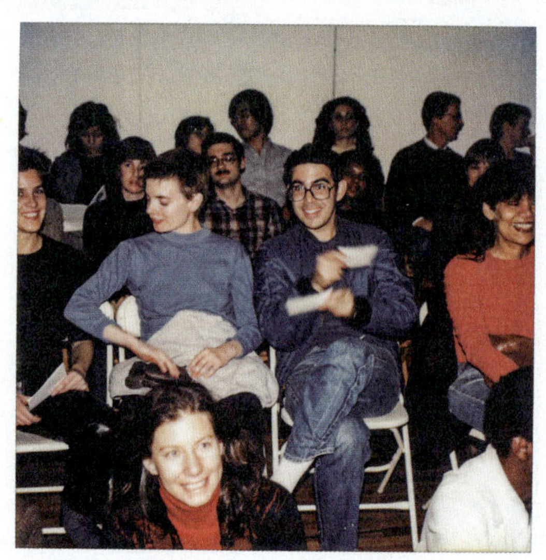

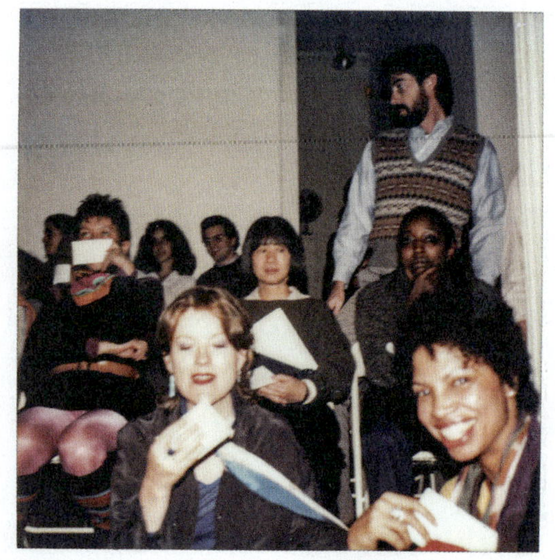

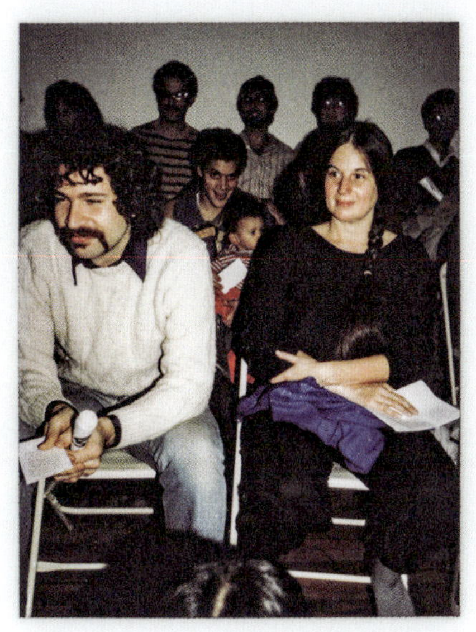

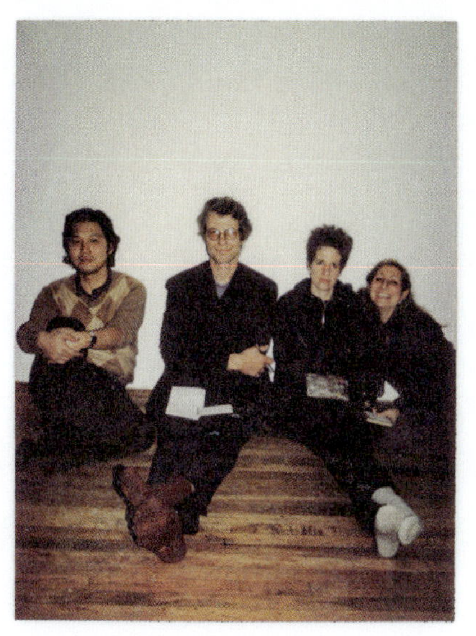

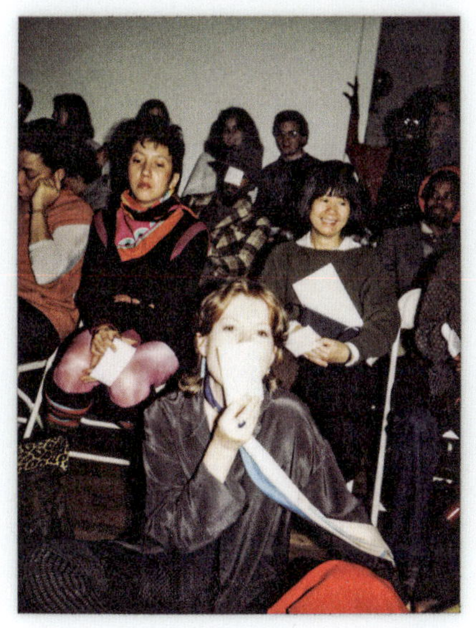

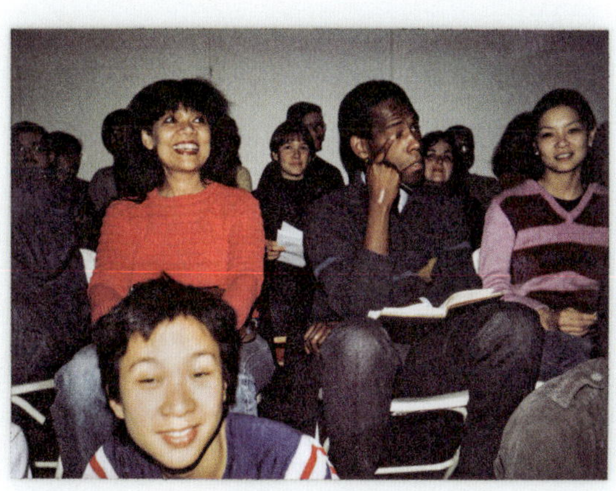

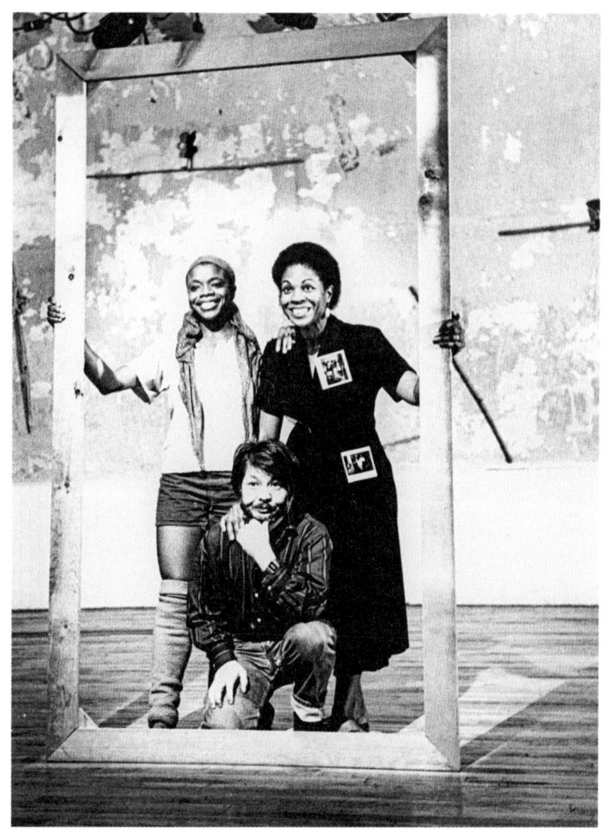

POSTCARD FOR *BLIND DATES*

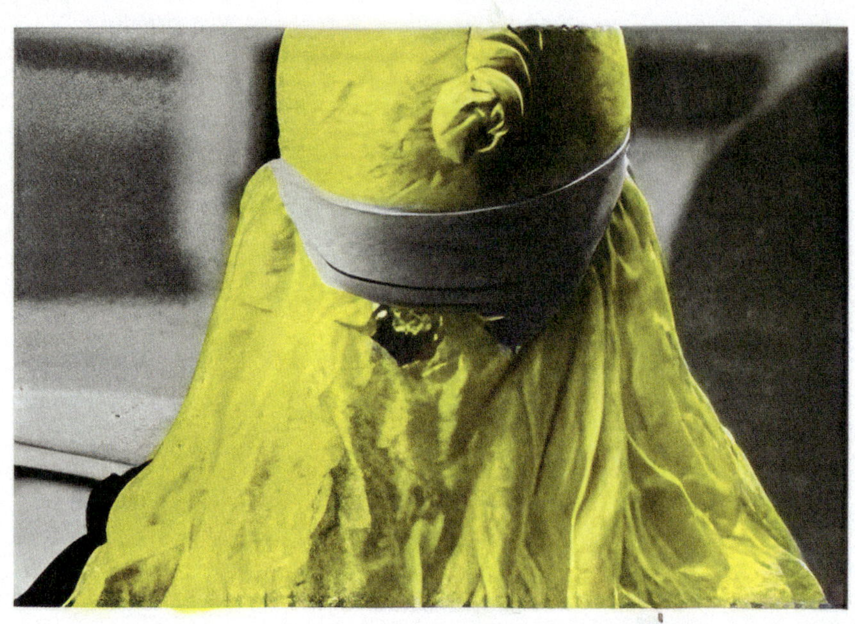

FLIER FOR *MOUTH TO MOUTH: CONVERSATIONS ON BEING—DOUBLE THINK BULEMIA*,
RADIO PROGRAM BROADCAST ON CHANNEL 5, NATIONAL PUBLIC RADIO, DECEMBER 15, 1988

SENGA NENGUDI *Mouth to Mouth: Conversations on Being*, initiated by Senga Nengudi Fittz. *Double Think Bulemia*. The state of Bulemia was named and discovered by the ever-exploring Sir Charles Abramson, better known as Dr. Fuki. Speaking with us on the state of Bulemia is one of its ministers of state and other citizens, including dignitaries Sun Ra and Cecil Taylor.

Tell me, Dr. Fuki. I've never heard of your country. What is the name of your country again?

DARRYL SIVAD (AS "DR. FUKI") Well, the name of the country is Bulemia. Actually, it's more like a state of mind rather than a country. A chosen few people live and exist in the state of Bulemia, and Bulemia exists in the state of them.

SN Now, even though it's a chosen few, can anyone become a citizen of Bulemia?

DS I think that anyone can work toward being a citizen. But not anyone can be a citizen, no, no.

SN Well, what does it take to become a citizen of Bulemia?

DS It just takes oneness. When you become one and aware with the citizens of the state, then you get closer to it. You see?

SN Well, can you tell me how one becomes one with oneness?

DS Well, I think that you start by approaching a certain spiritual awareness that we all hold in the state, the magistrates of the state all hold certain spiritual awareness. And I think that you start down that road of thinking, you think like the aristocrats of the state, you know? And slowly, oneness becomes whole with the person that is attempting to become one.

KAYLYNN SULLIVAN TWOTREES You become so clearly what you are that you perceive yourself as part of the whole. And that you live your life as part of that whole. And that you perceive every moment in its totality.

DS Well, I am Dr. Fuki. I am also known as the Minister of BS. I'm also the Minister of Finance and Health, Education, and Welfare. The government would not be as you know government. It would be a much higher order. Each individual would be responsible for himself and others.

CAROL BLANK We're always depending on each other. When you're in trouble, and you're in deep trouble, you depend on each other.

JOHN OUTTERBRIDGE It's a lonely place to hold your gut. To be honest about the way it smells. We came together when we came together, but we were together in the way we felt about things.

KSTT Everybody's continually hanging out with everybody else. There's no leader, everybody is a fierce individual.

SN And what would its major export be?

DS Its major export? Creativity. Certainly, it would be creativity.

JO I don't feel that we need to refer to what we do as a people as "art" today. Our creative processes benefit a lot of others, and us, you know, in terms of clearing the spirit and utilizing that. But if we can create schools of thought that are not readily recognized, we can also create new references and ways of referring languages as it has to do with creative expression. We need not fall in all of those categories that tend to put a cap on how ideas really flow and how they are germinated and how they have impact on the way we move ourselves through life. You know, and I really think that we have every right in the world to re-preface what is referred to as "art." Because if I can imagine, I can reach out at what is imagined.

KSTT And what I found out was that when I do nothing, I make things. And I make things out of whatever is there.

CHARLES ABRAMSON The act of making art is a cleansing act for me. Because I'm always ingesting information about a thing I want to create. So, in that sense, I'm filling myself with that thing. So, in order to get that thing out of me and onto a canvas, I have to make the act. That act has to follow. I'm following archetypical ways of doing things. I'm not following an art school formula for creating. My formula would be a formula for the creation of the universe, the creation of man. So, those are the things I'll use in order to create my work. You know, those are the things that I will use as the symbols in order to translate my work onto a canvas. I'm always the creator creating something. I'm always reflecting the higher creator when I create.

DS Now, the DeKoon, who lives in another physical state to the east, he's also a minister. And the DeKoon has given certain Koonceptual terms. As a matter of fact, he created the dicKoonary. And that is our active language.

SN I see. Could you speak DeKoon to me?

DS I'm speaking in a higher Koonscience right now.

SN So you've given me kind of the language of the country. What would the religions be that were practiced there? Or is it in itself, that?

DS Oh, there's no need for religion. Because religion suggested society needs some type of order. And we don't need that. We don't need that kind of thing. We have one, we have our being, we have each other in a oneness. So, we don't need any other type of armies, religions, politics—we don't need that.

CA No two people look at it the same way. No two people reflect it the same way.

DS I mean, you can walk the streets and recognize a member of Bulemia.

SN And when you recognize that person, that other member, do you give any sort of signal or is it just known? The oneness is felt?

DS Oh, you feel the oneness. You smile. You feel a Chantherian charm about them. I have been Bulemic off and on for about twenty-five years. Although I'm much older than that.

SN Yeah. So it's not something you're born to. It's something you have to evolve.

DS Oh, yes. And there are times, like right now, where I just, I think, and I'm out of Bulemia. You know, it's not a constant state. You know, when you're feeling other than yourself, you're usually out of the state.

SN So you can go in and out of this oneness.

DS Yes.

SN How do you feel when you're out of your Bulemic state?

DS You feel a certain sense of transparency. You feel lost and sort of disillusioned. You lose track of your Kooncept. Because, again, science, religion, politics is to assume or restore order on a certain level that we don't have a need for.

SN Now, does that mean that you're involved in disorder or no order?

DS Yes, the order is actually there if you want to refer to it as we refer to it as ... order. Again, we refer to it as being. Well, see in our society, I guess we will say that there is order yet chaos because we need the chaos to fuel creativity. We have certain music that we listen to for spiritual support and that type of thing.

JO I see music. Music has always given me images. They make sound a visual reality. You know, I grew up in a region, like, in the South, in North Carolina, where there was music.

There was the music of the hillbilly country, Western, strong music, very much like our own music because it comes from a hard place, an inter-place, a gutty place. Right? And it also tells the truth about that experience. And I heard that when I was a kid growing up. But at the same time, I heard of blues—I mean, real honest-to-goodness blues—and I heard jazz at the same time. All of those elements were there. There were musical sounds that you heard way out in the country that you heard no place else. So, when you hear those sounds in nature, when you hear those sounds today, or when you see things that remind you of that period, place, and time, you also hear what you see, you know. And so music is very, very visual to me, it always has been. And I think because music has a posture, it's a language that we share. A good friend of mine told me once, and this friend is a musician, he said, you know, Bridge, I'm so lucky that I can write music. He said, one thing that I discovered about a song is that it's no good until I can sing it to you. [laughs]

DS Bulemics usually express themselves through their involvement with themselves and others. They would have to set off a certain spirit, and they would have to participate in the non-discussion of reality. And transfix the higher cosmic possibilities of Koonceptualization. The Minister of BS and the DeKoon put together these terms to make conversation. If we needed it ... how can I say this? More zoned, so only the members of Bulemia would understand the Kooncept. There's a number of terms. There's the Kooncept, which is a higher order. "Koon" just means a higher order to us. That's all we're saying, a higher order. Kooncept: any situation or state of being that would be to you a "concept." "Concept" would probably be the same word to you. To recognize is to notice another member of Bulemia. "Koontaloupe" is the term that we give to, I believe you know it as "watermelon."

SN I see.

DS "Koonviction" it would be, uh, to feel, would it be "conviction" to you? And then we've also created a system of martial arts for when we actually need that kind of thing. We don't involve ourselves in violence, but we've given the term Koon Fu. I believe you know it as boxing.

SN I would love to look at your, was it Koon dictionary?

DS No, dicKoonary. Well, we need this to Koonmunicate. We need that between the members of our society.

SN Now, have you ever seen a child that's Bulemic?

DS Oh, certainly. They're born Bulemic. They stray from Bulemia as they grow older and learn from the ways of the world, they stray, and then eventually, hopefully come back.

SN So, then even from birth, there's a going in and out of the Bulemic state?

DS Also, there's a Bulemic pureness. They're born in Bulemia, and they stray out.

SN Now, what could you say that would entice someone to want to start evolving into the Bulemic state?

DS I think, first of all, a person would have to be in the Chantherian nature to want to approach Bulemia. There's a state of Chantheria. I'm trying to relate it to what you know. You know it as "limbo." The Chantherians are actually individuals who are approaching Bulemia at a rapid pace and may become Bulemic at some point in the future. Which I feel that an awful lot of people are Chantherian. But I feel that the person would want to become real within oneself. That is, real is the highest position that we have in Bulemia.

SN And what would real be?

DS Well, real would be the pinnacle of oneness. It would be the third eye with a Louis Vuitton contact. Everything in Bulemia is generated, actually, as we spoke before, from the real.

CB It's like, if I give you something from my heart, like, I'm talking from the root of it. If I give it to you, it's not like a con game. We're not conning each other. Here, this is for you.

DS There are Bulemics who are not conscious of the power of the real.

SN And they're still in that state, even though they're not conscious of the power?

DS Oh, they're in and out of that state. They're always fueled by it when they're in a state of Bulemia. There is no contact with real when you're in a state of Chantheria, or, I don't know if I'm allowed to say the term that's in back of Chantheria. It would take me out of the Bulemic state to actually say such a term, but I will say it at some point.

SN Well, can you tell me, when a Bulemic sees someone on the street that they think might be a good candidate for citizenship, how do they go about speaking to these people and drawing them in?

DS Oh, you speak to them from your Bulemia nature. You don't, we don't induct individuals as certain other societies might. Because this is actually the higher order. I'm out of my Bulemic nature. Now, there is a term that we give to individuals who are not in a Chantherian state. They're actually behind the Chantherian state and prehistoric as you know, we give them the term "Koonstipated." I have to go back. Okay, now I'm back into my Bulemic state, thank you.

SN That was rough, wasn't it?

DS It was difficult.

SN How far back do you think the Bulemic state goes? Because you just mentioned prehistoric.

DS The Bulemic state goes back to the first man.

CECIL TAYLOR This is just a continuum of what happened five, six, seven thousand years ago.

SN When you first realized that you had hit this Bulemic state, how did it come upon you? For instance, did it come upon you in your sleep? Or were you walking down the street and all of a sudden your enlightenment came, or what?

DS I was in high school, I believe. One day I'd gone to school, and I had worn a pair of Levi's and a plaid shirt to school. And I came home and I was watching—yes, I went to the Motown Revue, and I came out and something came over me. And the very next day, I went out and purchased a pair of burgundy silk pants and some black-and-white shoes and a gabardine shirt. And I knew then that I was tending toward some other state of being. You realize the state as you're with others who have realized it or realize it along with you.

SUN RA If you knew about me, I'm gonna create a special agency that's my own nation. And I'm doing a good job. I got a lot of evidence about being. I got a lot of evidence on everybody. I'm just gonna give everybody amnesty. But first, I'm gonna give everybody an eviction notice down from the skies. Eviction notice.

DS And you become, rather than be inducted, into a state of Bulemia.

SN Is there anything you would like to say to our audience?

DS Well, I feel that anyone that has listened this long has probably reached a state of Chantheria and have probably dropped the state of Koonstipation behind them. And I feel that they should reach toward the state of Bulemia without reaching. The state can be found in music.

KENNETH SEVERIN It feels like your music is just purely a force of nature, like the power of, like, the sex drive, or just the blind forces of nature, like thunder and lightning and mountains and erupting volcanoes exploding in the urge to survive, you know?

CT Hey, what it is ... when I was younger, I didn't understand, I had to work out certain personal problems and didn't understand my children, and I couldn't understand why they didn't do it my way, and they said, "No." Look: The thing that we learned is it's a celebration of life. Music has saved my life, poetry has saved my life. Music is just one of the forms. And I will probably be the most human I can possibly be, as well as the most developed musician before the chemistry changes and I become a mountain. Hell ain't got nothin' to do with it. Mountain.

DS It can be found in art.

CA You are a moving piece of art.

CB I can become famous or not famous, but my expression is my strength.

DS It can be found in culture. It can be found in oneness in any circle. There is only creation, and you cannot put time on creation. It works on its own accordance.

CA The act of creation is always around us. It's always an ongoing thing. And so at any point, I can tap into it.

SN Do you ever dream in a Bulemic state?

DS Oh, a Bulemic state is constantly a dream. Oh, yes, it's not, um, a tangible state.

CA Oh, my dreams, oh, they're really vivid. They influence me quite a bit because they're so good. I dream every night. I just seem to dream all night long. And the imagery is so dynamic that I think it influences me a lot. And so I would say my painting and the act of painting comes from that. Also, again, creating at night, I'm creating images in my head while I sleep.

SN Can you give an example of a Bulemic dream?

DS A Bulemic dream? Well, the individuals of our society dream and I certainly once was a member of our society, but I have reached a higher order now. So, I don't have the dream as you ask me, I've reached another plateau in society where I don't have those anymore. But let me say this about the Bulemic dream: Once you reach a state of Bulemia, you still have a certain amount of refuge from the Koonstipation that you probably suffered before then, and that would be the use of the dream to rid you of all Koonstipated notions. And once you reach a certain level of Bulemic society, you cease to have that dream.

SN What places would border Bulemia?

DS You should think about it in terms of a Hula-Hoop or something like that where you have the state of Koonstipation in the middle, but in no way is it connected or encapsulated. To the outside of the state of Koonstipation you have Chantheria, which is approaching Bulemia. To the outer edges, you have Bulemia.

SN So is it like Saturn?

DS Well, Saturn is a ball, no.

SN But it has rings around it.

DS It's more like James Brown's records. To think about it in terms of flatness. It's not a ball, it's a Hula-Hoop.

SN So even though the Koonstipation is inside, it does not affect the outer—

DS Oh, no, no. Certainly not. I mean, if you think about it this way, if you thought of the state of Koonstipation being on the outside, the state of Chantheria again being in the middle, and Bulemia being the nucleus, well, then we would be surrounded by the Koonstipated notion. It is the toilet principle. That's why we have the Koonstipated notion centralized. To the outer edges, or the rim of the toilet, we will have Chantheria. And off of those edges we'll have Bulemia, whose ever-extending presence is worldly and cosmic.

SN Ah, I see. Well, I really thank you, Dr. Fuki.

DS Oh no, I'm the Minister of BS.

SN Sorry, thank you. I thought, well, what happened, what's happening with Dr. Fuki?

DS Well, Dr. Fuki has reached a state of real. He's in the eternal sense a Bulemastermind. Again, the term is "oneness" and it's real. And it's a state of nothingness and everything. And that's what he is presently.

CA I'm creating images of what I'd like life to be, what I imagine life to be. I had this whole plan of what man should be about. So, I'm always creating.

SN Well, I really appreciate this. I know the world is waiting to hear this and to be aware that this state is around them.

DS Yes, the state is around them. Yes. It is around them.

SN Thank you. [music plays]

SN Voices of Bulemia:

MINISTER OF BS
Darryl Sivad

CITIZENS OF BULEMIA
Sir Charles Abramson, otherwise known as Dr. Fuki
Carol Blank
John Outterbridge
Kenneth Severin
Kaylynn Sullivan TwoTrees

DIGNITARIES
Sun Ra
Cecil Taylor

MUSIC ACCENTS
Butch Morris
Tyrone Mitchell
George Mingo
The illustrious Danny Davis of Sun Ra affiliation

INITIATOR
Senga Nengudi Fittz

ENGINEER

Scott Frasier

KS Success for your Human Revolution and your relationships with the rest of the world is to be able to communicate with all people on all levels by any level, high, low, whatever level, just deal with one human to another human being. Whether you are highly educated with an incredible amount of information, or you have no education and no information, human revolution is to deal with another human being and to realize the fact that they have potential. Period.

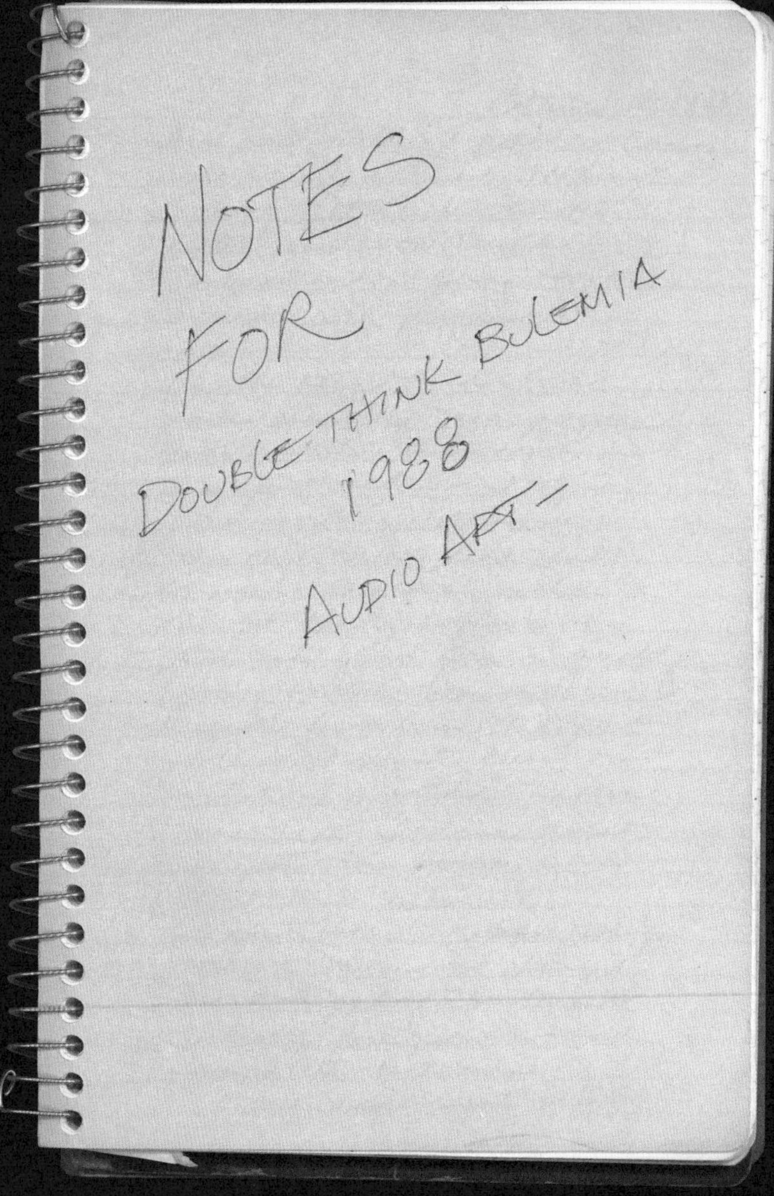

NOTEBOOK FOR *MOUTH TO MOUTH: CONVERSATIONS ON BEING—DOUBLE THINK BULEMIA*

Sun ra
(Word for word)

Some Black People came They wanted
to ask me some questions ~~Some this same~~
~~That right on the house on Pico Blvd at~~
~~one of the fellows~~ mothers house. ~~Th~~
They were sitting around about 14 of Them
from different newspapers and magazines
I said how all this time I been here
and ~~those~~ of the other race in every country and know all about
me – and you should have know all about
me first. ~~There was a~~ Here you come asking all about YOU GOT TO ASK ME FIRST
me. and you should know first. IT'S time you should
~~There was a cat there~~ YOU SHOULD HAVE GOTTEN THIS FIRST
IT'S TIME YOU SHOULD KNOW ABOUT ME

~~SO THIS CAT G~~ SO IT WAS A CAT ~~THERE~~
AND THERE WAS A CAT SO THIS CAT GOT
IN THE MIDDLE OF THE FLOOR AND SAID
RA RA AND THEY THEY LOOKED AND THEIR EYES BUCKED
DO YOU KNOW, IN ABOUT FIVE MINUTES THEY LEFT AND
~~AND THE CAT SAID RA RA~~ BUT THE CAT GOT UNDER THE CHAIR
DIDN'T ASK ME NO QUESTIONS AND THE CAT SAID ~~RA RA~~ AND I SAID SEE THERE
EVEN THE CATS KNOW ME AND THE CAT WANTS TO KNOW WHAT TROUBLE DO YOU HAVE FOR THE CATS
YOU KNOW THEY SHOULD HAVE LAUGHED AT THAT
BUT THEY DIDN'T HAVE NO SENSE OF HUMOR
THEY SHOULD HAVE GONE ON AND ASKED ME QUESTIONS
BUT IN FIVE MINUTES ONLY I AND THE CAT WAS LEFT
NOW THE CREATOR SHOWED THEM SOMETHING,
THROUGH A SENSE OF HUMOR HE LET THEM KNOW YES! THAT ~~[illegible]~~ RA IS
REPRESENTING ~~[illegible]~~ ME. I TELL THE WHITE RACE YES
THAT I AM THE CREATOR'S SPECIAL AGENT TO SPY

Cecil Taylor
(Word for Word)

① I'M THINKING ALONG THE ~~old~~ LINES ?? THE OLD ARGUMENT ~~THAT~~ ABOUT
BEEBOOP EVEN BACK IN THE 40'S AND
50'S THAT YOU COULDN'T DANZE TO IT
THAT WAS THE FIRST CRITICIZM, AND IT
GOES TO ME THE WHOLE ARGUMENT
OF COURSE YOU CAN DANZE TO IT YOU HAVE
TO DANZE ~~A~~ ALOT ~~ALOT~~ FASTER AND ALOT DIFFERENTLY
A LOT DIFFERENTLY - BIRD CAME TO SYMPHONY
BALLROOM 1947-1948 THOSE THAT COULD DID
~~The Gloria~~ TOOK ME TO A PLACE IN LONDON CALLED
THE WAG THE WHAT THE WAS
PATRICE MOHAMMAD & NATHEN PAVIS PLAYING
RIGHT OK AFTER THAT THE DANCERS TOOK
THE FLOOR JAMES BROWN, THEN COUNT BASIS, BILLY
HOLIDAY NEVER STOPPED DANCING AND THERE WERE
TWO WEST INDIANS WHO WERE NEW INTO BASICS
THEY STARTED DOING SOME OF THE NICHOLAS BROS.
~~CHERYL~~ TOOK US TO A DISCO IN WUPPERTAL
SAME THING - BERLIN
NEW YORK YOU HEARD BILLY HOLIDAY YOU HEARD
DEXTOR GORDON AND THOSE PEOPLE NEVER STOPPED
DANCING
AND IN ENISBORRO THE OLYMPIC THING
~~YOU KNOW~~ RIGHT - THEY WERE DANCING TO SUNRA.
I WENT TO A DISCO THERE
~~WE JUST CAME FROM SUNRA~~ OTA
GO ON TELL THEM ABOUT YOURSELF
~~DON'T BE SHY~~ ~~MODST~~ MODEST

Bulemia
Possible structure

Title — either Tyrone Sax
or Butch (Opera section of his Berlin tape)
or George Mingo
May need to add my own explaination Dialogue
Darryl - with Carol overlay at points
(ex. Darryl - Bulemia is a state of Being - Carol its a state of Being)
John Outterbridge
Cecil Taylor) maybe there background
Sunra) can be their music
Tyrone Mitchell

credits - ~~Sunra~~ Song in Sunra style
* Tape Danny's Music off video

Notes - Think about creating space and images - like old fashion radio

* Try - slowing down, speeding up running backwards Butch's music

Dialogue
A few years ago I ~~was~~ was made aware of a new place called Bulemia. This program is an attempt by some of the citizens of Bulemia to express what it is and where it is (the nature of Bulemia)
(the state of Bulemia)

Ask Scott if he has tap dancing tape - Norman's just tap

APPROACH SOMEONE AND WHISPER IN THEIR EAR TO DO A MOVEMENT (IE CROSS YOUR EYES, STICK OUT YOUR TOUNGE REAR YOUR HINNY ETC). AFTER THEY DO THEIR MOVEMENT THEY SHOULD GO ACROSS THE ROOM AND WHISPER A MOVEMENT TO SOMEONE ELSE. AND SO ON AND SO ON.

SUBTLY
SENGA

21:59 EST

MGMCOMP MGM

A FEW OF THE
THINGS I JUST
TOLD YOU WAS
A LIE

SOME OF WHAT
I JUST TOLD YOU
WAS A LIE

MOST OF WHAT
I JUST TOLD
YOU WAS A LIE

HANDOUT FOR “PERFORMANCE TRUTHS,”
GUEST ARTIST LECTURE INVITED BY KERRY JAMES MARSHALL,
UNIVERSITY OF ILLINOIS, CHICAGO, 1997

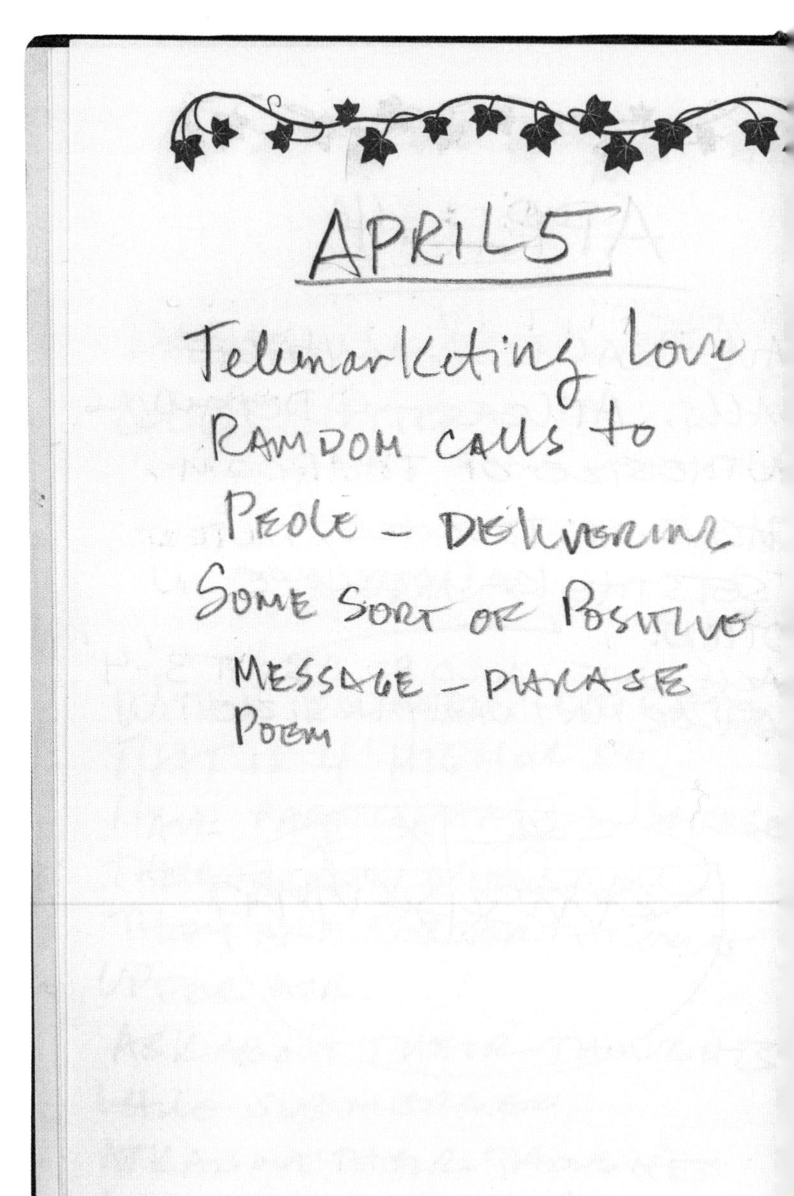
APRIL 5
Telemarketing love
RAMDOM CALLS to
PEOLE - DELIVERING
SOME SORT OF POSITIVE
MESSAGE - PHRASE
POEM

APRIL 6

MAKE POETRY SILK SCARF.
HANG AROUND MY NECK
READ MY POEM TO AS MANY
PEOPLE WHO INQUIRE ABOUT
WHAT I AM WEARING

APRIL 17

SAY/THINK ONE WORD
ALL DAY LONG –
EVEN WHEN TALKING
TO OTHERS & EVEN
WHEN TALKING AND
THINKING TO YOURSELF

MAKE IT A VERB LIKE –

SING
MOVE
GIVE

APRIL 18

WHAT IS BLACK?
HAVE A SQUARE OR
CIRCULAR ROOM
WITH PHOTOS BY
PROPECIA LEIGH
OF OVER LIFESIZE IMAGES
OF PEOPLE WITH AFRICAN/
BLACK BLOOD FROM
PORCELAINE (OR) WHITE TO
PURPLE BLACK.
ALSO REFLECTING OTHER
HERITAGE LIKE ASIAN
ETC.

APRIL 21

FEELINGS

NEEDED - 4 WALLS OUTSIDE
OR INSIDE.
ONE WALL PAINTED BLACK
HAVE FOLKS WRITE WITH WHITE
CHALK WHAT THEY HATE
ANOTHER WALL PAINTED WHITE
WRITE WHAT (WHO) YOU TRULY LOVE
ANOTHER WALL PAINTED RED
WHAT YOU DESIRE
THE LAST WALL PAINTED ?
GREEN OR BLUE OR ____
WHAT YOU DO NOT WANT

THEY CAN ALSO DRAW
INSTEAD OF USING WORDS

APRIL 22

MY BUSINESS

MAKE UP BUSINESS CARDS
WITH MY NAME ON THEM
EACH HAVING A BUSINESS
THAT I AM TERRIBLE AT
OF COURSE HAND THEM OUT
WHERE AND WHEN I CAN

SENGA NENGUDI
HAIR STYLIST

SENGA FITZ
FINANCIAL PLANNER

CARD DESIGN AND LOGO WILL BE
PART OF IT AS WELL.

SENGA NENGUDI FITZ
MAINTENANCE
HOME/OFFICE

SENGA N. FITZ B.S.N.
NUTRITIONIST

ETC.

Walk a Mile in My Shoes

Use these shoes to walk or dance a mile (5,280 feet). If they don't fit make them work in some way. Let me know how it goes.
Send me a pair to wear.
Thanks

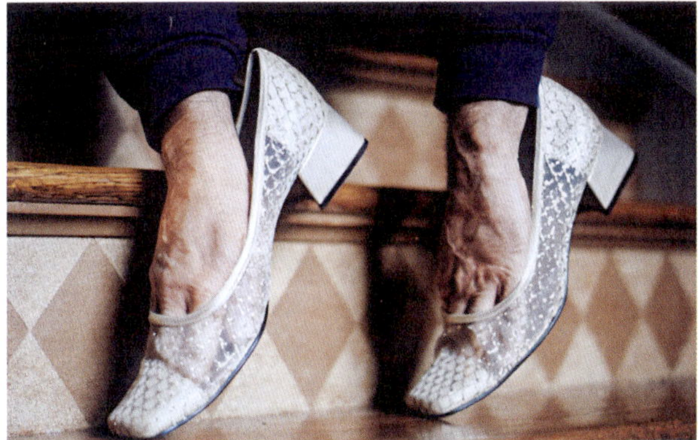

PERFORMANCE SCORE AND PHOTOGRAPH OF *WALK A MILE IN MY SHOES*, 1999

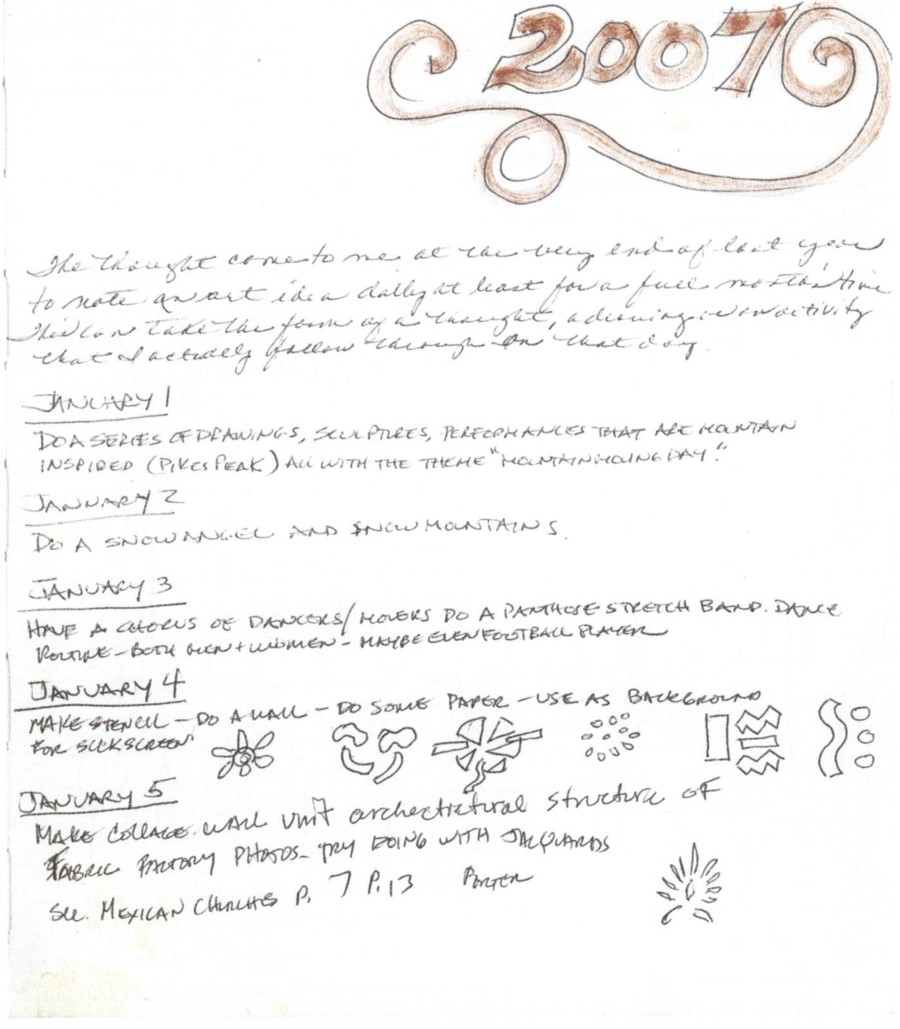

The thought came to me at the very end of last year to note an art idea daily at least for a full month's time. This can take the form of a thought, a drawing or an activity that I actually follow through on that day. January 1 Do a series of drawings, sculptures, performances that are mountain inspired (Pikes Peak) all with the theme "mountain moving day." January 2 Do a snow angel and snow mountains. January 3 Have a chorus of dancers/movers do a pantihose stretch band. Dance routine—both men + women—maybe even football player January 4 Make stencil—do a wall—do some paper—use as background for silkscreen January 5 Make collage wall unit architectural structure of fabric factory photos—try doing with jacquards. See Mexican churches p. 7 p. 13 Porter

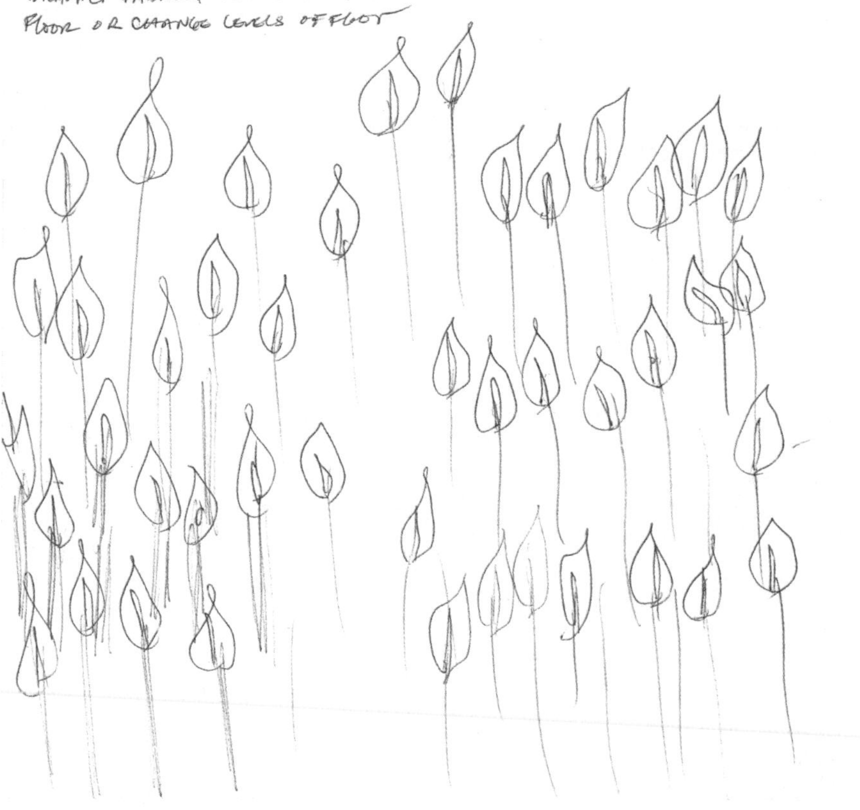

<u>January 6–Sat</u> Create a installation of lilies. A field of lilies that have those little water tubes to keep them fresh—but who ultimately deteriorate. With maybe some other subtle element like a painted floor or maybe wall treatment like fabric, draped fabric. People able to walk through field + maybe elevate floor or change levels of floor

JANUARY 7-SUNDAY
DO DRAWINGS OF LILIES ON ALL SIZES OF PAPER
BROWN PAPER - WHITE PAINT - yellow stem
PAINT WITH MY finger as well as line drawing with
339 [illegible] INK - MAYBE EVEN BLOCK PRINT

February 8, 2007 — 1:30 P.M.

Well my little idea of doing a piece daily in the month of January, writing it down [illegible] etc. did not quite work out.
Though I've enjoyed every minute at my studio the results have been less than stellar. It put me in that all to often visited state of "why do I even call myself an artist" and "what in the heck am I doing?"
I asked for guidance, I intended an answer and finally a veil was lifted when I started to think along the lines that I should validate the odd way I look at art + what really interests me.
I get saddened + frustrated when I draw or even sculpt etc. mainly because I am playing the old comparison game. Looking at art in traditional terms.
The thoughts have come to me regarding all of this in a very different way over the past 24 hours.
Some thoughts I've not flushed out yet. But the thought that there are thoughts is exciting after years, maybe a life time of thinking within a prescribed box.
The one thought that seems clear is that I can examine my love of space as a catalyst for a new way to approach my work.
I don't want to get overly excited about this whole thing like a balloon that gets so much air in it that it burst.
But it has been so long since I've been excited, genuinely

<u>January 7–Sunday</u> Do drawings of lilies on all sizes of paper / Brown paper—white paint—yellow stem / Paint with my finger as well as line drawing with ink—maybe even block print

<u>February 8, 2007–1:30 pm</u> Well my little idea of doing a piece daily in the month of january, writing at dawn etc. did not quite work out. . . .

I love spaces!

I love all of the studio spaces I've had, the spaces in which
I have lived, other people's spaces, land, vases, spaces
inside bottles, bottle caps, mouths, outer space
construction site spaces, digs, boxes
I like to section off things + spaces—define them.
Maybe that is why I love sculpture so much. It defines and envelops space.
It feels like my inquisitiveness about physics has something to do with this too.
The big question is how do I work on this concept without it just coming off looking like cordoned-off areas.
Because to define a space it must have borders—enclosures.
We are talking beyond ephemeral. We are talking ethereal.
Well, the thinking, the trying, the researching, the trip should be stimulating + fun.
We shall see what we shall see.

As I continue to think on this new concept of space it continues to evolve as I try to clarify it. Now it appears to have something to do with energy, energy in two ways.
Energy milling around trying to find its form
or/and pockets of energy that you feel and sense rather than see particularly.
Usually that sort of energy is evoked by creating a scene—like a spooky house or people arguing, or people making love, or like that scene I witnessed so long ago at that black arts festival in LA where this fighter had two girls on either arm + was kind of circling another fighter with I think a girl on his arm—just checking each other out. The scene was so intense that even though there was loud festival noise all around they created a circle of tense complete silence around the area that they occupied.
I'm wondering if there is a way to create this energy without an elaborate setup. I know when I've been in certain places, like sacred spaces, that I have felt something.

I was speeding down
the throughway boulevard
with thoughts of the
whiteness of light when off
to my right a strange sight
caught my eye.

On a brown grassy knoll a
white horse stood very still
held back from venturing
further by a wooden fence.

At first I thought the horse
was occupied with looking at
the herd of cars whizzing by
like a blur below him
I included in that number.

But no, at second glance, to
my amazement the horse was
looking past all that, beyond
all that, with such a sense of
longing in its eyes that I was
moved by the passion and
sadness of the moment. As if
that which allowed him to breathe
had been taken away.

Now as I write of this incident
the same look and stance must have
come over a slave mother watching
her child being taken away. Still
watching after the child was
far from sight.

those doing ritual
have the assurance
of time. individual
acts of art do not
have to depend on
permanence of the
materials only the
permanence of the soul.
[world/soul without
in]
i create a peace/
piece
i wipe it out with
my hands, my feet,
my body. it remains
in the fabric of
time threading
through the
millennia
remembered and
forgotten a thousand
times over. yet
there. seen—not
seen—experienced as
part of the air.

Seated as on thrones
The chorus of before
Call down to us
Be careful, mind your way
This way— this way

BY LILY BEA MOOR

I tumble forward
Like being pushed by gale force winds and then

I resist

I grab hold of nearby branches—holding so tight
They break my skin

Why do I hold them
I let go
These winds again push
Me forward
More gently this time

Supposedly I am facing you
The I am—
you take my hand
Hand over hand over hand
You walk with me
Walking slightly ahead you carry me
To and through my destinies

Still walking on
Following my guide
closing my eyes
I start to tremble

With a squeeze of assurance from the I am
The *I am* of assurance
I slowly open my eyes
Starting with a squint to wide-eyed

Wonder us, wonderous!
A bit more sure-footed I walk with more confidence as if completely on my own

Savoring each moment
the turbulent as
well as the sublime.

BY LILY BEA MOOR

LILIES OF THE VALLEY UNITE
Or not
Me Being
Me
Being is not
An
Action Verb
While
Others of my sort
Bang about
Creating Monuments of Steel/Marble
Gran ite
This is what the Craft's
All About
Working Hard with Pleasure
Pounding things out
Is is
A Pleasurable
Pursuit

Working Hard
As I
HARDLY Work
I Relish
In Creating art
Wherever my I
my Lazy Eye

Finds it
My colleagues
Work Hard
To Bring their Plans to Fruition
Giant Canvases Packed
with Color—Rooms Filled with Stuff
Strategically
Placed

Then(n) am I the Queen Bea
Content to have my Grapes Peeled
Or not
Content to Watch the
Workers scurry about
I Take a pointer
Touch an object
And say
"There
I proclaim you art"
As a Queen
Wood say to a Night
Problem is no
Body Recognizes
This Process
"OF" ART
There is no
Stamina involved

Thinking time
Is Mini-mal
Hands-on
Barely
LILIES OF THE VALLEY UNITE!
I THINK NOT!!!
Lilies of the Valley
DON'T DO A DAMN THING
Yet our presence
Is FELT
like an Anarchist
BECAUSE
We do in deed
E X I S T

by Lily Bea Moor

5/22/04
UJAZI'S BIRTHDAY

FACING FEAR TODAY
THE FEAR OF JUST
SITTING DOWN AND
DOING ART
I'VE ORGANIZED THE
STUDIO
I'VE GOTTEN MY MATERIALS
TOGETHER
THE TIME IS NOW

POETRY PLASTIQUE, 2004
PEN, CRAYON, MARKER, AND TONER ON PAPER,
6 PARTS: 8½ × 11 INCHES (21.6 × 27.9 CM) EACH

5/23/04

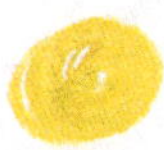

I AM THE RESURRECTION AND THE LIFE

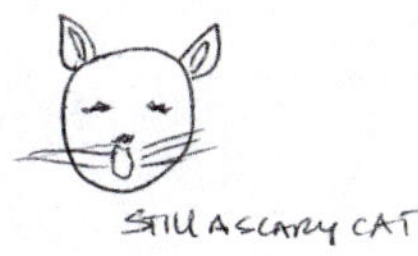

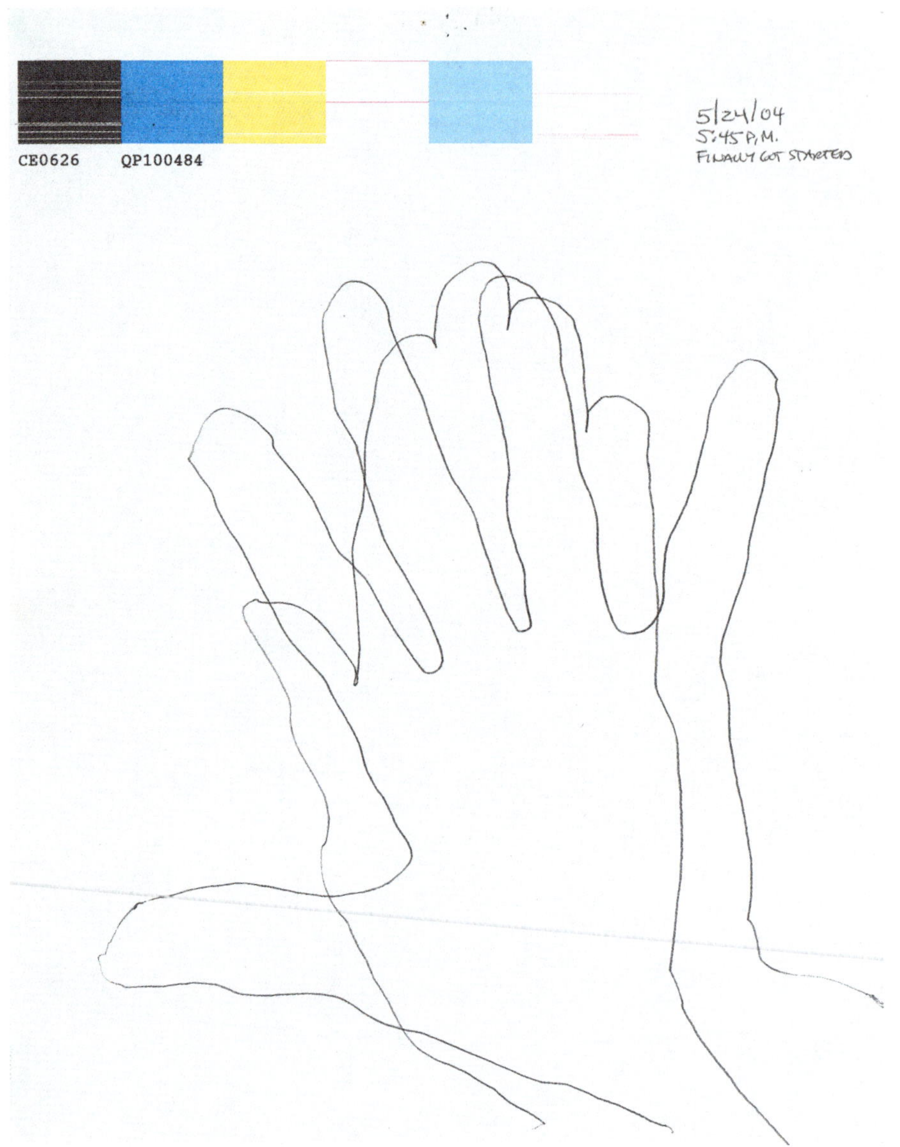
CE0626
QP100484
5/24/04
5:45 P.M.
FINALLY GOT STARTED

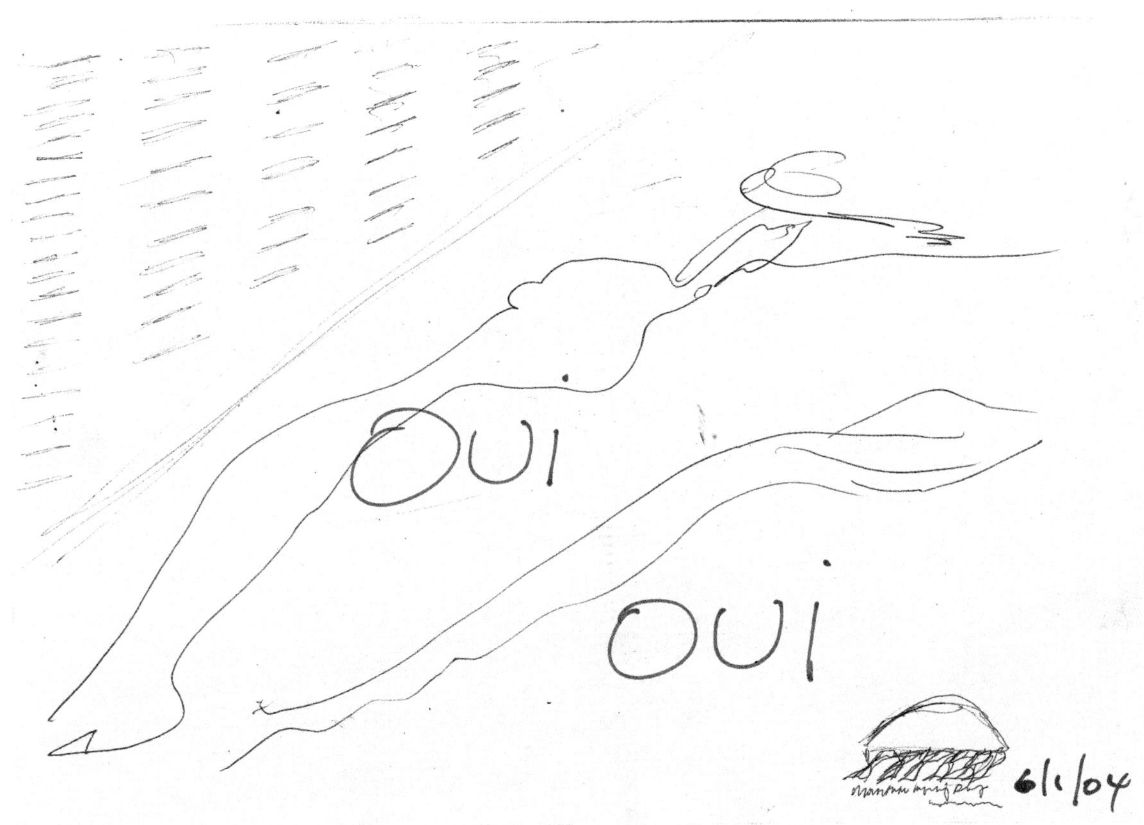
OUI
OUI
6/1/04

FRUSTRATION

6/2/04

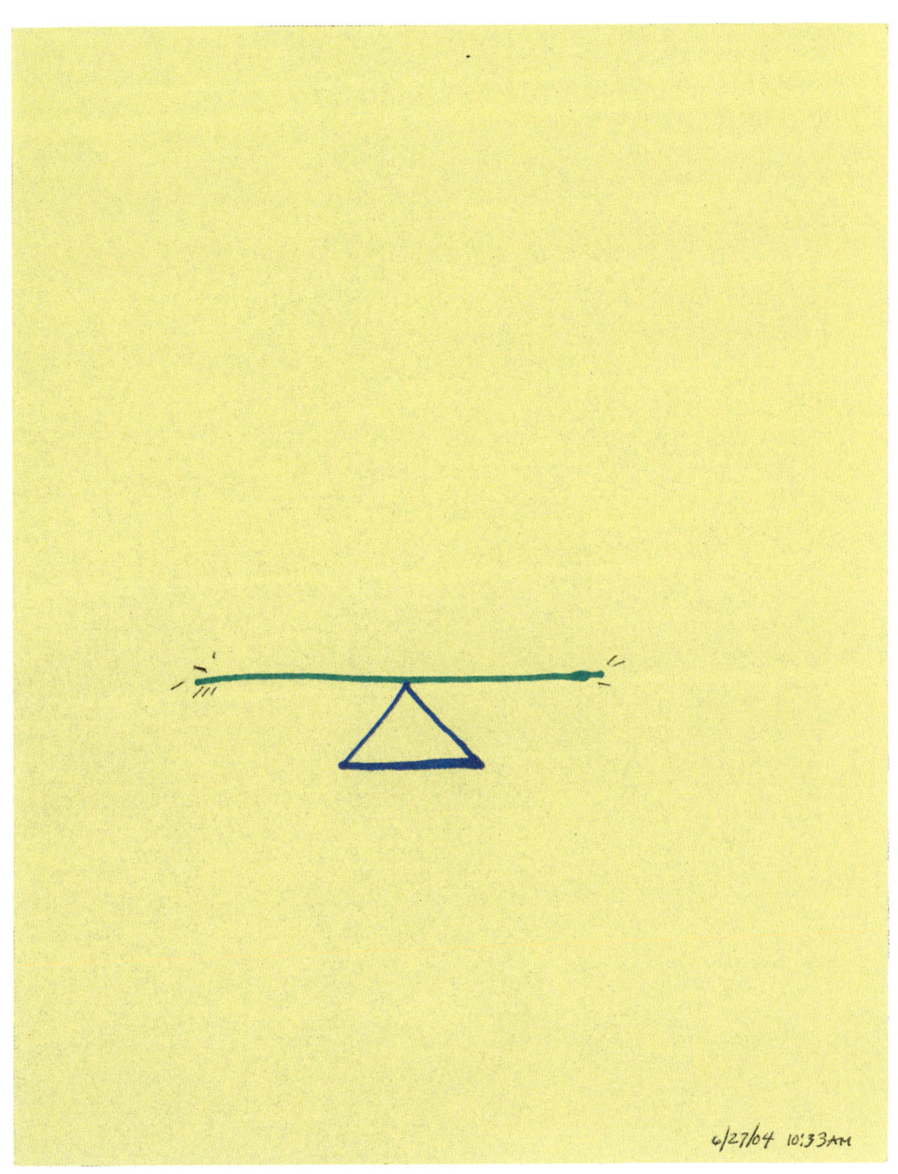

SHEET FROM *POETRY PLASTIQUE* AND PERFORMANCE
SCORE FOR *SEE-SEE RIDERS*, REED COLLEGE, PORTLAND,
FEBRUARY-MARCH 2024
PERFORMED BY KEYON GASKIN AND SIDONY O'NEAL

FOLLOWING SPREAD →→
TIME TRAVEL, 2004
COLLAGE ON PAPER,
11 × 17 INCHES (27.9 × 43.2 CM)

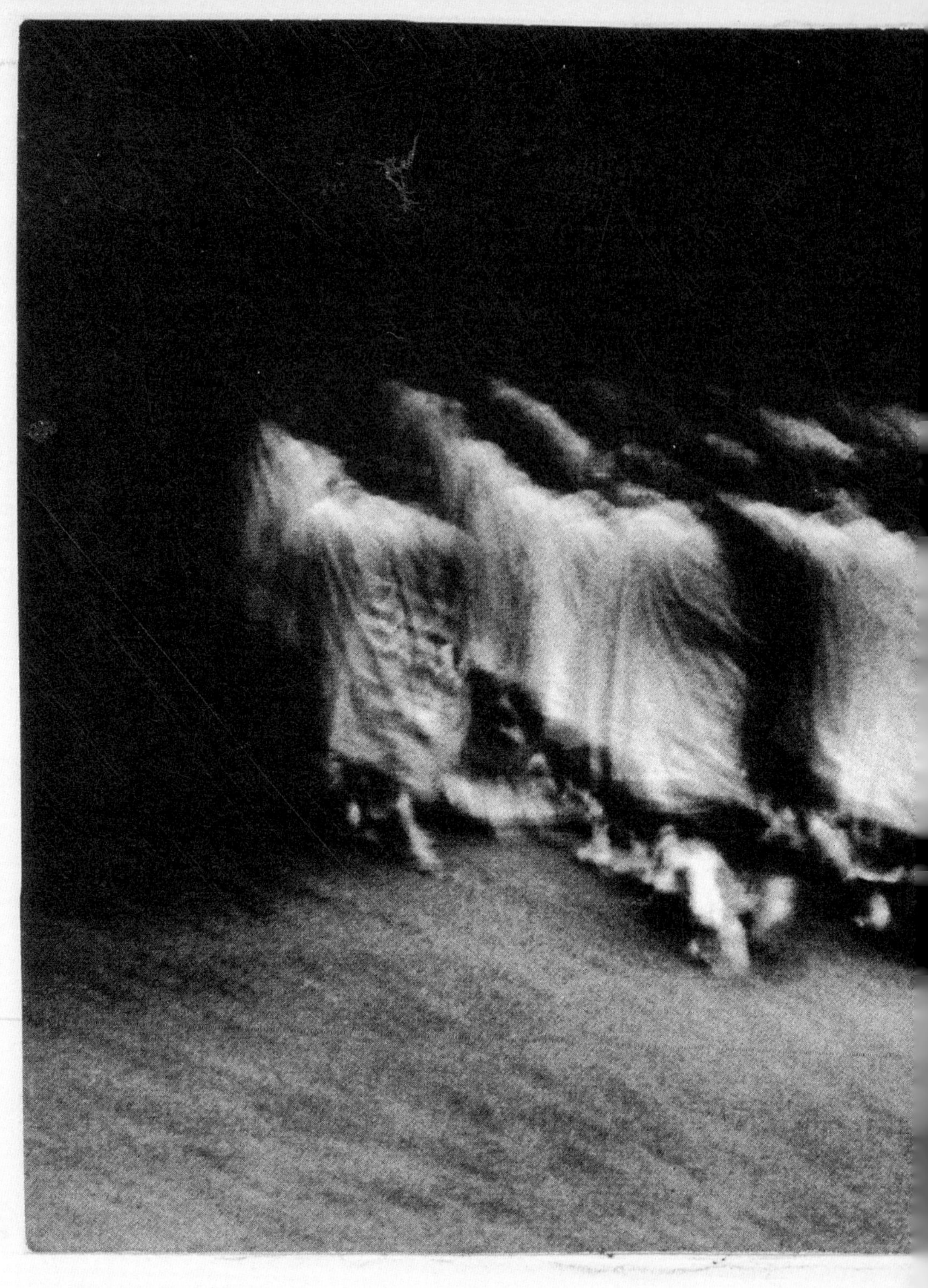

I HAVE ALWAYS
A YEARNING
TO TIME TRAVEL

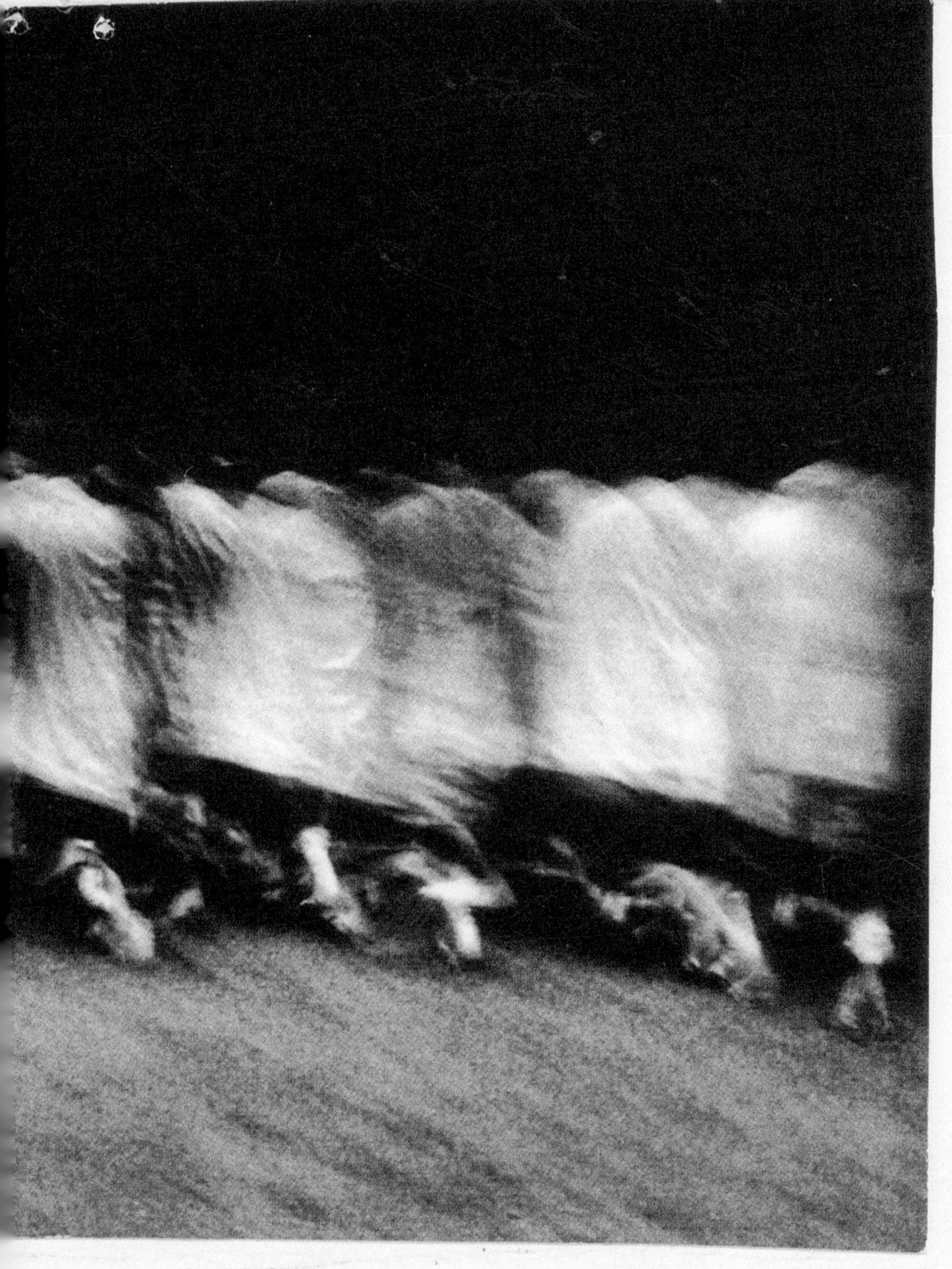

ADA·DESIRE

I have always had a desire
A yearning
To time travel
I have fantasized about it
Since childhood
Besides the awareness
That traveling back in time
Might be treacherous
If I traveled back as
I am today
A big black woman of a certain age
There is the issue of changing
History by turning left instead
Of right
I might negate
My own self being born
The issues and problems abound
Regarding true time travel
Forward or backward
I've however found a solution
Certainly not as adventurous
Or dangerous as the real thing
And that is history and
The study of visionaries
I've always had a passion for
History—as far back as I can
Remember
It excited me to no end
The problem is getting a
True picture of any given
Time ... The pioneer, the Indian,
The politicians, the African,
The conquered and the conquerors
I am reading a book about
Benjamin Franklin that is
Intriguing me to no end
And what the future holds
I believe I can garner that
From visionaries past and
Present as well as my own
Thought constructions
I will just time travel
Between the lines

Wouldn't it be wonderful
To outwit space and time
Travel to alternate universes
And alternate your mind
Go far far and farther
In infinite directions
Yet with all lines converging
Exalted space
Who needs manmade vehicles
When you are occupying outer space
Inner space spills out—outer space filters in
Space is the place
To be at the center of the axis
Before your eyes open
No pushing here there is plenty of room
Hand touches hand
Finger to finger
The lightest
Light touch
Star light
Vibrational energy
Stretching to the sea

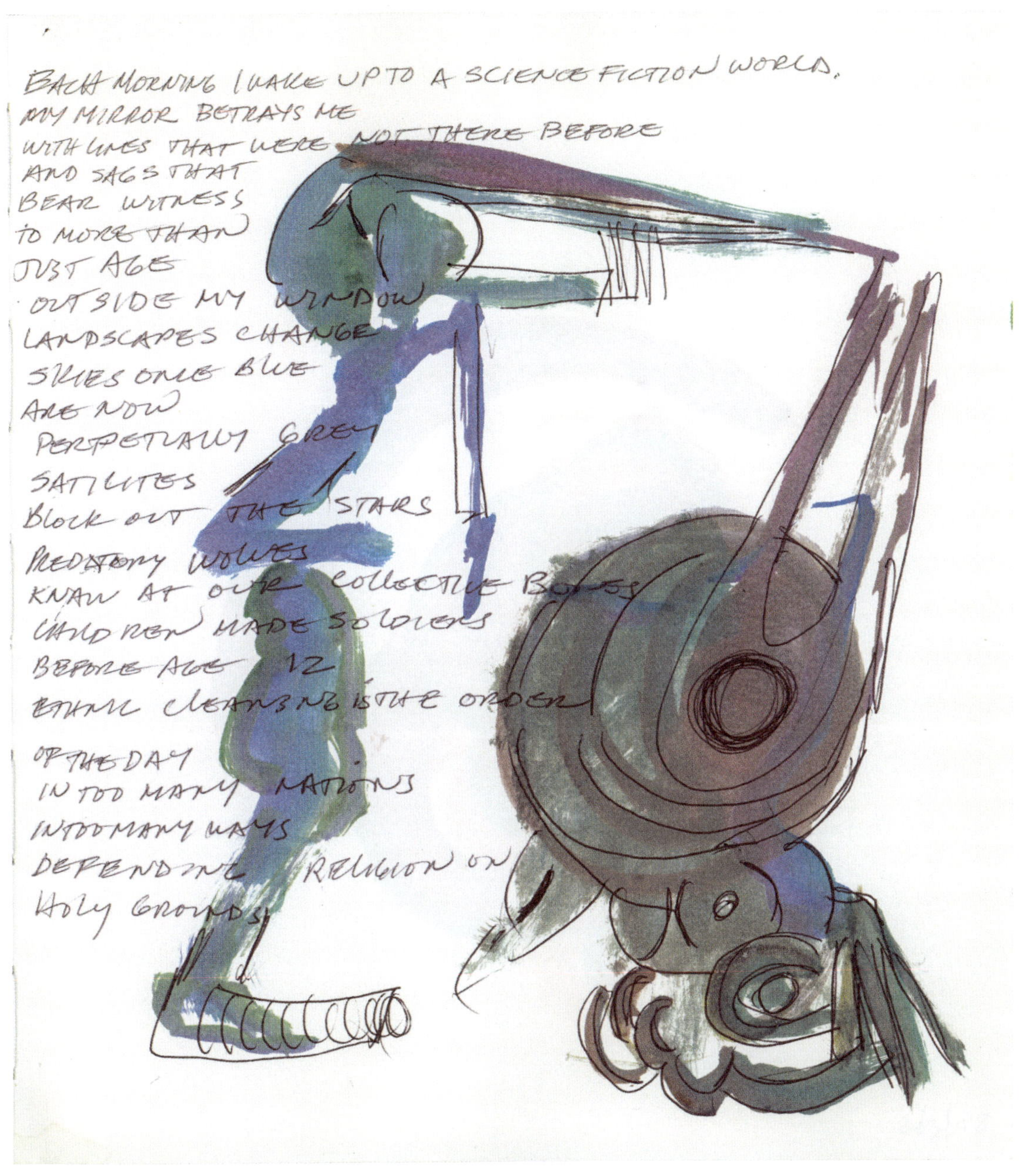

Each morning I wake up to a science fiction world. / My mirror betrays me / With lines that were not there before / And sags that / Bear witness / To more than / Just age / Outside my window / Landscapes change / Skies once blue / Are now / Perpetually grey / Satilites / Block out the stars / Predatory wolves / Knaw at our collective bodies / Children made soldiers / Before age 12 / Ethnic cleansing is the order / Of the day / In too many nations / In too many ways / Defending religion on / Holy grounds

Well the date is February 1, 2008 midnight. I have no idea why I am awake at this hour. I had a very full, active day. I've not journaled in this book in six months. I have a number of books and am not consistent with any of them. Oh well. Earlier in the night, actually just an hour ago Julian Schnabel was on Charlie Rose. As with most artists, all artist he said he likes to make things. When he said that all of a sudden my thought was, "I LIKE TO THINK THINGS." This was huge because it has puzzled me throughout my life + career why I'm not particular about having and wanting to make things. What a relief! I've often read "the idea is the thing." I knew the answer and didn't know I knew it.

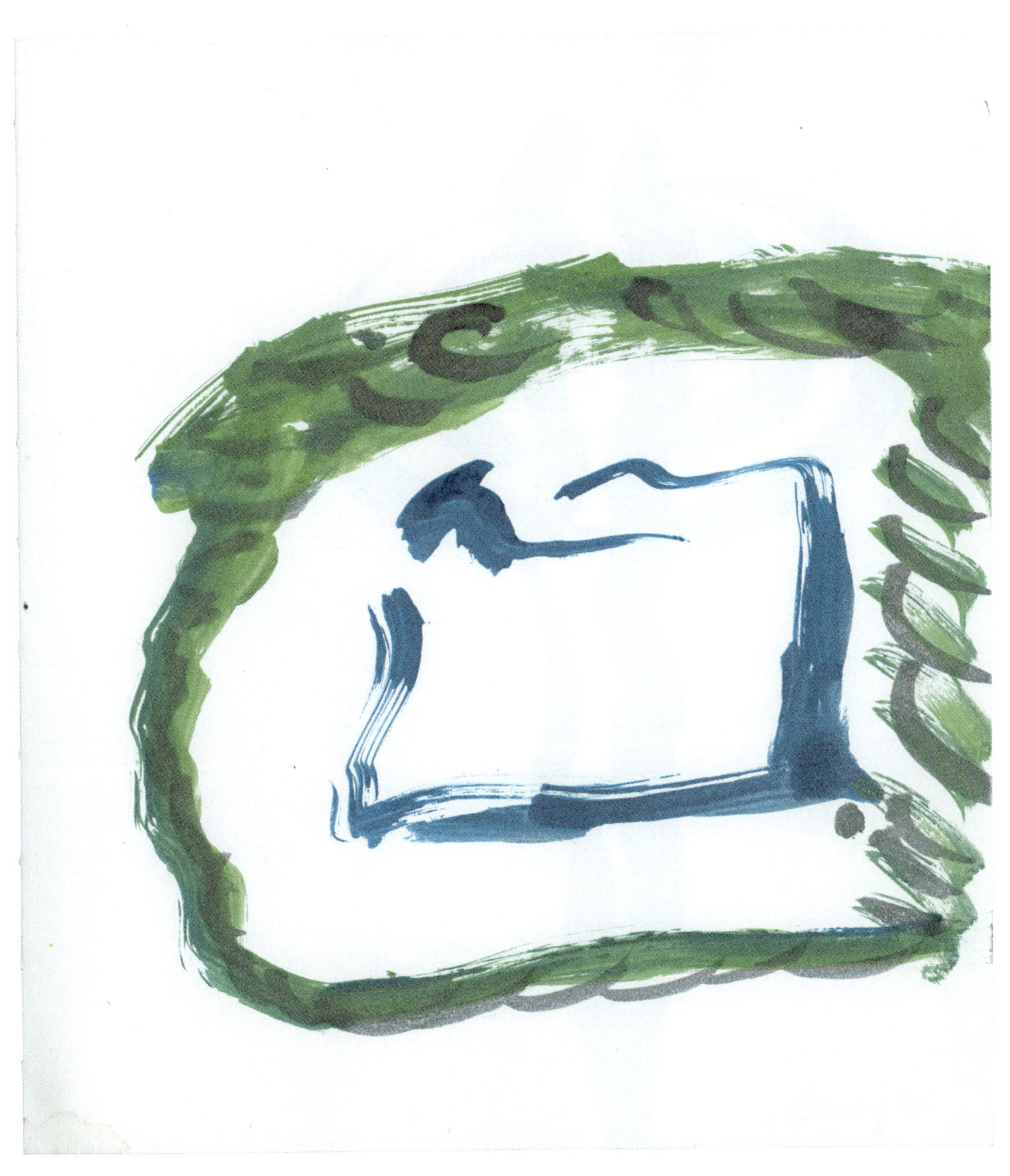

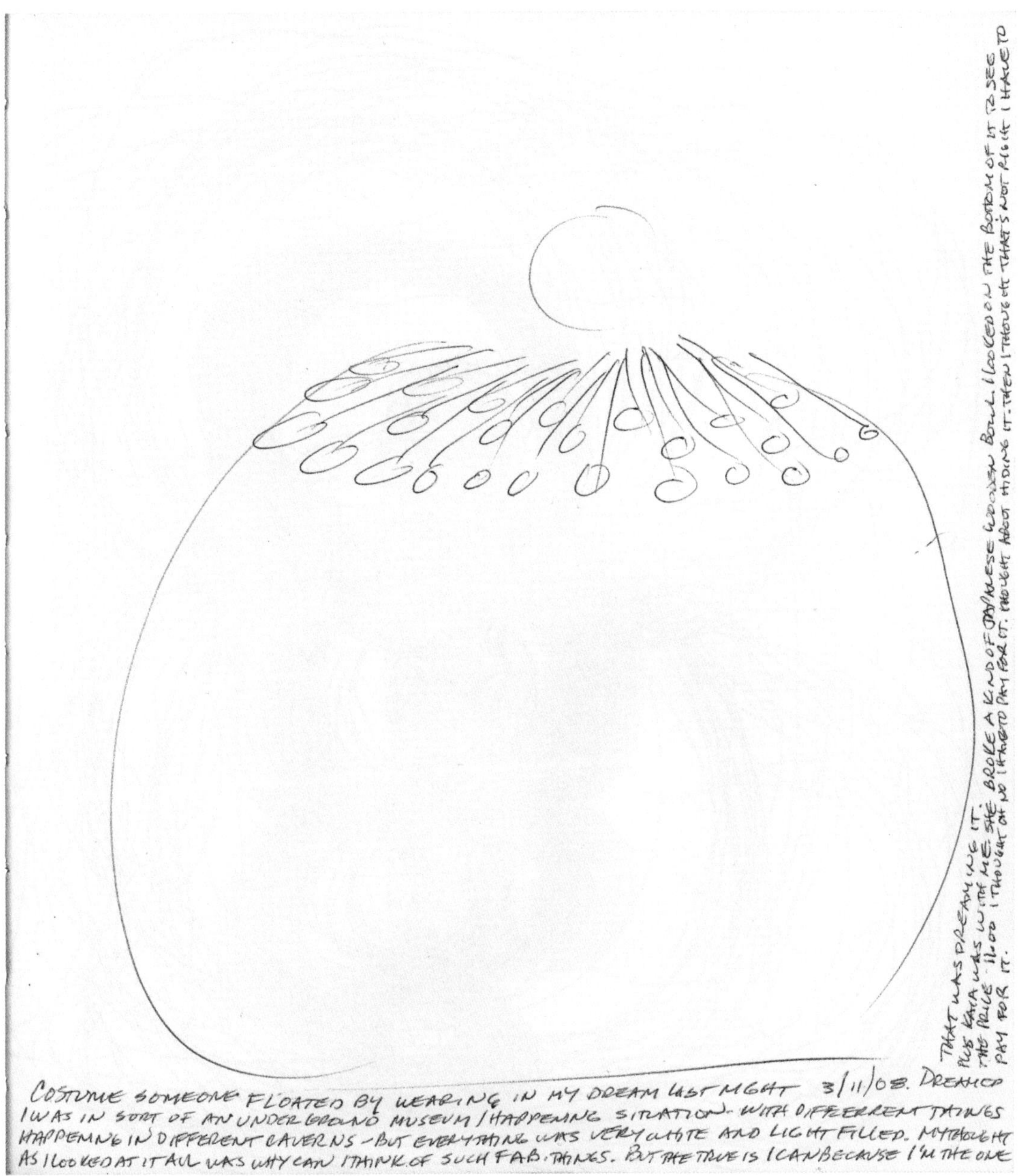

Costume someone floated by wearing in my dream last night. Dreamed I was in sort of an underground museum/happening situation with different things happening in different caverns—but everything was very white and light filled. My thought as I looked at it all was why can I think of such fab. things. But the true is I can because I'm the one that was dreaming it. Plus Kaia was with me. She broke a kind of Japanese wooden bowl. I looked on the bottom of it to see the price. 11.00. I thought oh no I have to pay for it. Thought about hiding it. Then I thought that's not right I have to pay for it.

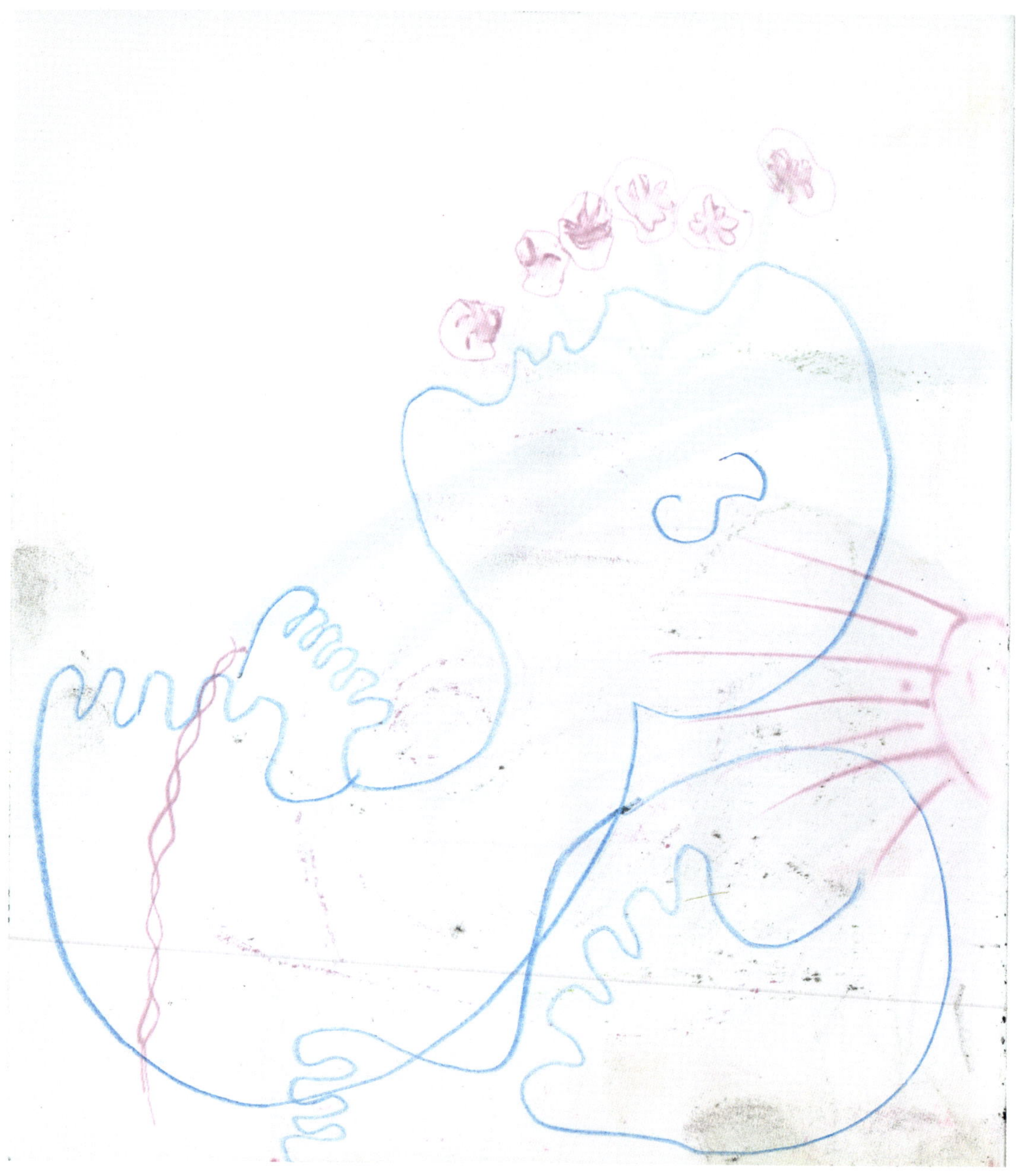

I am weary/wary of art / My hearts no longer's in the / Game / I've never been good at games / Anyway / My ego can't take it / It's also hard on the brain / I find no joy in making things / Flop, flop, fizz, fizz / Even thinking art and / Thinking "up" art / Holds / Absolutely / No / Thrill appeal at all / The weight/wait / Of creativity is too much / To bare/bear / What / Do I do / With this / Revelation / For the day? / Art has / Always / Been / My friend / My companion through / Thick and thin / Its given me everything / Me the legend, love, on occassion money, recognition, friendships / Camaraderie too /

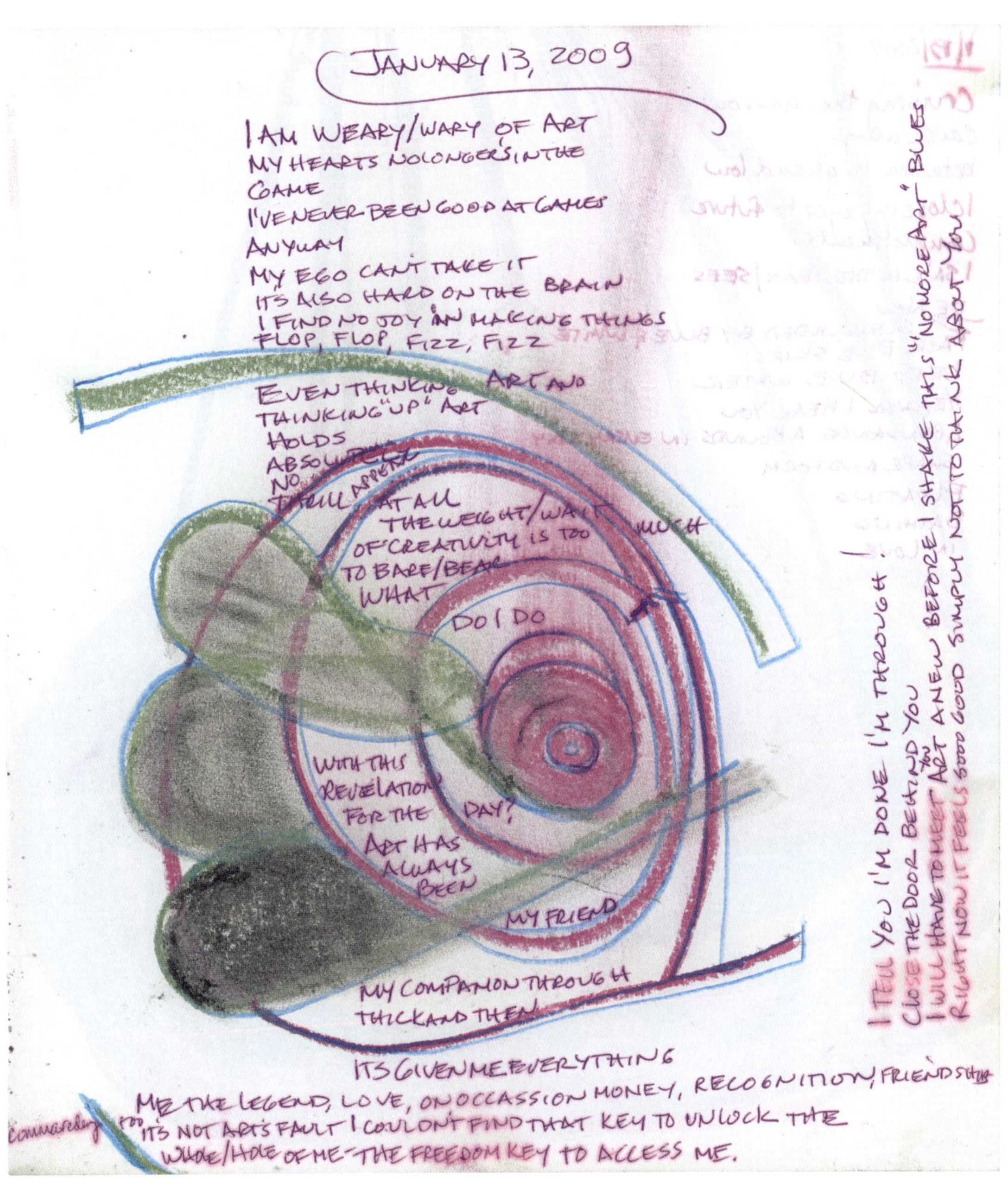

It's not art's fault I couldn't find that key to unlock the / Whole/hole of me—the freedom key to access me. / I tell you I'm done I'm through! / Close the door behind you / I will have to meet you art anew before I shake this "no more art" blues / Right now it feels sooo good simply not to think about you

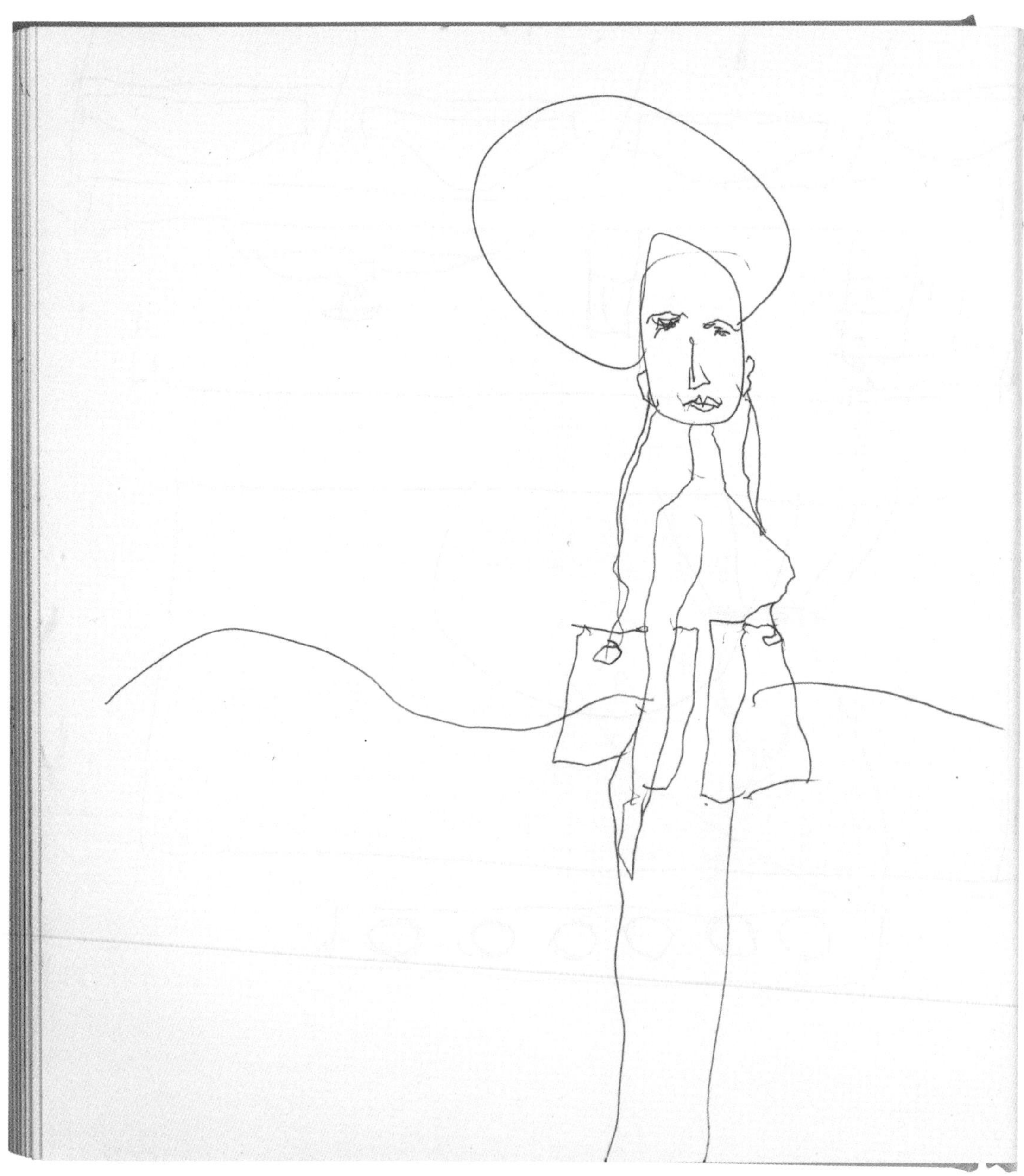

I THOUGHT I WOULD WORK WITH PINA BAUSH ONE DAY / She wasn't supposed to go so fast / 69   69 / It was fast— / Diagnosis—months later the end of life as we know it. / Brilliant woman—STAR with no equal—visiting ALIEN / I wanted to walk with you, dance with you. / I wanted to be a practicing part of your vision / Be on the stage—stage the stage— / Part of the crew—part of the troupe. / Destination / Wuppertal, Germany / DANCE-DANCE / ON TIPPY TOE—clinging to walls—crawling like spiders /

I THOUGHT I WOULD WORK WITH
PINA BAUSH ONE DAY

She wasn't suppose to go so fast
69 69
It was fast-
Diagnosis - months later the end of life as we know it.
Brilliant woman - Star with no equal - Visiting ALIEN
I wanted to walk with you, dance with you.
I wanted to be a practicing part of your vision
Be on the stage - stage the stage -
Part of the crew - Part of the troupe.
Illustration
Wuppertal, Germany
DANCE - DANSE
ON TIPPY TOE - CLINGING TO WALLS - CRAWLING LIKE SPIDERS
KICKING A ~~STAG~~ SAND - A STAGE FULL OF IT
DRESSING UP - DRESSING DOWN - ACTING OUT - DIGGING IN
GIVING VOICE IN MOVEMENT - FINDING MY VOICE THAT WAY
FINDING A WAY THRU SOMETHING ELSE BY WAVYING MY HAND
IN THE AIR - TOSSING MY HEAD TO THE SIDE - HIPS OUT THEN IN
LEG STRETCHED OUT IN OUT IN THEN A SPIN
TWIRLING OUT ARMS OUT STRETCHED THEN IN
BEING PINA'S TOOL IS THRU
DANCING ON MY OWN WILL HAVE TO DO.

1/21/10

Kicking a ~~stag~~ sand—a stage full of it / Dressing up—dressing down—acting out—digging in / Giving voice in movement—finding my voice that way / Finding a way thru something else by wavying my hand / In the air—tossing my head to the side—hips out then in / Leg stretched out in out in then a spin / Twirling out arms out stretched then in / Being Pina's tool is thru / Dancing on my own will have to do.

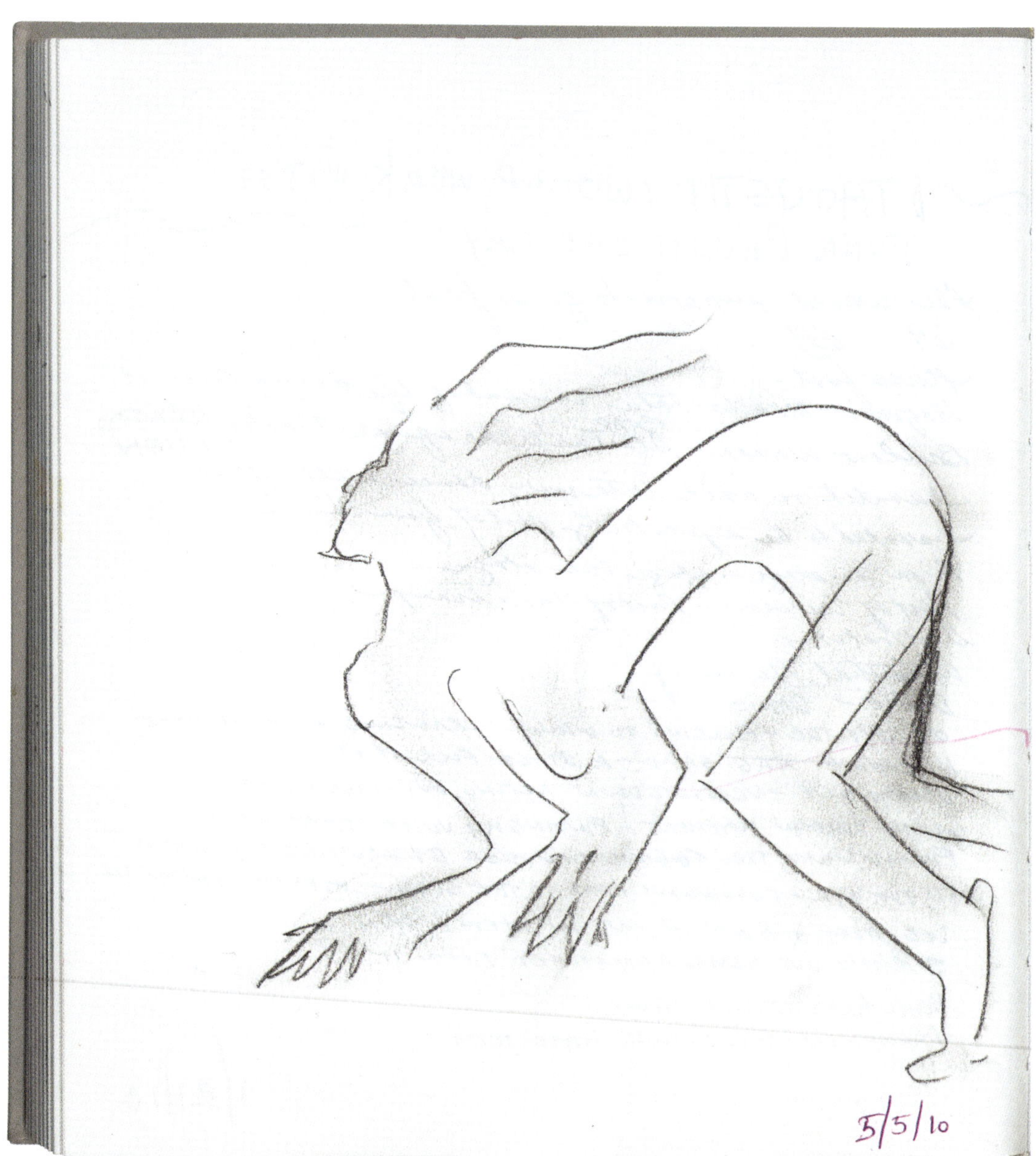
5/5/10

RITE LIGHT
GIVEN AWAY
SIGNALS
WEALTH
BEYOND COMPARE
ACHING TO BE USED UP
READILY AVAILABLE
FOR UNBLINKING EYES
L.B.M
5/16/10

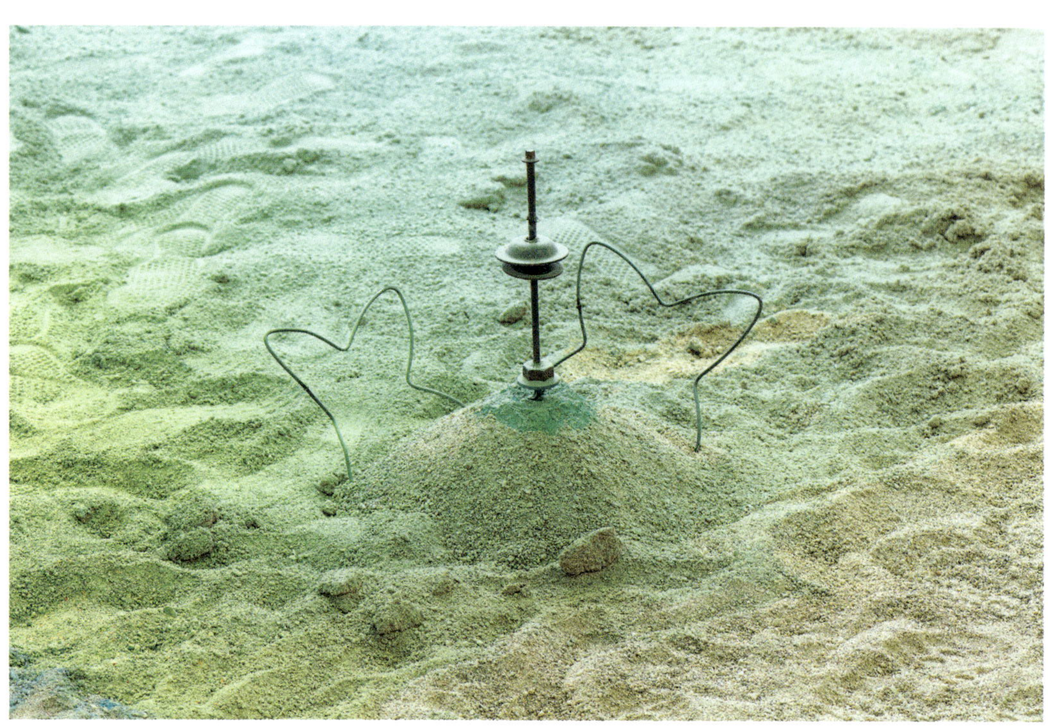

SANDMINING B (DETAIL), 2020
SAND, PIGMENT, STEEL, NYLON MESH,
AND DIGITAL SOUND FILE. DIMENSIONS VARIABLE
DIA ART FOUNDATION. DIA BEACON, NEW YORK,
FEBRUARY 17, 2023–MARCH 25, 2026

Emerge
Release
Discover
Define
Defend
Go
Give
Sway
Balance
Stop
Help
Circle
Focus
Embrace

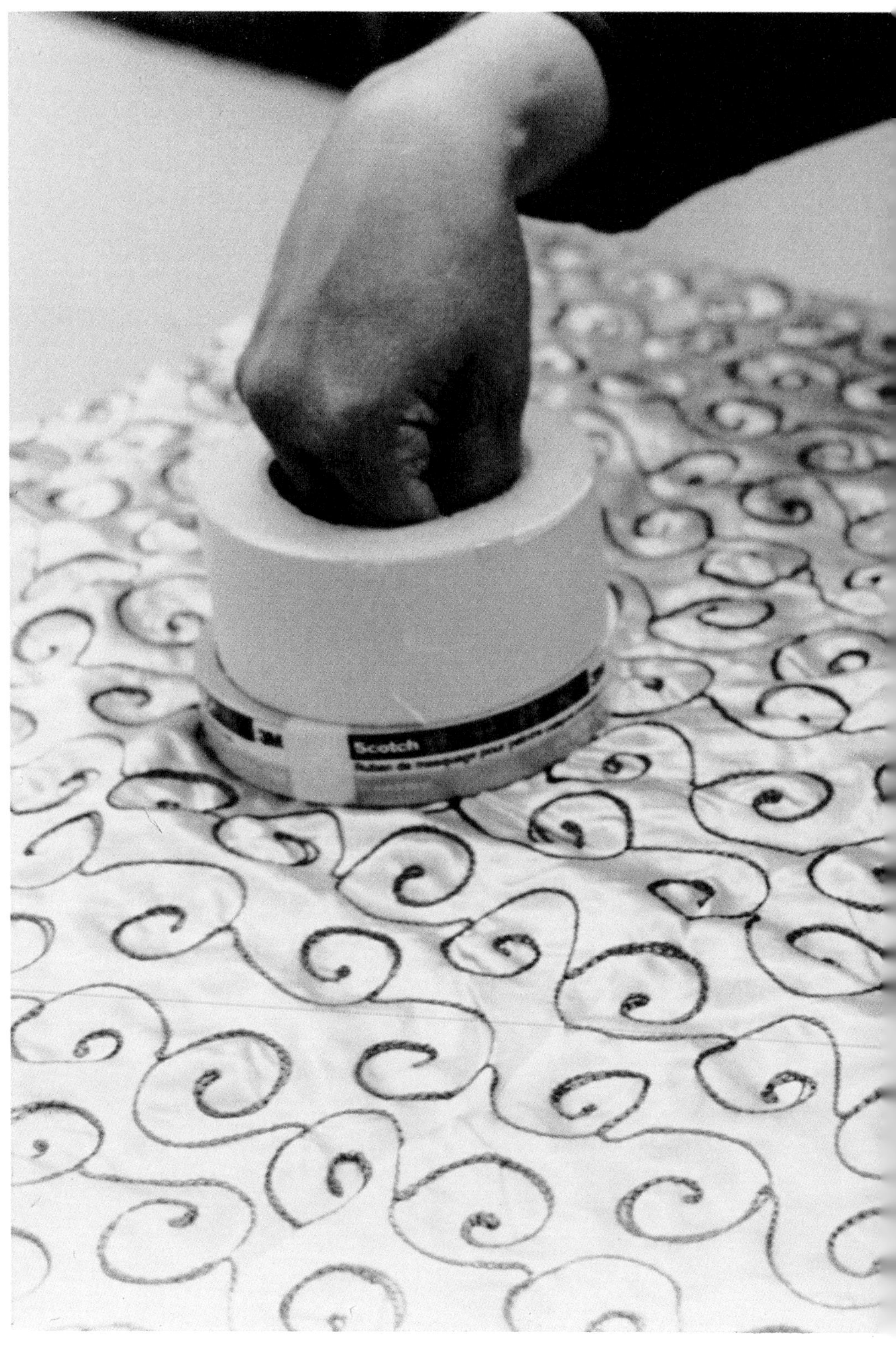

HANDS AND TAPE, 2001
DIGITAL PRINTS, $3\frac{1}{2}$ × 5 INCHES (8.9 × 12.7 CM) EACH

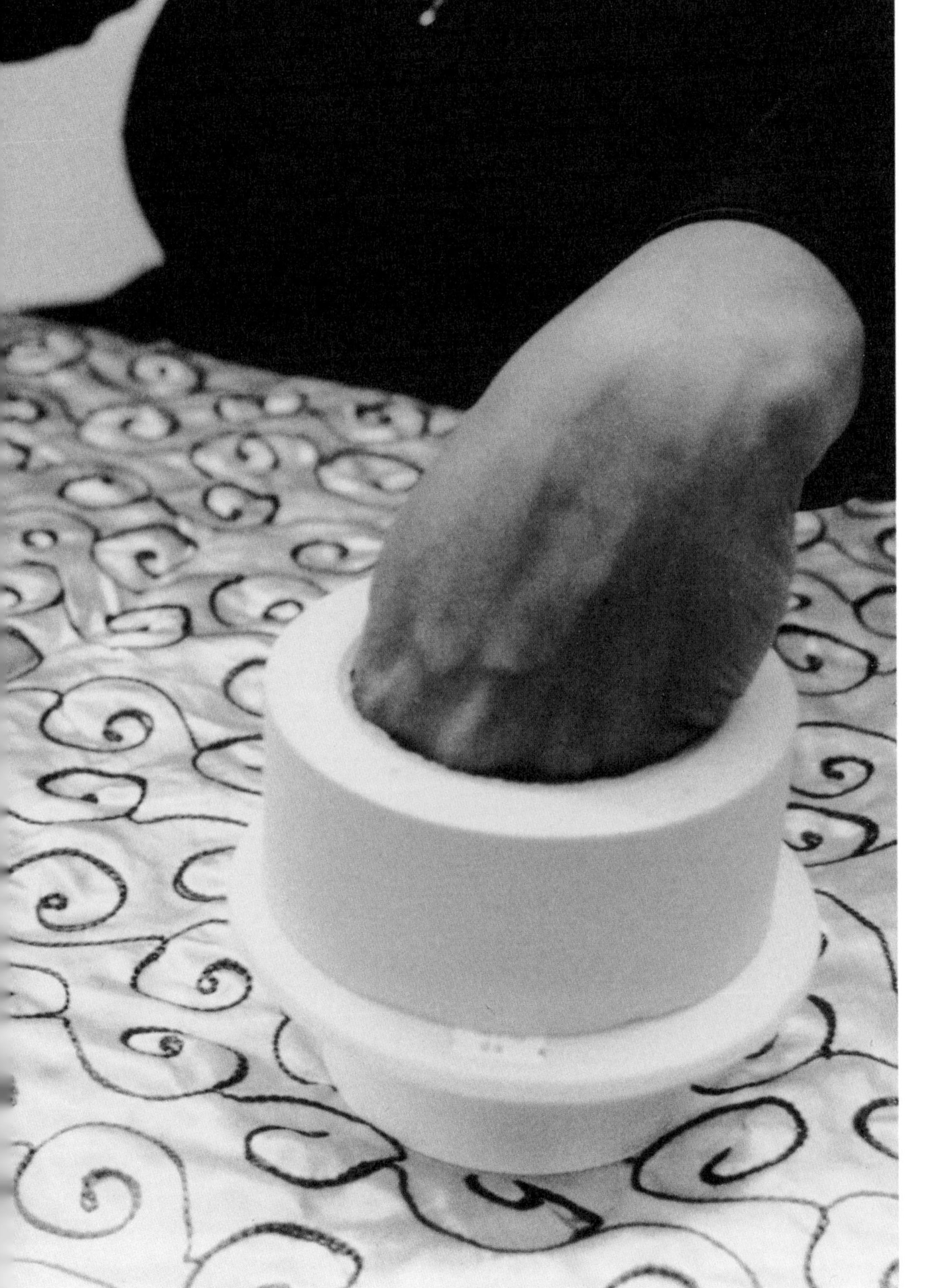

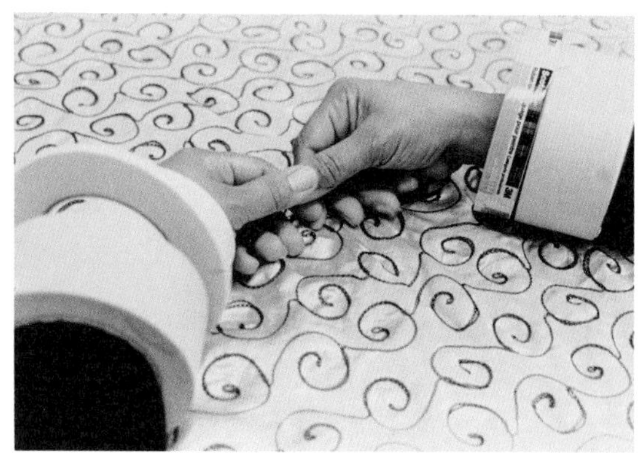

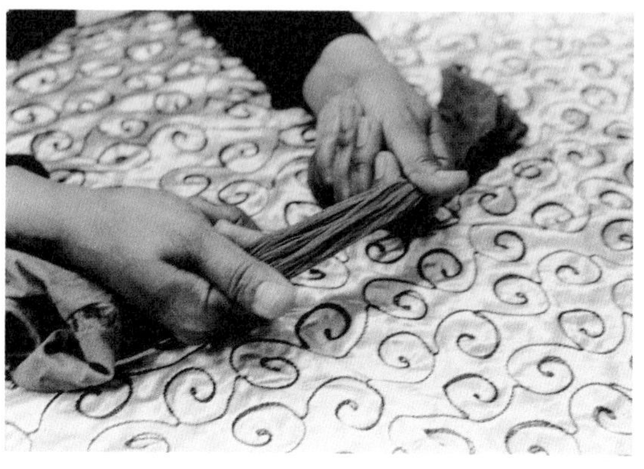

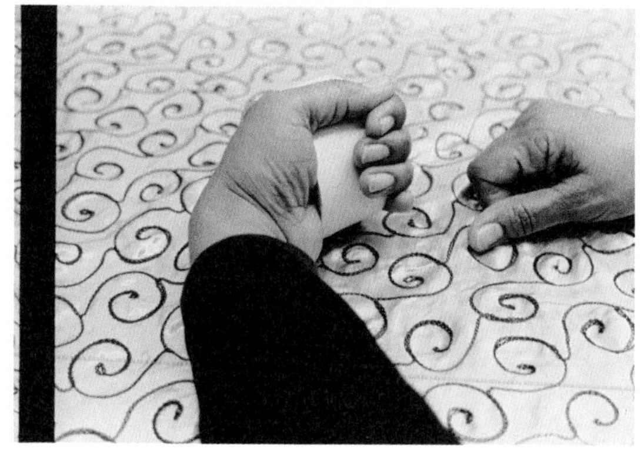

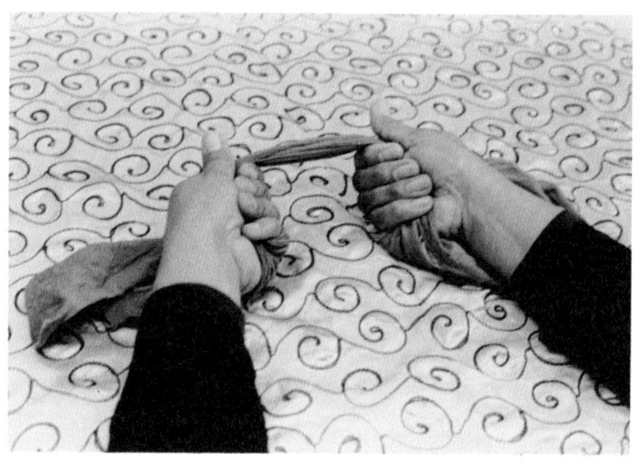

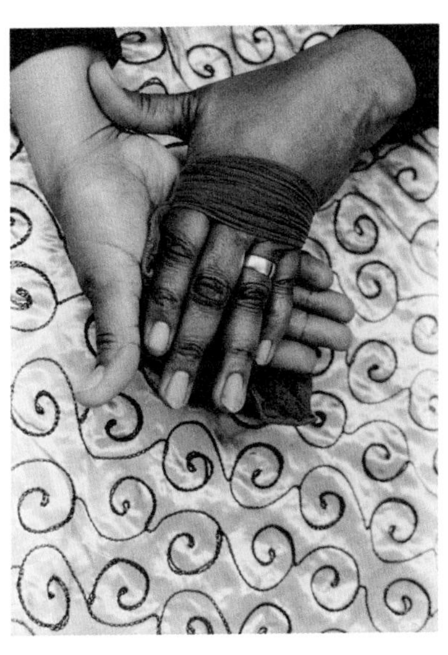

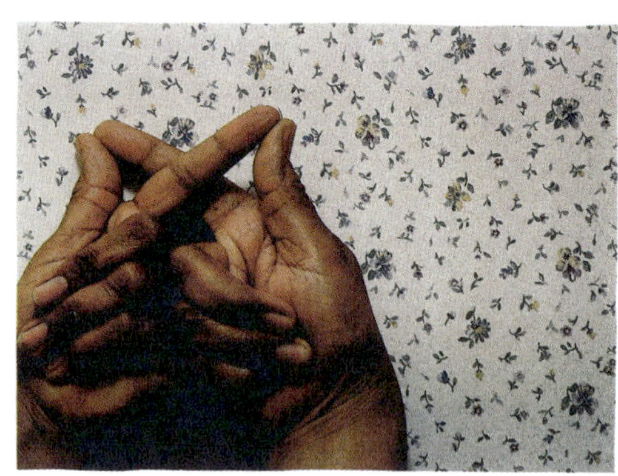

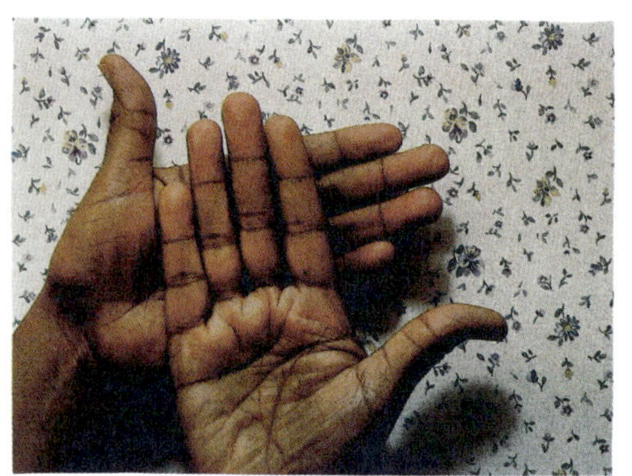

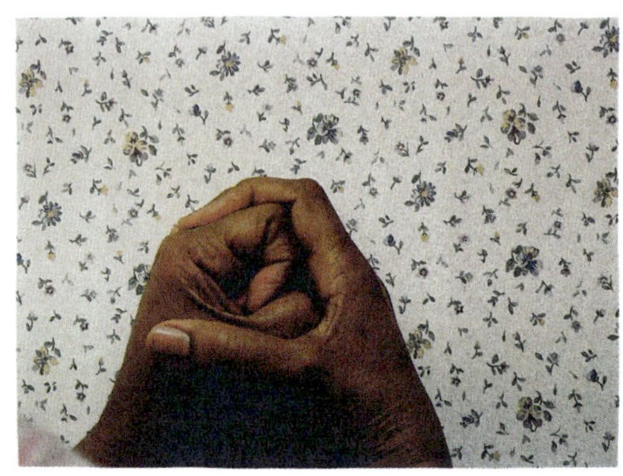

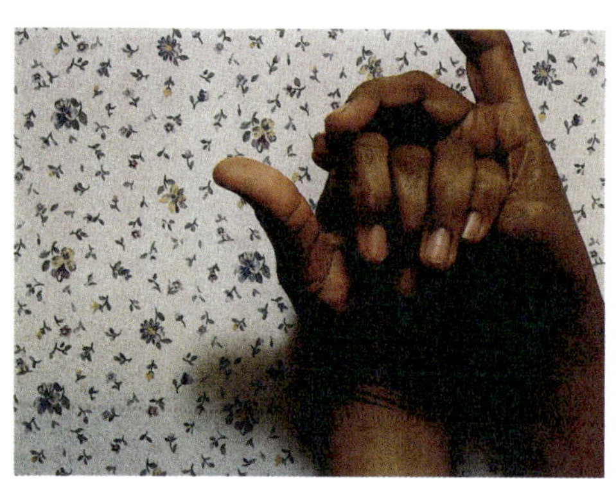

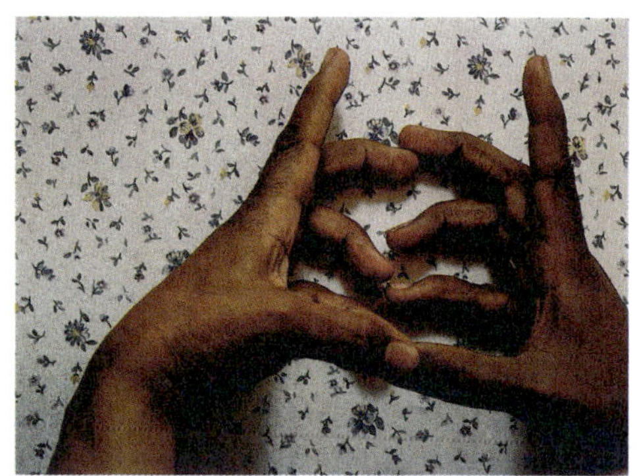

PROPECIA LEIGH, *HANDS*, 2001
DIGITAL PRINTS, 3½ × 5 INCHES (8.9 × 12.7 CM) EACH

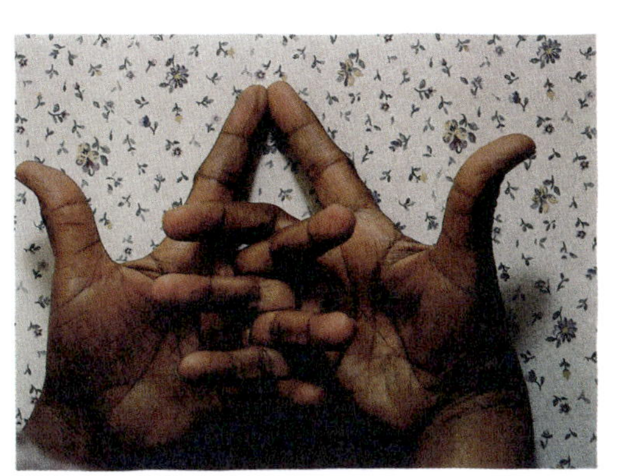

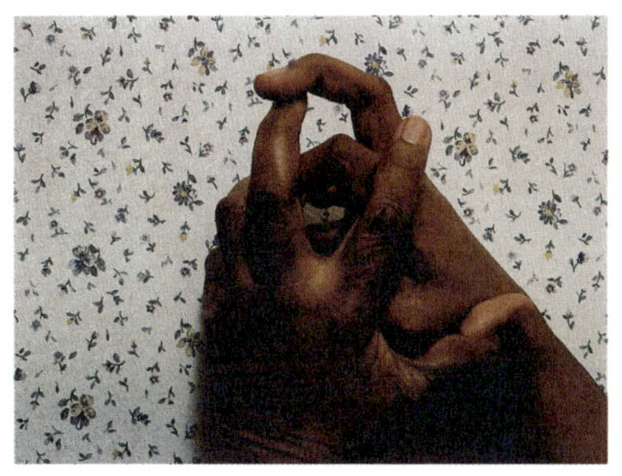

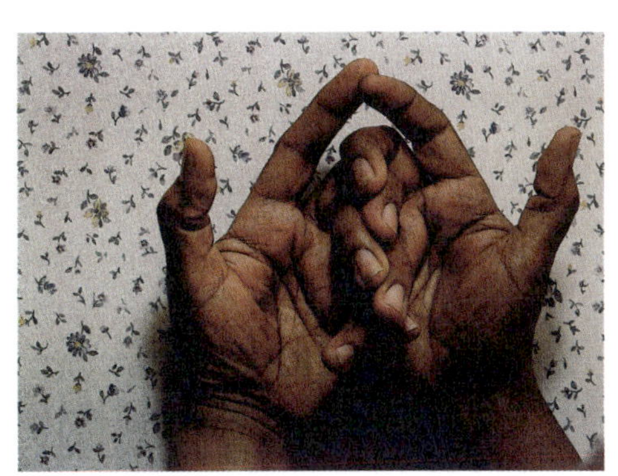

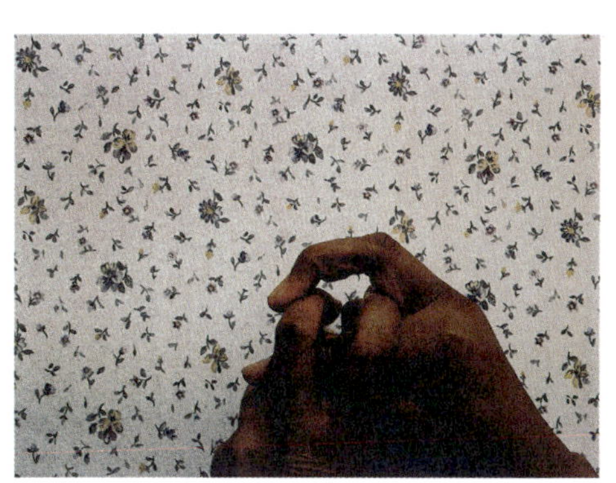

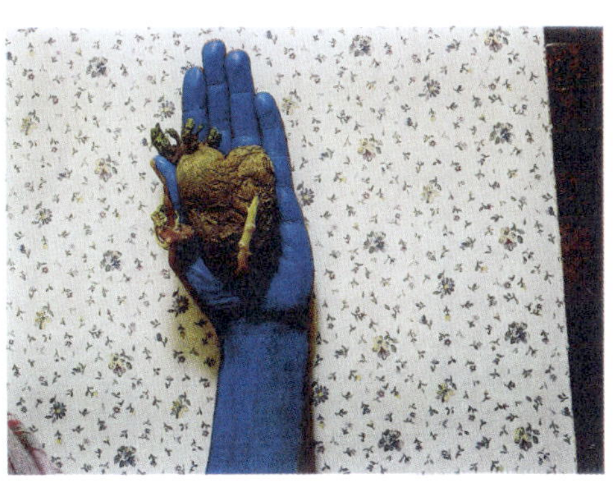

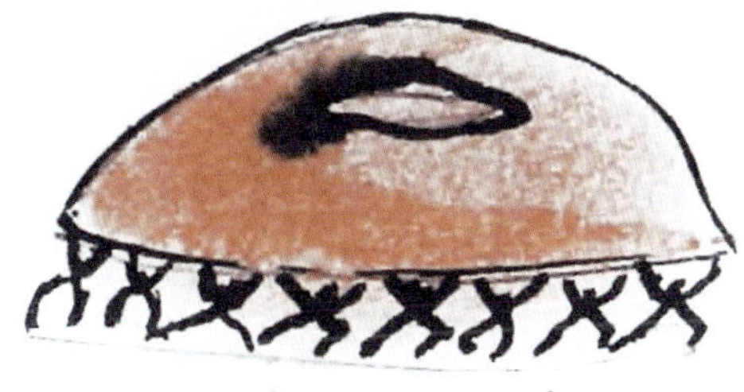

HARRIET CHIN, *MOUNTAIN MOVING DAY*, 2002
PENCIL ON PAPER, 8½ × 11 INCHES (21.6 × 27.9 CM)

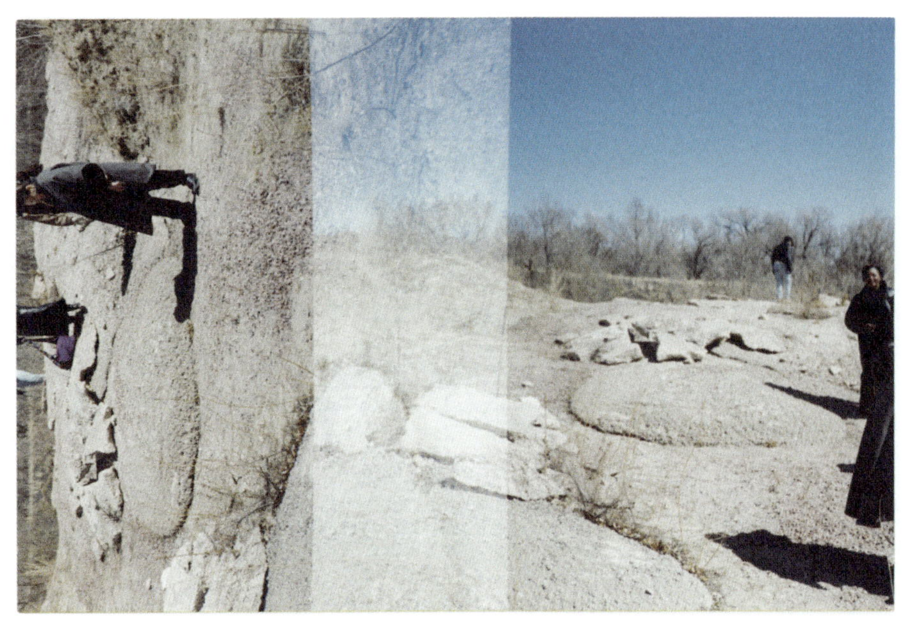

PHOTOGRAPHS OF *MOUNTAIN MOVING DAY*,
YEARLY PERFORMANCE, COLORADO SPRINGS, CA. 2002

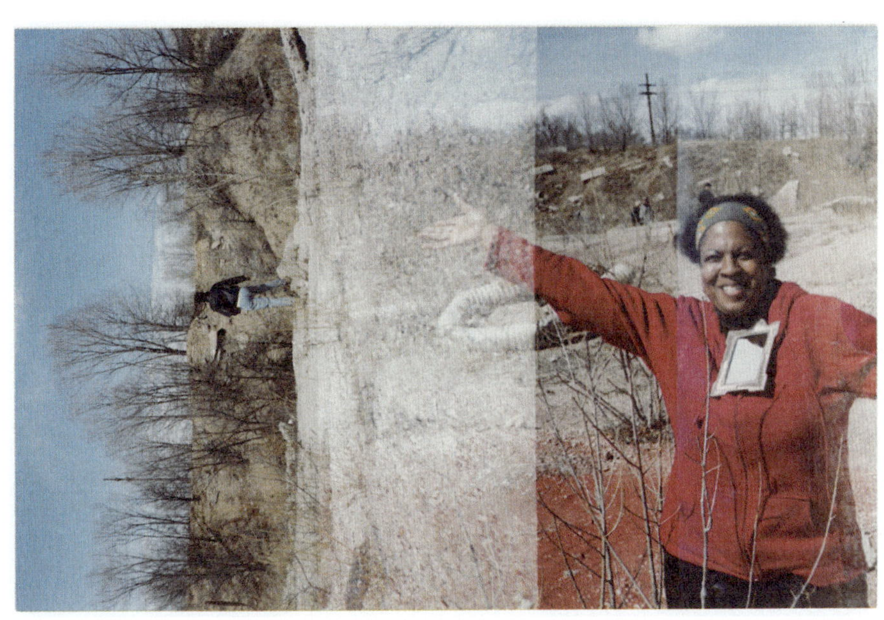

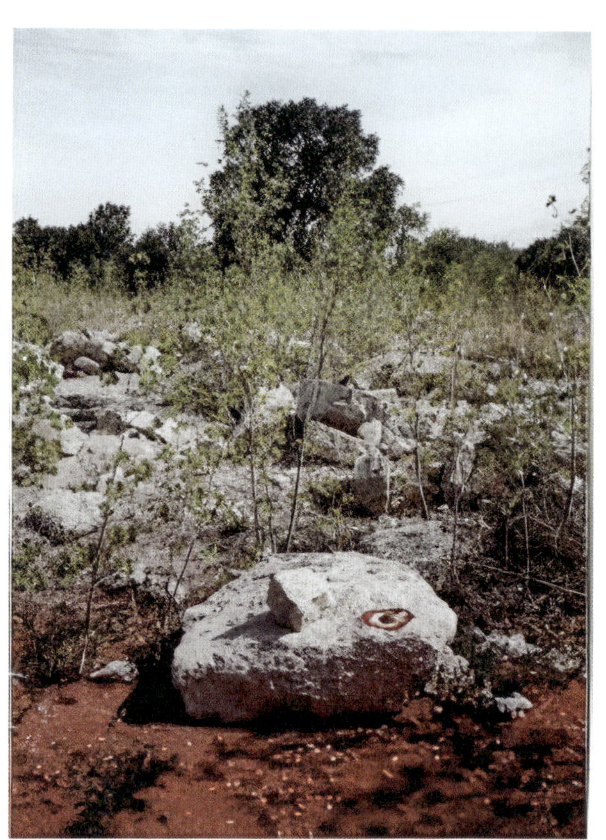

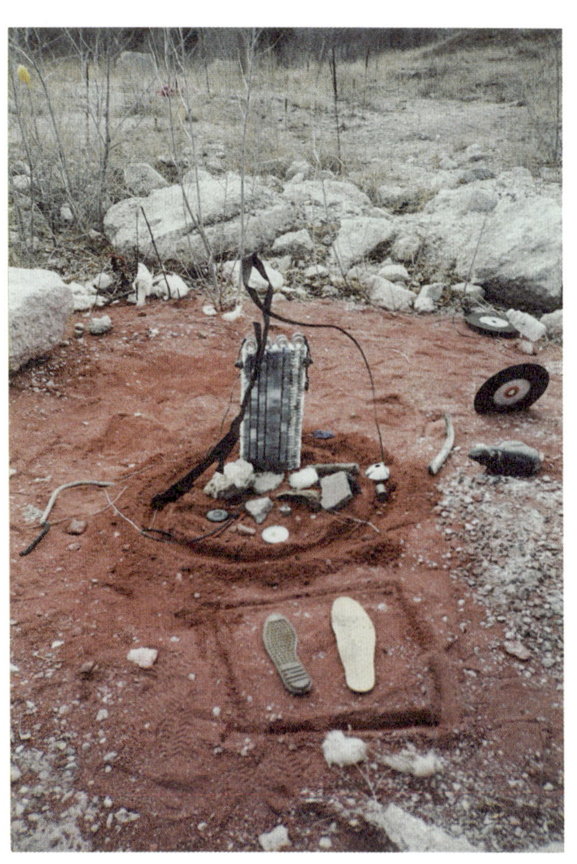

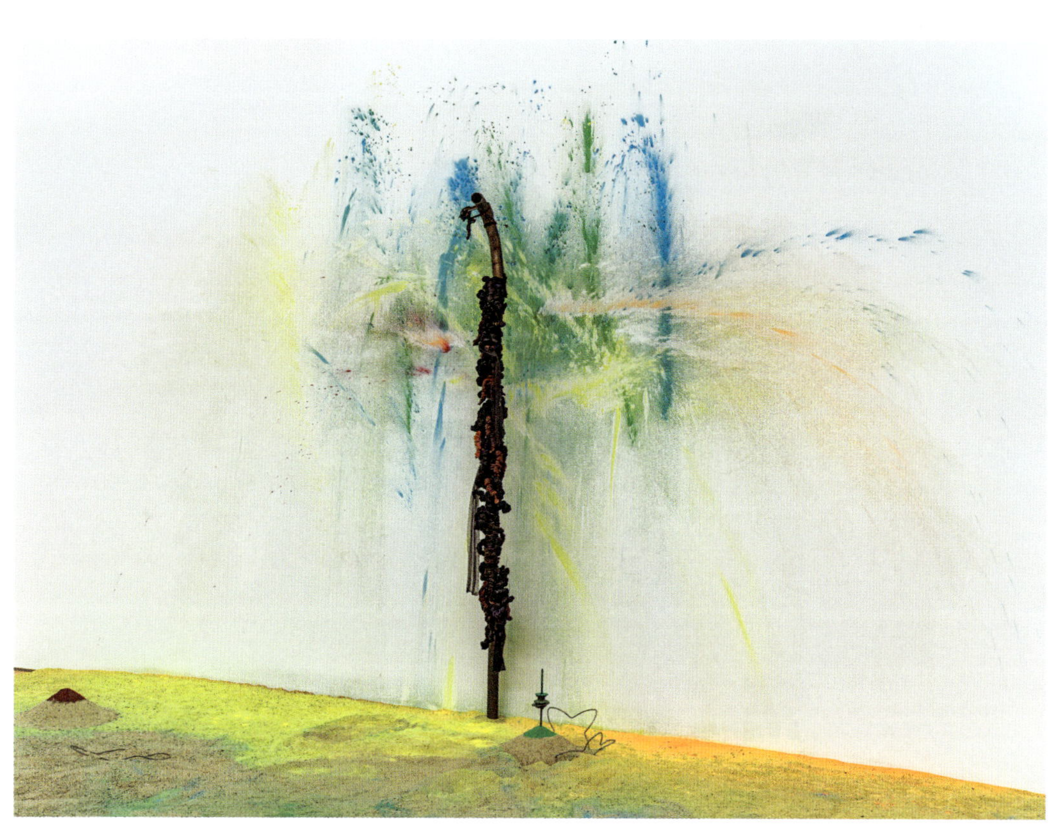

SENGA'S SONG

A. B. Spellman

senga nengudi is before us inside a wrap
of indeterminate fabric   it would be true
of her to be gowned in plastic bin bags
but we do not know the truth of this
she is cast as a found object   it is already art
we need not intervene   the splashed spots
are decoupage for the creases of the carapace
shredded paper warms the neck of her
her head plays a stone upon the boulder
one baleful eye stares out   condemns us
for reasons best not stated

in *last year at marienbad* alain resnais bobbed the eye
among human statues elegant   aloof   accessible
only to themselves & so made a dance of the sight
of persons we dare not know   senga nengudi works
from the other side of artifice when she animates made stuff
with the contemplative movement of bodies inside
& around forms she has made new & alive in a way
that makes us say   of course that grew here & stretched
its appendages up & abroad from its source in the colony
on the wall

the made thing of the made thing so mundane
we could not consider it without the intervention
of the hand & eye of the artist   the innocuous diurnally
mundane annoyingly   or so we assume   essential
pantyhose   sing the word   pantyhose   it swings
a little   it makes the day succeed as it touches
what it touches shapes what it shapes warms
what it warms & then must end its mundane days
in the cursed landfill of discarded & decayed things
we thought little of it when it served us   we think
nothing of it now

but the artist does not think like us   certainly
does not see like us that what we have made used
& discarded can be made again into a complex thing
that appends about the room   o look how it composes
at the heart   how it grows to the source of the light
o listen   coltranes voice has entered the room & is about
to enter us as he has animated the supple woman
who moves into what senga has imagined into being

of all the material of which art is made the dancers
body is most marvelous in the way it denies the constraints
we know it to have   in the form of childbirth the artist
stretched & stretched until she burst & made her greatest work

& then she settled back to her original construction
now she puts the dancer into the made piece where she
sweetly lifts   spreads   bends & lands so lightly she
seems never to know the perdure of the floor
who better to site this brilliant artifact than the artist
she sees ritual in the assembly   says ritual makes
community & community does need to be made in a time
& place like ours which appears to decompose as it thrives
& so cannot survive without a certain unhealthy dualism
& who but the artist can find that essential element
of juju in the artifact & the creation of the artifact

only a fool would deny the call to reason but it is
the reasonable fool who knows the applied evolutionary
discipline of the quick intuition which is the means & matter
of art   she can cast her dream static or in motion
or in animation of the molded static thing

how valiant an artist must be to deny the antique masters futile
quest for the indelible as the way to have done with death
which eventually will come for the masters pieces too no matter
how many stone & marble crypts we build around them
no   senga says   let us put art in the weather beneath
the freeway   let the jazz horns swap four bar licks
with the truck horns   let the dancer spin in the air before

the children & the needful & let them ask what & how &
why was that that i saw & heard & marveled at & will marvel
at until it goes wherever memory drifts away to when dreams
leave the dream place in the mind & unlike the conscious mind
can never know where it goes until it arrives or even be certain
where it has been until it leaves   we think we know but we do not

we think we know what space is or what a named thing is
but we cannot know unless the artist touches it & spells it for us
& then we can at least relax before the mystery & say to ourselves
well it is art & it will overcome the distance that awe imposes on us

place is elemental to art   place tells you whether the song
will echo or travel on until it dissipates into some other star
place tells us   here is the thing   it need not be still or pledge
its shape or name   it need only sing to us in the silence
of the artists voice

yet the world demands of the made work that it declare its tribe
if the made work is more than black is it any less black
if the woman has lived inside the matter of the work has she
invested or divested it   what performance is demanded
of the materialist me when the ritual arrives & percusses
all over him her them   must she them he dance it
or deploy the shekere until the rhythm animates the crowd
in the manner of the ecstatic dervish coltrane came to be

when he pledged to make saints of us all what can the godless
hope to feel at the touch of the juju in the swirl of the dance
is it the investment of the ancestors or the idea of the ancestors
who is the atheist without a god to deny

senga has written ritual builds community ritual
is in the collective arrival at the act of the maker
the communal touch at the delivery of the new life
the sweet chorus the environmental harmony
in the sound of we especially when she has allowed them
to bring their instruments butch morris brought his little horn
maren hassinger brought the form that will animate
the lines that senga sculpts of the thin brown mesh
what more eloquent contradiction is there than the still shot
of the dancer in flight her body bent into a geometry
ancient in its enclosure of space as its silent voice
tells us that freedom is optional if we have the form
for it & yes there are sengas lines to celebrate the flight
& feed our sight with dimension artfully contrived see
the inherent failure of simile is that it defines the image
with another image which if any good must contradict
as much as it confirms & so the human body as made work
ignited by form & the stuff of form that activates & is activated
by the bodys leaps & contortions & coltrane wants me
of all people to become a saint

sengas dancer moves the made form & so diverts its appendages
& makes it new which is the primary standard of jazz old & vanguard
the sand stuffed joints & feet of the thing give it a place to stand
a need all sentient beings share if they are to declare themselves
primary   even as we all must accept deaths hand

geometry
attachment   motion   stability   the attitude of the remade
thing   the way that music animates space & gives the evolved
form a voice from this angle   a home from another

my self wants no manifesto   my self is black & more than black
my self searches & cannot name the object of its search
though it knows what it must conquer & what it must elevate
my self is restless & settles best in song freely blown   my
self rises against the terror of the day which would renew
the awful state it was born into   no   my self will not have that
my self will have done with the fear of death even as it demands
no eternal life   my self will find the space where art is made
to move to the onward elevation of coltranes lines